The Green & the Red

The Green & the Red
Irish Divisions During the First World War

The Tenth (Irish) Division in Gallipoli

Bryan Cooper

With the Ulster Division in France

A. P. I. Samuels & D. G. Samuels

The Green & the Red
Irish Divisions During the First World War
The Tenth (Irish) Division in Gallipoli
by Bryan Cooper
With the Ulster Division in France
by A. P. I. Samuels & D. G. Samuels

FIRST EDITION

First published under the titles
The Tenth (Irish) Division in Gallipoli
and
With the Ulster Division in France

Leonaur is an imprint
of Oakpast Ltd

Copyright in this form © 2014 Oakpast Ltd

ISBN: 978-1-78282-325-4 (hardcover)
ISBN: 978-1-78282-326-1 (softcover)

http://www.leonaur.com

Publisher's Notes
The views expressed in this book are not necessarily those of the publisher.

Contents

The Tenth (Irish) Division in Gallipoli 7
With the Ulster Division in France 185

The Tenth (Irish) Division in Gallipoli

MULES IN THE ANZAC SAP

Contents

Foreword	13
Introduction	17
Author's Preface	19
The Formation of the Division	21
Mudros and Mitylene	40
The 29th Brigade at Anzac	59
Sari Bair	75
Suvla Bay and Chocolate Hill	92
Kiretch Tepe Sirt. August 15th-16th, 1915	112
Kaba Kuyu and Hill 60	129
Routine	144
Last Days	158
Retrospect	167
Appendix	176

So they gave their bodies to the common weal and received, each for his own memory, praise that will never die, and with it the grandest of all sepulchres, not that in which their mortal bones are laid, but a home in the minds of men, where their glory remains fresh to stir to speech or action as the occasion comes by.—Thucydides.

It seems as if this poor Celtic people were bent on making what one of its own poets has said of its heroes hold good for ever: 'They went forth to the war but they always fell.'—Matthew Arnold.

To
The Glorious Memory
Of the
Officers, Non-Commissioned Officers
And Men
Of the
Tenth Irish Division
Who Laid Down Their Lives in
Gallipoli
And
To Those Who Mourn for Them

Foreword

I have been asked to write a short foreword to the following pages, and I do so with the utmost pleasure. By the publication of this little book, Major Bryan Cooper will be performing a most valuable service, not only to his own country, Ireland, but to the Empire.

The history of the 10th (Irish) Division is, in many respects, unique. It was the first Irish Division raised and sent to the Front by Ireland since the commencement of the war. Not alone that, but it was the first definitely Irish Division that ever existed in the British Army.

Irish Divisions and Irish Brigades played a great part in history in the past, but they were divisions and brigades, not in the service of England, but in the service of France and other European countries and America.

The creation of the 10th (Irish) Division, therefore, marks a turning point in the history of the relations between Ireland and the Empire.

In many respects, the 10th (Irish) Division, notwithstanding the extraordinary and outstanding gallantry that it showed in the field, may be said to have been unfortunate. No division in any theatre of the war suffered more severely or showed greater self-sacrifices and gallantry. And yet, largely, I fancy, by reason of the fact that its operations were in a distant theatre, comparatively little has been heard of its achievements; and, for some reason which a civilian cannot understand, the number of honours and distinctions conferred on the division has been comparatively small. And yet we have the testimony of everyone, from the generals in command down, that the division behaved magnificently, in spite of the most terrible and unlooked-for difficulties and sufferings.

Before they went into action, their artillery was taken from them, and they landed at Suvla and Anzac without a single gun.

They were a division of the new army entirely made up of men who had no previous military experience, and who had never heard a shot fired. Yet, the very day they landed, they found themselves precipitated into the most tremendous and bloody conflict, exposed to heavy shrapnel and machine-gun fire, on an open strand, where cover was impossible.

To the most highly trained and seasoned troops in the world, this would have been a trying ordeal; but, to new troops, it was a cruel and terrible experience. And yet the testimony all goes to show that no seasoned or trained troops in the world could have behaved with more magnificent steadiness, endurance, and gallantry. Without adequate water supply—indeed, for a long time, without water at all, owing to mismanagement, which has yet to be traced home to its source—their sufferings were appalling.

As Major Bryan Cooper points out, it is supposed to be a German military maxim that no battalion could maintain its morale with losses of twenty-five *per cent*. Many of the battalions of the 10th Division lost seventy-five *per cent*., and yet their morale remained unshaken. The depleted Division was hastily filled up with drafts, and sent, under-officered, to an entirely new campaign at Salonika, where it won fresh laurels.

Another cruel misfortune which overtook them was, that, instead of being allowed to fight and operate together as a unit, they were immediately split up, one brigade being attached to the 11th Division, and entirely separated from their comrades.

There has been some misapprehension created, in certain quarters, as to the constitution of this 10th Division and its right to call itself an Irish Division. Major Bryan Cooper sets this question at rest. What really occurred was, that, quite early in the business, when recruiting for the 10th Division was going on fairly well in Ireland, for some unexplained reason, a number of English recruits were suddenly sent over to join its ranks. They were quite unnecessary, and protests against their incursion into the division fell upon deaf ears. As it happened, however, it was found that a considerable number of these English recruits were Irishmen living in Great Britain, or the sons of Irishmen, and, when the division went to the Front, Major Bryan Cooper states that fully seventy *per cent*, of the men, and ninety *per cent*, of the officers, were Irishmen. That is to say, the division was as much entitled to claim to be an Irish Division in its constitution as any division either in England, Scotland, or Wales is entitled to claim that it is an English,

Scotch, or Welsh Division.

Men of all classes and creeds in Ireland joined its ranks. The list of casualties which Major Bryan Cooper gives is heart-breaking reading to any Irishman, especially to one like myself, who had so many personal friends who fell gallantly in the conflict.

Irishmen of all political opinions were united in the division. Its spirit was intensely Irish. Let me quote Major Bryan Cooper's words:—

> It was the first Irish Division to take the field in war. Irish Brigades there had often been. They had fought under the Fleur-de-Lys or the Tricolour of France, and under the Stars and Stripes, as well as they had done under the Union Jack. But never before in Ireland's history had she seen anywhere a whole Division of her sons in the battlefield. The old battalions of the Regular Army had done magnificently, but they had been brigaded with English, Scotch, and Welsh units. The 10th Division was the first division almost entirely composed of Irish Battalions who faced an enemy. Officers and men alike knew this, and were proud of their destiny. As the battalions marched through the quiet English countryside, the drums and fifes shrieked out 'St. Patrick's Day' or 'Brian Boru's March,' and the dark streets of Basingstoke echoed the voices that chanted ' God Save Ireland,' as the units marched down to entrain. Nor did we lack the green. One unit sewed shamrocks into its sleeves. Another wore them as helmet badges. Almost every company cherished somewhere an entirely unofficial green flag, as dear to the men as if they were the regimental colours themselves. They constituted an outward and visible sign that the honour of Ireland was in the division's keeping, and the men did not forget it.

The men who had differed in religion and politics, and their whole outlook on life, became brothers in the 10th Division. Unionist and Nationalist, Catholic and Protestant, as Major Bryan Cooper says— "lived and fought and died side by side, like brothers." They combined for a common purpose: to fight the good fight for liberty and civilisation, and, in a special way, for the future liberty and honour of their own country.

Major Bryan Cooper expresses the hope that this experience may be a good augury for the future.

For my part, I am convinced that nothing that can happen can deprive Ireland of the benefit of the united sacrifices of these men.

I congratulate Major Bryan Cooper on his book. The more widely it is circulated, the better it will be for Ireland and for the Empire.

J. E. Redmond

St, Patrick's Day, 1917

Introduction

I have been asked to contribute a short introduction to this account of the doings of the 10th (Irish) Division in Gallipoli.

I commanded the division from the time of its formation until it left Gallipoli Peninsula for Salonika, and I am extremely glad that some record has been made of its exploits. I do not think that the author of this book intends to claim for the division any special pre-eminence over other units; but that he puts forward a simple account of what the first formed Irish Service Battalions suffered and how creditably they maintained the honour of Ireland.

Memories in war-time are short, and it may be that the well-earned glories of the 16th and Ulster Division have tended to obliterate the recollections of Suvla and Sari Bair. (The division has also the distinction of being the only troops of the Allies that have fought in Bulgaria up to date.)

In case these things are forgotten, it is well that this book has been written, for never in history did Irishmen face death with greater courage and endurance than they did in Gallipoli and Serbia in the summer and winter of 1915.

During the period of its formation the division suffered from many handicaps. To the difficulties which are certain to befall any newly created unit were added others due to the enormous strain that the nation was undergoing; arms and equipment were slow in arriving; inclement weather made training difficult, and for sake of accommodation units had had to be widely separated in barracks all over Ireland. All these difficulties were, however, surmounted, partly by the genuine keenness of all ranks, but in the main by the devoted work of the handful of regular officers and N.C.O.'s who formed the nucleus of the division.

No words can convey how much was done by these men, naturally disappointed at not going out with the original Expeditionary Force. They nevertheless threw themselves whole-heartedly into the work before them, and laboured unceasingly and untiredly to make the new units a success, they were ably seconded by retired officers who had rejoined, and by newly-joined subalterns, who brought with them the freshness and enthusiasm of youth.

Nor were the men behindhand. Though the monotony of routine training sometimes grew irksome, yet their eagerness to face the enemy and their obvious anxiety to do their duty carried them through, and enabled them to become in nine months well-trained and disciplined soldiers.

When they reached Gallipoli they had much to endure. The 29th Brigade were not under my command, so I cannot speak from personal knowledge, but I believe that every battalion did its duty and won the praise of its generals.

Of the remainder of the division I can speak with greater certainty. They were plunged practically at a moment's notice into battle, and were placed in positions of responsibility and difficulty on a desolate sun-baked and waterless soil, where they suffered tortures from thirst. In spite of this, and in spite of the fact that they were newly formed units mainly composed of young soldiers, they acquitted themselves admirably. No blame or discredit of any kind can possibly be attached to the rank and file of the 10th Division. Whatever the emergency, and however great the danger, they faced it resolutely and steadfastly, rejoicing when an opportunity arose that enabled them to meet their enemy with the bayonet.

Ireland has had many brave sons; Ireland has sent forth many splendid regiments in past times; but the deeds of the men of the 10th (Irish) Division are worthy to be reckoned with any of those of their predecessors.

(Sd.)   Bryan Mahon

Author's Preface

This book (which was written in haste during a period of sick leave) does not profess to be a military history; it is merely a brief attempt to describe the fortunes of the rank and file of the Tenth (Irish) Division. The division was so much split up that it is impossible for any one person to have taken part in all its actions; but I went to Gallipoli with my battalion, and though disabled for a period by sickness, I returned to the Peninsula before the division left it, so that I may fairly claim to have seen both the beginning and the end of the operations. I have received great assistance from numerous officers of the division, who have been kind enough to summarise for me the doings of their battalions, and I tender them my grateful thanks.

Captain Fish has also very kindly allowed me to use three more of his sketches, which, though deprived of the charm of colour possessed by the originals, give a far better idea of the scenery of Gallipoli than can be obtained from any photograph. Having shared the life led by Captain Fish's battalion in Gallipoli, I cannot help admiring the manner in which he managed to include a paint-box and a sketchbook in the very scanty kit allowed to officers. My comrade, Francis Ledwidge, who himself served in the ranks of the division, summed up the object of our enterprise in beautiful lines. In them he has fulfilled the poet's mission of expressing in words the deepest thoughts of these who feel them too sincerely to be able to give them worthy utterance.

In dealing with the general aspect of the Gallipoli Expedition, I have tried to avoid controversial topics. As a general rule, I have followed the version given by Sir Ian Hamilton in his despatch, which is still the only official document that exists for our guidance. I am conscious that the book, of necessity, has omitted many gallant deeds, and has dealt with some units more fully than with others.

I can only plead in extenuation that I found great difficulty in getting detailed information as to the doings of some battalions, and that to this, rather than to prejudice on my part, is due any lack of proportion that may exist. It is by no means easy for an Irishman to be impartial, but I have done my best.

Bryan Cooper

March 1st, 1917

P.S.—Since this was written Francis Ledwidge has laid down his life for the honour of Ireland, and the world has lost a poet of rare promise.

The Irish in Gallipoli

Where Aegean cliffs with bristling menace front
The treacherous splendour of that isley sea,
Lighted by Troy's last shadow; where the first
Hero kept watch and the last Mystery
Shook with dark thunder. Hark! the battle brunt!
A nation speaks, old Silences are burst.

'Tis not for lust of glory, no new throne
This thunder and this lightning of our power
Wakens up frantic echoes, not for these
Our Cross with England's mingle, to be blown
At Mammon's threshold. We but war when war
Serves Liberty and Keeps a world at peace.

Who said that such an emprise could be vain?
Were they not one with Christ, who fought and died?
Let Ireland weep: but not for sorrow, weep
That by her sons a land is sanctified.
For Christ arisen, and angels once again
Come back, like exile birds, and watch their sleep,

Francis Ledwidge

France
24th February, 1917

CHAPTER 1

The Formation of the Division

The army, unlike any other profession, cannot be taught through shilling books. First a man must suffer, then he must learn his work and the self-respect which knowledge brings.—Kipling.

Within ten days of the outbreak of the war, before even the Expeditionary Force had left England, Lord Kitchener appealed for a hundred thousand recruits, and announced that six new divisions would be formed from them. These six divisions, which were afterwards known as the First New Army, or more colloquially as K.1, were, with one exception, distributed on a territorial basis. The Ninth was Scotch, the Eleventh North Country, the Twelfth was recruited in London and the Home Counties, and the Thirteenth in the West of England.

The exception was the Fourteenth, which consisted of new battalions of English light infantry and rifle regiments. The Tenth Division in which I served, and whose history I am about to relate, was composed of newly-formed or "Service" battalions of all the Irish line regiments, together with the necessary complement of artillery, engineers, Army Service Corps, and R.A.M.C. They were distributed as follows:—

29th Brigade.
5th Service Battalion, Royal Irish Regiment.
6th   *ditto*   Royal Irish Rifles.
5th   *ditto*   The Connaught Rangers.
6th   *ditto*   The Leinster Regiment.

The 5th Royal Irish Regiment afterwards became the Divisional Pioneer Battalion, and its place in the 29th Brigade was taken by the 10th Hampshire Regiment.

30th Brigade.
6th Service Battalion, Royal Dublin Fusiliers.
7th   ditto   ditto
6th Service Battalion, Royal Munster Fusiliers.
7th   ditto   ditto

31st Brigade.
5th Service Battalion, Royal Inniskilling Fusiliers.
6th   ditto   ditto
5th Service Battalion, Royal Irish Fusiliers.
6th   ditto   ditto

It will be seen that the 29th Brigade consisted of regiments from all the four provinces of Ireland, while the 30th Brigade had its depots in the South of Ireland, and the 31st in Ulster. The Divisional Troops were organised as follows:—

Artillery.
54th Brigade R.F.A.
55th   „   R.F.A.
56th   „   R.F.A.
57th (Howitzer) Brigade R.F.A.
Heavy Battery R.G.A.

Engineers.
65th Field Company R.E.
66th   ditto   R.E.
85th   ditto   R.E.
10th Divisional Signal Company.
10th Divisional Train.
10th Divisional Cyclist Company.
30th Field Ambulance, R.A.M.C.
31st   ditto
32nd   ditto

A squadron of South Irish Horse was allocated as Divisional Cavalry, but this only joined the division at Basingstoke in May, and was detached again before we embarked for Gallipoli.

Fortunately, one of the most distinguished of Irish generals was available to take command of the division. Lieut.-General Sir Bryan Mahon was a Galway man who had entered the 8th (Royal Irish) Hussars from a Militia Battalion of the Connaught Rangers in 1883. For ten years he served with his regiment, acting as adjutant from 1889 to 1893, but recognising that British cavalry were unlikely to see much active service, he transferred to the Egyptian Army in the latter year. He served with the cavalry of this force in the Dongola Expedition in 1896, and was awarded the D.S.O. For his services in the campaign, which ended in the capture of Khartoum, he received the brevet rank of Lieutenant-Colonel.

He next commanded the mounted troops which achieved the defeat and death of the *Khalifa*, and for this he was promoted to Brevet-Colonel. He was then transferred to South Africa, where he commanded a mounted brigade and had the distinction of leading the column which effected the relief of Mafeking, being created a Companion of the Bath for his services on this occasion. After the South African War he returned to the Soudan as Military Governor of Kordofan. His next commands were in India, and he had only vacated the command of the Lucknow Division early in 1914. While holding it in 1912 he had been created a K.C.V.O.

At the time he took over the 10th Division he was fifty-two years of age. His service in Egypt and India had bronzed his face and sown grey in his hair, but his figure and his seat on a horse were those of a subaltern. He scorned display, and only the ribbons on his breast told of the service he had seen. A soft cap adorned with an 8th Hussar badge, with a plain peak and the red band almost concealed by a khaki cover, tried to disguise his rank, but the manner in which it was pulled over his eyes combined with the magnificent chestnut he rode and the eternal cigarette in his mouth, soon made him easily recognisable throughout the division.

Experienced soldier as he was, he had qualities that made him even better suited to his post than military knowledge, and in his years in the East he had not forgotten the nature of his countrymen. The Irish soldier is not difficult to lead: he will follow any man who is just and fearless, but to get the best out of him, needs sympathy, and this indefinable quality the general possessed. It was impossible for him to pass a football match on the Curragh without saying a pleasant word to the men who were watching it, and they repaid this by adoring their leader. Everything about him appealed to them—his great reputation, the horse he rode, his Irish name, and his Irish nature, all went to their hearts. Above all, he was that unique being, an Irishman with no politics, and this, in a division that was under the patronage of no political party, but consisted of those who wanted to fight, was an enormous asset.

Fortunately, the Infantry brigadiers had also some knowledge of

Lieut.-General Sir Bryan Mahon,
K.C.V.O., C.B., D.S.O.

Irish troops. Brigadier-General R. J. Cooper, C.V.O., who led the 29th Brigade, had commanded the Irish Guards. Another Irish Guardsman, Brigadier-General C. Fitz-Clarence, V.C, commanded the 30th Brigade at the time of its first formation, but he was soon afterwards called to France to command the 1st Brigade in the Expeditionary Force, and met his death at the first battle of Ypres. His place was taken by Brigadier-General L. L. Nicol, who had done the bulk of his service in the Rifle Brigade, but had begun his soldiering in the Connaught Rangers. The 31st Brigade was commanded by Brigadier-General F. F. Hill, C.B., D.S.O., who had served throughout a long and distinguished career in the Royal Irish Fusiliers. The Divisional Artillery was at first under the command of Brigadier-General A. J. Abdy, but when this officer was found medically unfit for active service, he was replaced by Brigadier-General G. S. Duffus.

I must now describe the actual formation of the division, and in view of the fact that it was the beginning of one of the most gigantic military improvisations on record, it may be desirable to do so in some detail.

Fortunately there were some regular cadres available. In the first place, there was the Regimental Depot, where usually three regular officers were employed, the senior being a major. In almost every case he was promoted to temporary Lieutenant-Colonel, and given the command of the senior Service Battalion of his regiment. The other two officers (usually a captain and a subaltern) were also transferred to the new unit. Then, again, the Regular Battalion serving at home before embarking for France was ordered to detach three officers, and from ten to sixteen N.C.O.'s. In many cases these officers did not belong to the Regular Battalion, but were officers of the regiment who had been detached for service with some Colonial unit, such as the West African Frontier Force, or the King's African Rifles. Being on leave in England when war broke out, they had rejoined the Home Battalion of their unit, and had been again detached for service with the New Armies. Where more than one Service Battalion of a regiment was being formed, the bulk of these officers and N.C.O.'s went to the senior one.

There was yet another source from which regular officers were obtained, and those who came from it proved among the best serving in the division.

At the outbreak of the war all Indian Army officers who were on leave in England were ordered by the War Office to remain there and were shortly afterwards posted to units of the First New Army. Two of the brigade-majors of the division were Indian Army officers, who, when war was declared, were students at the Staff College, and nearly every battalion obtained one Indian officer, if not more. It is impossible to exaggerate the debt the division owed to these officers. Professional soldiers in the best sense of the word, they identified themselves from the first with their new battalions, living for them, and, in many cases, dying with them. Words cannot express the influence they wielded and the example they gave, but those who remember the lives and deaths of Major R. S. M. Harrison, of the 7th Dublins, and Major N. C. K. Money, of the 5th Connaught Rangers, will realise by the immensity of the loss we sustained when they were killed, how priceless their work had been.

A certain number of the reserve of officers were also available for service with the new units. It seemed hard for men of forty-five or fifty years of age who had left the army soon after the South African War, to be compelled to rejoin as captains and serve under the orders of men who had previously been much junior to them, but they took it cheerfully, and went through the drudgery of the work on the barrack square without complaining. Often their health was unequal to the strain imposed upon it by the inclement winter, but where they were able to stick it out, their ripe experience was most helpful to their juniors. The battalions which did not secure a regular commanding officer got a lieut.-colonel from, the reserve of officers, often one who had recently given up command of one of the regular battalions of the regiment.

Besides officers from the reserve of officers, there were also a considerable number of men who had done five or six years' service in the Regular Army or the militia and had then retired without joining the reserve. These were for the most part granted temporary commissions of the rank which they had previously held. A few were also found who had soldiered in Colonial corps, and eight or ten captains were drawn from the District Inspectors of the Royal Irish Constabulary. These united to a knowledge of drill and musketry a valuable insight into the Irish character, and as by joining they forfeited nearly £100 a year apiece, they abundantly proved their patriotism.

It will thus be seen that each battalion had a regular or retired regular commanding officer, a regular adjutant, and the four company commanders had as a rule had some military experience. The quartermaster, regimental sergeant-major, and quartermaster-sergeant were usually pensioners who had rejoined, while company sergeant-majors and quartermaster-sergeants were obtained by promoting N.C.O.'s who had been transferred from the regular battalion. The rest of the cadres had to be filled up, and fortunately there was no lack of material.

For about a month after their formation the Service Battalions were short of subalterns, not because suitable men were slow in coming forward, but because the War Office was so overwhelmed with applications for commissions that it found it impossible to deal with them. About the middle of September, however, a rule was introduced empowering the C.O. of a battalion to recommend candidates for temporary second-lieutenancies, subject to the approval of the Brigadier, and after this the vacancies were quickly filled. Some of the subalterns had had experience in the O.T.C., and as a rule these soon obtained promotion, but the majority when they joined were quite ignorant of military matters, and had to pick up their knowledge while they were teaching the men.

About the end of the year, classes for young officers were instituted at Trinity College, and a certain number received instruction there, but the bulk of them had no training other than that which they received in their battalions. They were amazingly keen and anxious to learn, and the progress they made both in military knowledge and in the far more difficult art of handling men was amazing. Drawn from almost every trade and profession, barristers, solicitors, civil engineers, merchants, medical students, undergraduates, schoolboys, they soon settled down together and the spirit of esprit de corps was quickly created. Among themselves, no doubt, they criticised their superiors, but none of them would have admitted to an outsider that their battalion was in any respect short of perfection.

I shall never forget the horror with which one of my subalterns, who had been talking to some officers of another division at Mudros, returned to me saying, "Why, they actually said that their colonel was a rotter!" Disloyalty of that kind never existed in the 10th Division. The subalterns were a splendid set, and after nine months' training compared well with those of any regular battalion. They believed in themselves, they believed in their men, they believed in the division, and, above all, in their own battalion.

I must now turn to the men whom they led. Fortunately, the inexperience of the new recruits was, to a large extent, counteracted by the rejoining of old soldiers. It was estimated that within a month of the declaration of war, every old soldier in Ireland who was under sixty years of age (and a good many who were over it) had enlisted again. Some of these were not of much use, as while living on pension they had acquired habits of intemperance, and many more, whose military experience dated from before the South African War, found the increased strain of army life more than they could endure. However, a valuable residue remained, and not only were they useful as instructors, and in initiating the new recruits into military routine, but the fact that they had usually served in one of the Regular battalions of their regiment helped to secure a continuity of tradition and sentiment, which was of incalculable value. In barracks these old soldiers sometimes gave trouble, but in the field they proved their value over and over again.

Of the Irish recruits, but little need be said. Mostly drawn from the class of labourers, they took their tone from the old soldiers (to whom they were often related), and though comparatively slow in learning, they eventually became thoroughly efficient and reliable soldiers.

There was, however, among the men of most of the battalions, another element which calls for more detailed consideration. Except among old soldiers and in Belfast, recruiting in Ireland in August, 1914, was not as satisfactory as it was in England, and in consequence, Lord Kitchener decided early in September to transfer a number of the recruits for whom no room could be found in English regiments to fill up the ranks of the 10th Division. The fact that this was done gave rise, at a later date, to some controversy, and it was even stated that the 10th Division was Irish only in name. This was a distinct exaggeration, for when these "Englishmen" joined their battalions, it was found that a large proportion of them were Roman Catholics, rejoicing in such names as Dillon, Doyle, and Kelly, the sons or grandsons of Irishmen who had settled in England.

It is not easy to make an accurate estimate, but I should be disposed to say that in the infantry of the division 90 *per cent*, of the officers and 70 *per cent*, of the men were either Irish or of Irish extraction. Of course, the 10th Hampshire Regiment is not included in these calculations. It may be remarked that there has never, in past history, been such a thing as a purely and exclusively Irish (or Scotch) battalion. This point is emphasised by Professor Oman, the historian of the Peninsular War, who states:

In the Peninsular Army the system of territorial names prevailed for nearly all the regiments, but in most cases the territorial designation had no very close relation with the actual *provenance* of the men. There were a certain number of regiments that were practically national, *i.e.*, most of the Highland battalions, and nearly all of the Irish ones were very predominantly Highland and Irish as to their rank and file: but even in the 79th or the 88th there was a certain sprinkling of English recruits. (*Wellington's Army*.)

Before leaving this subject it should be noted that the Englishmen who were drafted to the division in this manner became imbued with the utmost loyalty to their battalions, and wore the shamrock on St. Patrick's Day with much greater enthusiasm than the born Irishmen. They would have been the first to resent the statement that the regiments they were so proud to belong to had no right to claim their share in the glory which they achieved.

At first, however, they created a somewhat difficult problem for their officers. They had enlisted purely from patriotic motives, and were inclined to dislike the delay in getting to grips with the Germans; and being, for the most part, strong Trades Unionists, with acute suspicion of any non-elected authority, they were disposed to resent the restraints of discipline, and found it hard to place complete confidence in their officers. They also felt the alteration in their incomes very keenly. Many of them, before enlistment, had been miners earning from two to three pounds a week, and the drop from this to seven shillings, or in the case of married men 3s. 6d., came very hard. The deduction for their wives was particularly unwelcome, not because they grudged the money, but because when they enlisted they had not been told that this stoppage was compulsory, and so they considered that they had been taken advantage of.

However, they had plenty of sense, and soon began to realise the necessity of discipline, and understood that their officers, instead of being mercenary tyrants, spent hours in the Company Office at the end of a long day's work trying to rectify such grievances as non-payment of separation allowance. Regimental games helped them to feel at home. Some of them soon became lance-corporals, and before Christmas they had all settled down into smart, intelligent and willing soldiers. One English habit, however, never deserted them: they were unable to break themselves of grumbling about their food.

The division contained one other element to which allusion must be made. In the middle of August, Mr. F. H. Browning, President of the Irish Rugby Football Union, issued an appeal to the young professional men of Dublin, which resulted in the formation of "D" Company of the 7th Royal Dublin Fusiliers. This was what is known as a "Pals" Company, consisting of young men of the upper and middle classes, including among them barristers, solicitors, and engineers. Many of them obtained commissions, but the tone of the company remained, and I know of at least one barrister who had served with the Imperial Yeomanry in South Africa, who for over eighteen months refused to take a commission because it would involve leaving his friends. The preservation of rigid military discipline among men who were the equals of their officers in social position was not easy, but the breeding and education of the "Pals" justified the high hopes that had been formed of them when their regiment was bitterly tested at Suvla.

The Royal Artillery, Royal Engineers, Army Service Corps, and the Royal Army Medical Corps recruits who came to the division were, for the most part, English or Scotch, since no distinctively Irish units of those branches of the service exist. Generally speaking, they were men of a similar class to the English recruits who were drafted into the infantry.

A detailed description of the training of the division would be monotonous and uninteresting even to those who took part in it, but a brief summary may be given. The points of concentration first selected were Dublin and the Curragh, the 30th Brigade being at the latter place. At the beginning of September, the 29th Brigade were transferred to Fermoy and Kilworth, but the barracks in the South of Ireland being required for the 16th (Irish) Division, two battalions returned to Dublin, the 6th Leinsters went to Birr, and the 5th Royal Irish to Longford. The latter battalion soon became pioneers and were replaced by the 10th Hampshires, who were stationed at Mullingar. The 54th Brigade, Royal Field Artillery, were at Dundalk, and the remainder of the artillery at Newbridge and Kildare. The Engineers, Cyclists, and Army Service Corps trained at the Curragh, the Signal Company at Carlow, and the Royal Army Medical Corps at Limerick.

Naturally, the War Office were not prepared for the improvisation of units on such a large scale, and at first there was a considerable deficiency in arms, uniform, and equipment. Irish depots, however, were not quite so overwhelmed as the English ones, and most recruits arrived from them in khaki, although minor articles of kit, such as combs and tooth-brushes were often missing. The English recruits on the other hand, joined their battalions in civilian clothes, and were not properly fitted out till the middle of October. The Royal Army Medical Corps at Limerick also had to wait some time for their uniform.

The infantry soon obtained rifles (of different marks, it is true) and bayonets, but the gunners were greatly handicapped by the fact that the bulk of their preliminary training had to be done with very few horses and hardly any guns. Deficiencies were supplied by models, dummies, and good will; and considering the drawbacks, wonderful progress was made. Another article of which there was a shortage was great-coats, and in the inclement days of November and December their absence would have been severely felt. Fortunately, the War Office cast aside convention and bought and issued large quantities of ready-made civilian overcoats of the type generally described as "Gents' Fancy Cheviots." Remarkable though they were in appearance, these garments were much better than nothing at all, and in January the warmer and more durable regulation garments were issued. The men also suffered a good deal of hardship at first from having only one suit of khaki apiece, for when wet through they were unable to change, but they recognised that this discomfort could not be instantly remedied, and accepted it cheerfully.

Until the end of 1914, the bulk of the work done by the Infantry consisted of elementary drill, platoon and company training and lectures, with a route march once or twice a week. A recruits' musketry course was also fired. Plenty of night operations were carried out, two evenings a week as a rule being devoted to this form of work. The six battalions in Dublin were somewhat handicapped by lack of training ground, as the Phoenix Park became very congested. This deficiency was later remedied to a certain extent by certain landowners who allowed troops to manoeuvre in their demesnes; but considerations of distance and lack of transport made this concession less valuable than it would have been had it been possible to disregard the men's dinner hour.

Side by side with this strenuous work the education of the officers and N.C.O.'s was carried on. The juniors had everything to learn, and little by little the news that filtered through from France convinced the seniors that many long-cherished theories would have to be reconsidered. It gradually became clear that the experience of South Africa and Manchuria had not fully enlightened us as to the power of modern heavy artillery and high explosives, and that many established tactical methods would have to be varied. We learnt to dig trenches behind the crest of a hill instead of on the top of it; to seek for cover from observation rather than a good field of fire; to dread damp trenches more than hostile bullets. We began, too, to hear rumours of a return to mediaeval methods of warfare and became curious as to steel helmets and hand grenades.

Had these been the only rumours that we heard, we should have counted ourselves fortunate. Unhappily, however, in modern war there is nothing so persistent as the absolutely unfounded rumour, and in K. 1 they raged like a pestilence. We were all eager to get the training finished and settle to real work, and our hope's gave rise to the most fantastic collection of legends. The most prevalent one, of course, was that we were going to France in ten days' time, usually assisted by the corroborative detail that our billets had already been prepared, but this was run close by the equally confident assertion on the authority of a clerk in the Brigade Office, "that we were destined for Egypt in a week." It is to be hoped that after the war, some folk-lore expert will investigate legends of the New Armies. If he does so, he will be interested to find that France and Egypt were almost the only two seats of war which the division as a whole never visited.

In the NewYear, battalion training began, carried out on the occasional bright days that redeemed an abominable winter. At the beginning of February it was proposed to start brigade training, and in order to enable the 29th Brigade to concentrate for this purpose, various changes of station were necessary. Accordingly, the whole 29th Brigade moved to the Curragh, where one battalion was accommodated in barracks and the other three in huts. In order to allow this move to be carried out the 7th Royal Dublin Fusiliers, the Reserve Park Army Service Corps and the Divisional Cyclist Company were transferred to Dublin where they were quartered in the Royal Barracks.

Brigade field days, brigade route marches and brigade night operations were the order of the day throughout February, and a second course of musketry was also fired. Early in March the divisional commander decided to employ the troops at the Curragh in a series of combined operations. For this purpose he could dispose of two infantry brigades (less one battalion), three brigades of Royal Field Artillery, the heavy battery (which joined the division from Woolwich about this time), three field companies of Royal Engineers, while on special occasions the divisional Signal Company were brought over from Carlow and the cyclists from Dublin. He could also obtain the assistance of the two reserve regiments of cavalry which were stationed at the Curragh.

Though we criticised them bitterly at the time, these Curragh field-days were among the pleasantest of the division's experiences. By this time the battalions had obtained a corporate existence and it was exhilarating to march out in the morning, one of eight hundred men, and feel that one's own work had a definite part in the creation of a disciplined whole. The different units had obtained (at their own expense) drums and fifes, and some of them had pipes as well. As we followed the music down the wet winding roads round Kilcullen or the Chair of Kildare, we gained a recollection of the hedges on each side bursting into leaf, and the grey clouds hanging overhead, that was to linger with us during many hot and anxious days.

As a rule, these combined operations took place twice in the week. For the rest of the time ordinary work was continued, while on the 16th of April, Sir B. Mahon held a ceremonial inspection of the units of the division which were stationed at the Curragh, Newbridge and Kildare. The infantry marched past in "Battalion Mass," and the artillery in "Line Close interval." At this time, too, company commanders began to mourn the loss of many of their best men who became specialists. As mules, Vickers guns, signalling equipment, etc., were received, more and more men were withdrawn from the companies to serve with the regimental transport, the machine-gun section, or the signallers. The drain due to this cause was so great that the company commander seldom saw all the men who were nominally under his command except on pay-day.

While this process was going on the weaklings were being weeded out. A stringent medical examination removed all those who were considered too old or too infirm to stand the strain of active service, and they were sent to the reserve battalions of their unit. Men of bad character, who were leading young soldiers astray, or who, by reason of their dishonesty, were a nuisance in the barrack-room, were discharged as unlikely to become efficient soldiers.

But on the whole there was not much crime in the division. A certain amount of drunkenness was inevitable, but the principal military offence committed was that of absence without leave. This was not unnatural under the circumstances. Men who had not fully realised the restraints of discipline, and had been unable to cut themselves completely adrift from their civilian life were naturally anxious to return home from time to time. If they could not obtain leave, they went without it; when they got it, they often overstaffed it, but their conduct was not without excuse. One man who had overstayed his pass by a week, said in extenuation, "When I got home, my wife said she could get no one to plant the land for her, and I just had to stay until I had the garden planted with potatoes." And there is no doubt that in most cases of absence the relations of the absentee were responsible for it. It was not easy for men who had been civilians four months before to realise the seriousness of their offence while they saw the division, as they thought, marking time, and knew that their homes were within reach, and officers were relieved when at the end of April units received orders to hold themselves in readiness to move to a point of concentration near Aldershot.

This point of concentration proved to be Basingstoke, and by the end of the first week in May the whole division was assembled there. As we journeyed we read how the 29th Division had charged through the waves and the wire, and effected its landing at Cape Helles, and how against overwhelming odds the Australians and New Zealanders had won a foothold at Gaba Tepe. At that time, however, our thoughts were fixed on France.

At Basingstoke we were inspected and watched at work by the staff of the Aldershot Training Centre, and were found wanting in some respects. In particular, we were unduly ignorant of the art and mystery of bombing, and many hot afternoons were spent in a labyrinth of trenches which had been dug in Lord Curzon's park at Hackwood, propelling a jam tin weighted with stones across a couple of intervening traverses. Bayonet-fighting, too, was much practised, and the machine-gun detachments and snipers each went to Bordon for a special course. In addition, each brigade in turn marched to Aldershot, and spent a couple of days on the Ash Ranges doing a refresher course of musketry.

The most salient feature, however, of the Basingstoke period of training was the divisional marches. Every week the whole division, transport, ambulances and all, would leave camp. The first day would be occupied by a march, and at night the troops either billeted or bivouacked. On the next day there were operations: sometimes another New Army division acted as enemy, sometimes the foe was represented by the cyclists, and the pioneer battalion. As night fell, the men bivouacked on the ground they were supposed to have won, occasionally being disturbed by a night attack. On the third day we marched home to a tent, which seemed spacious and luxurious after two nights in the open. These operations were of great value to the staff, and also to the

BASINGSTOKE. A HALT

MUSKETRY AT DOLLY MOUNT

transport, who learned from them how difficulties which appeared insignificant on paper became of paramount importance in practice. The individual officer or man, on the other hand, gained but little military experience, since as a rule the whole time was occupied by long hot dusty marches between the choking overhanging hedges of a stony Hampshire lane.

What was valuable, however, was the lesson learnt when the march was over. A man's comfort usually depended on his own ingenuity, and unless he was able to make a weatherproof shelter from his ground sheet and blanket he was by no means unlikely to spend a wet night. The cooks, too, discovered that a fire in the open required humouring, and all ranks began to realise that unless a man was self-sufficient, he was of little use in modern war. In barracks, the soldier leads a hard enough life, but he is eternally being looked after, and if he loses anything he is obliged to replace it at once from the grocery bar or the quartermaster's store. On service, if he loses things he has to do without them, and in Gallipoli where nothing could be obtained nearer than Mudros and everything but sheer necessities had to be fetched from Alexandria or Malta, the ingrained carelessness of the soldier meant a considerable amount of unnecessary hardships. It would be too much to say that these marches and bivouacs eradicated this carelessness, but they did, at any rate, impress on the more thoughtful some of the difficulties to be encountered in the future.

The monotony of training was broken on the 28th of May when His Majesty the King visited and inspected the division. The 31st Brigade was at Aldershot doing musketry, but the 29th and 30th Brigades and the divisional troops paraded in full strength in Hackwood Park. His Majesty, who was accompanied by the queen, rode along the front of each corps and then took up his position at the Saluting Point. The troops marched past: first the Infantry in a formation (Column of Platoons) which enabled each man to see his Sovereign distinctly, followed by the Field Ambulances, the squadron of South Irish Horse, and the Artillery, Engineers and Army Service Corps. On the following day, His Majesty inspected the 31st Brigade as they were marching back from Aldershot to Basingstoke.

This inspection was followed by another one, as Field-Marshal Lord Kitchener, who had been unable to accompany His Majesty, paid the division a visit on June 1st.

It would be superfluous to describe both these inspections, since the same ceremonial was adopted at each, and since the 31st Brigade was absent on the 28th May, an account of the parade for Lord Kitchener may stand for both occasions. The inspection took place in an open space in Hackwood Park, the infantry being drawn up, one brigade facing the other two on the crest of a ridge, while the mounted troops in an adjoining field were assembled on a slope running down to a small stream. The scene was typically English; here and there a line of white chalk showed where a trench had broken the smooth green turf, and all around, copses and clumps of ancient trees, in the full beauty of their fresh foliage, spoke of a land untouched for centuries by the stern hand of war. Soon very different sights were to meet the eyes of the men of the 10th Division, and at Mudros, and on the sun-baked Peninsula, many thought longingly of soft Hampshire grass and the shade of mighty beeches.

Though the sun shone at intervals, yet there was a chill bite in the wind, and the troops who had begun to take up their positions at 10 o'clock were relieved when at noon the field-marshal's cortege trotted on to the review ground, and began to ride along the lines. The broad-shouldered, thick-set figure was familiar, but the face lacked the stern frown so often seen in pictures, and wore a cheerful smile. Yet he had good reason to smile. Around him were men—Hunter, Mahon, and others—who had shared his victories in the past, and before him stood the ranks of those who were destined to lend to his name imperishable glory. He, more than any other man, had drawn from their homes the officers and men who faced him in Hackwood Park, and trained and equipped them, until at last, after ten months' hard and strenuous work, they were ready to take the field. He looked on the stalwart lines, and all could see that he was pleased.

After he had passed along the ranks, he returned to the saluting point, and the march past began. The division had no brass bands, but each unit, in close column of platoons, was played past by the massed drums and fifes of its own brigade. First came the Royal Irish, swinging to the lilt of "Garry Owen," in a manner that showed that their C. O. and sergeant-major were old Guardsmen. Then followed the Hampshires, stepping out to the tune that has played the 37th past the saluting point since the days of Dettingen and Minden. Then again the bands took up the Irish strain, and the best of drum-and-fife marches, "St. Patrick's Day," crashed out for the Connaught Rangers. Then came a sadder note for the Leinsters' march is "Come Back to Erin," and one knew that many of those marching to it would never see Ireland again.

But sorrowful thoughts were banished as the quickstep of the Rifles succeeded to the yearning tune. After the Rifles had passed, the music became monotonous, since all Fusilier Regiments have the same march-past, and by the time the rear of the 31st Brigade had arrived, one's ears were somewhat weary of the refrain of the "British Grenadiers." At a rehearsal of the Inspection, the Dublin Fusiliers had endeavoured to vary the monotony by playing "St. Patrick's Day," but the fury of the Connaught Rangers, who share the right of playing this tune with the Irish Guards alone, was so intense that it was abandoned, and Munsters and Dublins, Inniskillings and Faugh-a-Ballaghs, moved past to the strains of their own march. "The British Grenadiers" is a good tune, and Fusilier regiments are not often brigaded together, so that this lack of variety is seldom noted, yet there are so many good Irish quick-steps unused that perhaps the Fusilier regiments from Ireland might be permitted to use one of them as an alternative.

After the infantry came the field ambulances, and after them the squadron of the South Irish Horse. These were followed by rank after rank of guns with the Engineers and Army Service Corps bringing up the rear. The long lines of gleaming bayonets, and the horses, guns, and wagons, passing in quick succession, formed a magnificent spectacle. Not by dragon's teeth had this armed force been raised in so short a time, but by unresting and untiring work.

As a result of these inspections the following orders were issued:—

> 10th Division Order No, 34.　　　　　　　　　1st June, 1915.
>
> Lieutenant-General Sir B. Mahon received His Majesty's command to publish a divisional order to say how pleased His Majesty was to have had an opportunity of seeing the 10th Irish Division, and how impressed he was with the appearance and physical fitness of the troops.
>
> His Majesty the King recognises that it is due to the keenness and co-operation of all ranks that the 10th Division has reached such a high standard of efficiency."
>
> The General Officer Commanding 10th Irish Division has much pleasure in informing the troops that Field-Marshal Earl Kitchener of Khartoum, the Secretary of State for War, expressed himself as highly satisfied with all he saw of the 10th Division at the inspection today."

After these two inspections the men began to hope that they would soon be on the move, but the regular routine continued, and all ranks began to get a little stale. The period of training had been filled with hard and strenuous work, and as the days of laborious and monotonous toil crept on, one felt that little was being gained by it. It is not an exaggeration to say that so far as physical fitness was concerned, the whole of the division which went as an organised whole to Gallipoli was in better condition at the end of April than when they left England. Infantry, engineers, and the Royal Army Medical Corps were all fully trained and qualified for the work they were called on to do. The transport were not, but then the transport were left behind in England. It is possible, too, that the artillery gained by the delay, but they did not accompany the division, and the two brigades that eventually landed in the Peninsula were completely detached from it. The staff certainty gained much experience from their stay at Basingstoke, but on reaching Gallipoli the division was split up in such a manner that the experience they had acquired became of little value.

Just as we were beginning to despair of ever moving, on the 27th of June the long-expected order arrived, and the division was warned to hold itself in readiness for service at the Dardanelles.

CHAPTER 2

Mudros and Mitylene

When in Lemnos we ate our fill of flesh of tall-horned oxen.
—Homer.

It will now be proper to describe the doings of the division in somewhat fuller detail. The immediate result of the warning received on June 27th, which was officially confirmed on July 1st, was to throw an enormous amount of work upon officers and N.C.O.'s. Already the gaps in our strength had been filled up by drafts drawn from the 16th (Irish) Division, and now it was necessary for the whole of the men to be re-equipped. Helmets and khaki drill clothing had to be fitted, much of the latter requiring alteration, while the adjusting of *pagris* to helmets occupied much attention, and caused the advice and assistance of men who had served in India to be greatly in demand. At the same time new English-made belts and accoutrements were issued, the American leather equipment, which had been given out in March and had worn very badly, being withdrawn.

We had gained one advantage from the numerous false alarms that rumour had sprung upon us, the men's field pay-books and field conduct-sheets were completely filled in and ready. This turned out to be extremely fortunate, as the company officers, sergeant-majors, and platoon sergeants found that the time at their disposal was so fully occupied that they would have had little leisure left for office work. The pay lists were closed and balanced, and sent with the cash-books to the regimental paymaster; any other documents which had not already been sent to the officer in charge of records were consigned to him, and at last we felt we were ready.

One symptom of the conditions under which we were going to fight was to be found in the fact that we lost some of our comrades.

The Heavy Battery and the squadron of the South Irish Horse were transferred to other divisions destined for France, while the transport, both divisional and regimental, was ordered to stand fast at Basingstoke. Worse than this, all regimental officers' chargers were to be handed over to the Remount Department. This indication that we were intended for a walking campaign caused considerable dismay to some machine-gun officers, who had invested in imposing and tight-fitting field boots, and were not certain whether they would be pleasant to march in. As for the men of the machine-gun detachments, their feelings were beyond expression. The knowledge that gun, tripod, and belts would have to be carried everywhere by them in a tropical climate deprived them of words. However, they were too delighted to be on the move at last to grumble for long.

In the week beginning July 5th the departure began. The trains left at night, and battalions would awake in the morning to find tents previously occupied by their neighbours empty. The weather had changed to cold showers, and the men marching through the night to the station had reason to be thankful that their drill clothing was packed away in their kit-bags, and that they were wearing ordinary khaki serge. The helmets, however, were found to keep off rain well. Units were so subdivided for entraining purposes that there was little ceremony and less music at the departure. The men paraded in the dark, marched through the empty echoing streets of the silent town, sometimes singing, but more often thoughtful. The memory of recent farewells, the complete uncertainty of the future, the risks that lay before us, alike induced a mood that if not gloomy was certainly not hilarious. The cheerful songs of the early training period were silent, and when a few voices broke the silence, the tune that they chose was "God Save Ireland." We were resolved that Ireland should not be ashamed of us, but we were beginning to realise that our task would be a stiff one.

The composition of the division was as follows:—

Divisional Staff.

G.O.C.: Lieut.-General Sir B. T. Mahon, K.CV.O., C.B., D.S.O.
Aide-de-Camp: Capt. the Marquis of Headfort (late 1st Life Guards).
General Staff Officer, 1st Grade: Lieut.-Col. J. G. King-King, D.S.O., Reserve of Officers (late the Queen's).
General Staff Officer, 2nd Grade: Major G. E. Leman, North

Staffordshire Regiment.
General Staff Officer, 3rd Grade: Captain D, J. C. K. Bernard, The Rifle Brigade.
A.A. and Q.M.G.: Col. D. Sapte, Reserve of Officers (late Northumberland Fusiliers).
D.A.A. and Q.M.G.: Major C. E. Hollins, Lincolnshire Regiment.
D.A.Q.M.G.1: Major W. M. Royston-Piggott, Army Service Corps.
D.A.D.O.S.: Major S. R. King, A.O.D.
A.P.M.: Lieutenant Viscount Powerscourt, M.V.O., Irish Guards, S.R.
A.D.M.S.: Lieut.-Col. H. D. Rowan, Royal Army Medical Corps.
D.A.D.M.S.: Major C.W. Holden, Royal Army Medical Corps.

29th Brigade.

G.O.C.: Brigadier-General R.J. Cooper, C.V.O. Brigade Major: Capt. A. H. McCleverty, 2nd Rajput Light Infantry.
Staff Captain: Capt. G.Nugent, Royal Irish Rifles.
Consisting of:—
10th Hampshire Regiment, commanded by Lieut. -Col. W. D. Bewsher.
6th Royal Irish Rifles, commanded by Lieut. Col. E. C. Bradford.
5th Connaught Rangers, commanded by Lieut.-Col. H. F. N. Jourdain.
6th Leinster Regiment, commanded by Lieut.-Col. J. Craske, D.S.O.

30th Brigade.

G.O.C.: Brigadier-General L. L. Nicol.
Brigade Major: Major E. C. Alexander, D.S.O.,
55th Rifles, Indian Army. Staff Captain: Capt. H. T. Goodland, Royal Munster Fusiliers.
Consisting of:—
6th Royal Munster Fusiliers, commanded by Lieut.-Col. V. T. Worship, D.S.O.
7th Royal Munster Fusiliers, commanded by Lieut.-Col. H. Gore.
6th Royal Dublin Fusiliers, commanded by Lieut.-Col.

P. G. A. Cox.
7th Royal Dublin Fusiliers, commanded by Lieut.-Col. G. Downing.

31st Brigade.

G.O.C.: Brigadier-General F. F. Hill, C.B.,D.S.O.
Brigade Major: Capt. W. J. N. Cooke-Collis, Royal Irish Rifles.
Staff Captain: Capt. T. J. D. Atkinson, Royal Irish Fusiliers.
Consisting of:—
    5th Royal Inniskilling Fusiliers, commanded by Lieut.-Col. A. S. Vanrenen.
    6th Royal Inniskilling Fusiliers, commanded by Lieut.-Col. H. M. Cliffe.
    5th Royal Irish Fusiliers, commanded by Lieut.-Col. M. J. W. Pike.
    6th Royal Irish Fusiliers, commanded by Lieut.-Col. F. A. Greer.

Divisional Troops.

5th Royal Irish Regiment (Pioneers) commanded by Lieut.-Col. The Earl of Granard, K.P.

Divisional Artillery.

Brigadier-General, R.A.: Brigadier-General G. S. Duffus.
Brigade Major: Capt. F. W. Barron, R.A.
Staff Captain: Captain Sir G. Beaumont.
Consisting of:—
    54th Brigade Royal Field Artillery, commanded by Lieut.-Col. J. F. Cadell.
    55th Royal Field Artillery, commanded by Lieut.-Col. H. R. Peck.
    56th Brigade Royal Field Artillery, commanded by Brevet-Col. J. H. Jellett.
    The 57th (Howitzer) Brigade, R.F.A., remained in England.

Royal Engineers.

Commanding Officer, Royal Engineers: Lieut.-Col. F. K. Fair.
Consisting of:—
    65th Field Company, R.E.
    66th   *ditto*
    85th   *ditto*

10th Signal Company, commanded by Capt. L. H. Smithers.

Royal Army Medical Corps.

30th Field Ambulance, commanded by Lieut.-Col. P. MacKessack.

31st Field Ambulance, commanded by Lieut.-Col. D. D. Shanahan.

32nd Field Ambulance, commanded by Lieut.-Col. T. C. Lauder.

10th Divisional Cyclist Corps, commanded by Capt. B. S. James.

There is one particular in which the British Army may fairly claim to be superior to any force in the world, and that is in embarkation. Years of oversea expeditions, culminating in the South African War, have given us abundant experience in this class of work, and the fact that even in a newly formed unit like the 10th Division every battalion contained at least one officer who had taken a draft to India, helped to make things run smoothly. The voyage itself was uneventful. For the most part the troopships employed were Atlantic liners, and the accommodation and food provided for officers might be called luxurious. There were, however, two flies in the ointment. The architect of the boats had designed them rather for a North Atlantic winter than for summer in the Mediterranean, and the fact that at night every aperture had to be tightly closed for fear lest a gleam of light might attract an enemy submarine, made sleep difficult.

The men, who were closely packed, found it impossible in their berths down below, and the officer of the watch was obliged to pick his way among hundreds of prostrate forms as he went from one end of the deck to the other. The second grievance was lack of deck space, which precluded anything in the shape of violent exercise. Attempts at physical drill were made wherever there was an inch of spare room, and for the rest lectures and boat drill whiled away the tedium of the day. Almost the only soldiers on board with a definite occupation were the machine gunners perched with their guns on the highest available points, and keeping a keen look-out for periscopes. Responsibility also fell upon the officer of the watch, who was obliged to make a tour of the ship, looking out for unauthorised smoking and unscreened lights every hour, and reporting "All correct" to the ship's officer on the bridge. For the rest, the foreseeing ones who had provided themselves with literature read; officers smoked and played bridge; men smoked, played "House" and dozed; but through all the lethargy and laziness there ran a suppressed undercurrent of suspense and excitement.

The bulk of the transports conveying the division called at Malta and Alexandria, on their way from Devonport to Mudros, but one gigantic Cunarder, having on board Divisional Headquarters, 30th Brigade Headquarters, the 6th Leinster Regiment, 6th and 7th Royal Munster Fusiliers, and detachments of the 5th Royal Irish Regiment (Pioneers), and 5th The Connaught Rangers, sailed direct from Liverpool to Mudros, and cast anchor there on July 16th. These troops were the first of the division to reach the advanced base of the Dardanelles operations, and it was with eager curiosity that they looked at the novel scene. They were in a land-locked harbour, which from the contour of the hills surrounding it might have been a bay on the Connemara coast had not land and sea been so very different in colour. Soft and brilliant as the lights and tints of an Irish landscape are, nothing in Ireland ever resembled the deep but sparkling blue of the water, and the tawny slopes of the hills of Lemnos. Northward, at the end of the harbour, the store-ships and water-boats lay at anchor; midway were the transports, and near the entrance the French and British warships.

On the eastern shore dust coloured tents told of the presence of hospitals; and to the west, lines of huddled bivouacs indicated some concentration of newly-arrived troops. The heart of the place, from which every nerve and pulse throbbed, was a big, grey, single-funnelled liner, anchored near the eastern shore. Here were the headquarters of the Inspector-General of Communications, and the Principal Naval Transport Officer; here the impecunious sought the Field Cashier; and the greedy endeavoured (unsuccessfully, unless they had friends aboard) to obtain a civilised meal. Next to her a big transport acted as Ordnance Store, and issued indiscriminately grenades and gum-boots, socks and shrapnel. At this time, no ferries had been instituted, and communication with these ships, though essential, was not easy. If you were a person of importance, a launch was sent for you; if, as was more likely, you were not, you chartered a Greek boat, and did your best to persuade the pirate in charge of it to wait while you transacted your business on board.

We had ample time to appreciate this factor in the situation as it was three days before we disembarked. During that time we succeeded in learning a little about the conditions of warfare in what we began to call "the Peninsula." Part of the 29th Division, which by its conduct in the first landing had won itself the title of "Incomparable," was back at Mudros resting, and many of its officers came on board to look for friends. Thus we learned from men who had been in Gallipoli since they had struggled through the surf and the wire on April 24th the truth as to the nature of the fighting there. They taught us much by their words, but even more by their appearance; for though fit, they were thin and worn, and their eyes carried a weary look that told of the strain that they had been through. For the first time we began to realise that strong nerves were a great asset in war.

At last the order for disembarkation came, and a string of pinnaces, towed by steam launches from the battleships, conveyed the men ashore. Kits followed in lighters, and wise officers seized the opportunity to add to their mess stores as much stuff as the purser of the transport would let them have. It was our last contact with civilisation.

On the beach there was a considerable amount of confusion. The western side of the harbour had only recently been taken into use by troops, and though piers had been made, roads were as yet nonexistent. Lighters were discharging kit and stores at half-a-dozen different points, and the prudent officer took steps to mount a guard wherever he saw any of his stuff. In war, primitive conditions rule, and it is injudicious to place too much confidence in the honesty of your neighbours.

At last the over-worked staff were able to disentangle the different units, and allot them their respective areas, and the nucleus of the division found itself installed in the crest of a ridge running northward, with the harbour on the east, and a shallow lagoon on the west. Across the lagoon lay a white-washed Greek village, surrounded by shady trees, in which divisional headquarters were established, and behind this rose the steep hills that divided Mudros from Castro, the capital of Lemnos. Further south was another village with a church; otherwise the only features of the landscape were a ruined tower and half-a-dozen windmills. Except at divisional headquarters there was not a tree to be seen. The ground was a mass of stones. Connaught is stony, but there the stones are of decent size. In Mudros, they were so small and so numerous that it took an hour to clear a space big enough for a bed. Between the stones were thistles and stubble, and here and there a prickly blue flower. In the distance one or two patches of tillage shone green, but except for these everything was dusty, parched and barren. On the whole an unattractive prospect.

However, it was necessary to make the best of it, and soon the bivouacs were up, though their construction was made more difficult by the complete absence of wood of any kind. The men had been instructed to supplement the blanket, which they had brought from England, by another taken from the ship's stores, and the hillside soon presented to the eye an endless repetition of the word "Cunard" in red letters. Officers soon found it impossible to obtain either shelter, tables, or seats sufficient for a battalion mess, and companies began to mess by themselves. Few parades could be held, for there were very few lorries and no animals at all in Mudros West, so that practically everything required by the troops had to be carried up from the beach by hand. Most of the camps were nearly a mile from the Supply Depot, so that each fatigue entailed a two-mile march, and by the time that the men had carried out a ration fatigue, a wood fatigue, and two water fatigues, it was hard to ask them to do much more. A few short route marches were performed, but most commanding officers were reluctant to impose on the men harder tasks than those absolutely necessary before they became acclimatised.

Already we were beginning to make the acquaintance of four of the Gallipoli plagues—dust, flies, thirst and enteritis. Our situation on the spur was exposed to a gentle breeze from the north. At first we rejoiced at this, thinking it would keep away flies and make things cooler; but soon we realised that what we gained in this respect we lost in dust. From the sandy beach, from the trampled tracks leading to the supply depots, from the bivouacs to windward, it swept down on us, till eyes stung and food was masked with it. It became intensified when a fatigue party or, worst of all, a lorry, swept past, and the principal problem confronting a mess-president was to place the mess and kitchen where they got least of it.

The flies were indescribable. For a day or v two they seemed comparatively rare, and we hoped that we were going to escape from them; but some instinct drew them to us, and at the end of a week they swarmed. All food was instantly covered with them, and sleep between sunrise and sunset was impossible except for a few who had provided themselves with mosquito nets. Not only did they cause irritation, but infection. There appeared to be a shortage of disinfectants, and it was impossible either to check their multiplication, or to prevent them from transmitting disease. They had, however, one negative merit: they neither bit nor stung. If instead of the common housefly we had been afflicted with midges or mosquitoes, our lot would have

SARI BAIR

MUDROS. THE AUTHOR'S BIVOUAC
(In the background is the officers mess)

been infinitely worse.

The third plague was thirst. In July, in the Eastern Mediterranean, the sun is almost vertical; and to men in bivouac whose only shelter is a thin waterproof sheet or blanket rigged up on a couple of sticks, it causes tortures of thirst. All day long one sweats, and one's system yearns for drink to take the place of the moisture one is losing. Unfortunately, Lemnos is a badly-watered island, and July was the driest season of the year. All the wells in the villages were needed by the Greek inhabitants: and though more were dug, many of them ran dry, and the water in those that held it was brackish and unsuitable for drinking. The bulk of the drinking-water used by the troops was brought by boat from Port Said and Alexandria, and not only was it lukewarm and tasteless, but the supply was strictly limited. The allowance per man was one gallon per day; and though on the surface this appears liberal, yet when it is reflected that in 1876 the consumption of water per head in London was 29 gallons,[1] it will be seen that great care had to be exercised.

Even this scanty allowance did not always reach the men intact, for the water carts of some units had not arrived, and so the whole of it had to be carried and stored in camp-kettles. In order to spare the men labour, arrangements were made by which these camp-kettles were to be carried in a motor-lorry; but on the primitive roads so much was spilt as to render the experiment futile. Even in carrying by hand, a certain amount of leakage took place. In order to control the issue of water, most of it, after the men had filled their water-bottles, was used for tea, which though refreshing, can hardly be called a cooling drink. However, Greek hawkers brought baskets of eggs, lemons, tomatoes and water melons. The last, though tasteless, were juicy and cool, and the men purchased and ate large quantities of them.

Possibly they were in part to blame for the fourth affliction that befell us in the shape of enteritis. Though not very severe, this affliction was widespread, hardly anyone being free from it. A few went sick, but for every man who reported himself to the doctor, there were ten who were doing their duty without complaining that they were indisposed. Naturally, men were reluctant to report sick just before going into action for the first time; but though they were able to carry on, yet there was a general lowering of vitality and loss of energy due to this cause, which acted as a serious handicap in the difficult days

---

1. Table in Humber's *Water Supply of Cities and Towns* (London, 1876).— Quoted by Hodgkin in *Italy and her Invaders,*"Vol. 4.

to come.

Some thought that this epidemic was caused by the food issued to the men, and it was certainly possible to imagine a diet more suited to a tropical climate than salt bully beef and hard dry biscuits. An issue of rice was, however, sanctioned, and this boiled with currants formed the men's usual midday meal—the inevitable stew of bully, cooked in a dixie with desiccated vegetables, being reserved till the evening. The rice would have been nicer had it been cooked with milk, but the small allowance of condensed milk available was needed for tea. The bully, too, could have been made more palatable had curry-powder been forthcoming, as the officers' messes which possessed this condiment found it invaluable in disguising the peculiar flavour. Tinned meat is not suited to tropical climates. However, very few officers' messes had brought much in the way of stores, as they were uncertain whether they would be able to carry them, and all officers soon found themselves reduced to the same rations as the men, supplemented by the few eggs and tomatoes obtainable from Greek hawkers. Except for these hawkers, Mudros West had no resources for shopping at this time. All villages were out of bounds, and there was at this period no canteen—even a Greek one.

One advantage, however, the place possessed: the bathing was magnificent. From 8 a.m. to 6 p.m. (or, as we were learning to call it, from 8 to 18 o'clock), it was forbidden, as the doctors feared sunstroke; but at six in the evening the bulk of the day's work over, everyone who could leave camp trooped down to a little bay. The men undressed on the shore, the officers on a small pier which ran out far enough to make a dive possible. The water was perfect—warm enough to make it possible to stay in for an hour, and yet cool and refreshing after the heat and dust of the day. The western sun, no longer blazing fiercely overhead, made dressing and drying a pleasure; and the walk up the hill to the evening meal in the twilight made one feel that the world was not such a bad place after all. There was more cheerfulness and laughter at the bathing place than anywhere else in Mudros. Many friendships were made there, some soon to be severed by Death, and men who had begun to harp on the truth of Kipling's words:

Comfort, content, delight,
The ages slow brought gain.
They vanished in a night:
Ourselves alone remain."

.... were forced to admit that pleasure and happiness had not completely vanished from the world.

While the first comers were becoming hardened to the discomforts of the Island, the remainder of the division began to arrive. They had called at Alexandria, the base of the Mediterranean Expeditionary Force, and had left there the details allotted to the base and the bulk of their kit, wagons and water-carts. The artillery had also been ordered to remain in Egypt till further orders. The rest of the 29th Brigade, with their brigade headquarters, arrived between the 23rd and 29th of July, and they were followed by the rest of the pioneer battalion, the Field Companies of the Royal Engineers, the Signal Company, who found their motorcycles more hindrance than help on the roadless island, the cyclists, and the field ambulances. These last no sooner arrived than they were called on to receive patients, for the prevalent malady had already knocked some men out. It was a severe test, but the doctors and orderlies rose to it splendidly, providing for their patients from their own private stores when government supplies were not available.

The newly-arrived units were for the most part employed on fatigues. Everything needed on the Peninsula had to be carried up to camp: everything else, including the base kits of the units who had not called at Alexandria, had to be carried back again to the beach, where a dump was being formed inside a barbed wire fence. Officers were ordered to lighten their valises, so that they could be carried with ease by one man, and there was much cogitation as to what should be taken and what left behind. As a matter of fact, we saw so little of our valises after landing in the Peninsula that the careful distinction established between essentials (bedding, spare socks and shirt) and non-essentials (spare coat and breeches and boots) was wasted. Most of us determined to rely on our packs, which, we stuffed with a mackintosh, razor, soap, sponge, and (in my own case) a couple of books.

From this packing, however, the 29th Brigade were distracted by Brigade night operations, which took the form of an attack on a hill five miles away. The march in the dark over broken and stony ground proved very trying to the men, who had not recovered the condition which they had lost on the voyage, and many of them dropped off to sleep as soon as they halted. It became clear to us that our task was likely to be an arduous one.

Meanwhile, we began to wonder as to the whereabouts of the remainder of the division, since half of the 30th Brigade and the entire 31st had not landed. The transports conveying them had reached Mudros, but owing to the shortage of water it had been decided not to land them there, but to send them to Mitylene. The fact that it was found impossible to concentrate three divisions at Mudros simultaneously, illustrates the enormous increase that has taken place in the numbers employed in modern war. The most famous military expedition of ancient history had its rendezvous and base at Lemnos before it proceeded to attack Troy, and it would appear probable that Mudros Bay, the largest and best harbour on the island, was the one used by the fleet of Agamemnon.

There seems no reason to suppose that the water supply there has diminished, and it is certain that as the time needed for the voyage was longer, the sailing ships and oared galleys in which the Greek host made their way to the Trojan plain, must have been furnished with a copious supply of drinking water before they set sail. Homer does not record the fact that they suffered from thirst, and so it is clear that the whole army was able to subsist on what proved insufficient for less than 50,000 British soldiers. The theory of Professor Delbrück[2] that the numbers taking part in ancient battles were grossly exaggerated, seems to rest on some foundation.

In some respects the units that went to Mitylene were more fortunate than the rest of the division. They did not disembark, but remained on board the liners which had brought them out from England, thus securing good food and immunity from dust and flies. Mitylene, moreover, is far more beautiful than Mudros, and its smiling farms set in the midst of fruit trees and olive groves, were more welcome to the eye than the bare stony hills of Lemnos. There was, too, a larger and more friendly Greek population. Boats from the shore came out loaded with melons, grapes, and other varieties of fruit, so that those men who were possessed of money could get a change of diet. The worst that the 31st Brigade and 6th and 7th Dublin Fusiliers had to complain of, was dullness. Except for bathing and an occasional route march on shore, there was but little to break the monotony of shipboard life; and after a week or so in harbour, everyone was beginning to be a little "fed-up."

They disliked, too, the fact that they appeared to have lost the rest of the division, and had no information about their future movements; but they were no worse off in that respect than the rest of us. All that

---

2. *Numbers in History*, by Dr. Hans Delbrück, London University Press, 1914.

we knew was, that we were part of the 9th Corps, commanded by Lieut.-General Sir F. Stopford. We knew little of him, but we knew that he was an Irishman and were prepared to take him on trust. Battalion commanders had been issued with sets of maps which, when put together, covered the whole of the Gallipoli Peninsula and part of the Asiatic coast; but possibly this was only a "blind." Rumours, of course, were plentiful and very varied: a strong favourite was one which may conceivably have been encouraged by those in authority, and which suggested that we were intended to make a descent on Smyrna. The fact that the remainder of the division were known to be at Mitylene tended to confirm this, though there were sceptics who flouted this view and declared that we were to land near Enos in order to co-operate with the Bulgarian Army.

We had already been informed by irresponsible individuals that Bulgaria had declared war on Turkey. All these rumours undoubtedly tried the nerves of the troops, but secrecy was absolutely essential. The Island was not entirely under Allied control, a considerable part of the population were Turks, and any leakage of information would have proved fatal to the general's plans. As it was, we could see in the evening, as the ferry boats sailed out with their loads of reinforcements past the cheering battleships, bonfires kindled on the heights in order to inform the enemy on the mainland of the numbers and strength of the troops being moved. Some of us, as we watched them, recalled the beacons which signalled to Argos from the same peaks the news that Troy had fallen, and wondered if the day was soon to come when they would announce the capture of Constantinople.

In order that the movements of the division may be understood, it is now necessary to give a short summary of the plan of campaign adopted by General Ian Hamilton; but it must be borne in mind that at the time regimental officers and men knew nothing of what was intended.

The objective of the Mediterranean Expeditionary Force was to secure the high ground commanding the Narrows of the Dardanelles, and to silence or capture the Turkish batteries which barred its passage to the Fleet. In order to achieve this object. Sir Ian Hamilton had at the end of April landed the bulk of his forces at the Southern extremity of the Gallipoli Peninsula. The landing was achieved by the 29th Division, much assisted by a subsidiary landing on the Asiatic coast executed by a French Division. On the following day the French re-embarked and joined the British in Gallipoli.

At this period Sir Ian Hamilton had at his disposal at Cape Helles the 29th Division, the 43rd (East Lancashire) Territorial Division, the Royal Naval Division, and two French divisions. With these troops, he made repeated assaults on the Turkish positions, on Achi Baba, but although he succeeded in considerably enlarging the area held by him, the main Turkish defences remained intact. Reinforcements in the shape of the 52nd (Lowland) Territorial Division and the 29th Indian Brigade hardly did more than compensate for wastage due to wounds and disease; and by the beginning of July it was clear to the commander-in-chief that, in spite of the desperate courage displayed by his troops, little was to be gained by keeping on hammering at Achi Baba. If it were won it would only be at a terrific cost, and its capture would not mean decisive victory, as behind lay another and taller mountain, Kilid Bahr, which barred the way to Maidos and the Narrows.

Fortunately, Cape Helles was not the only foothold that we had gained in the Peninsula. While the landing there was taking place on April 25th the Australian and New Zealand Army Corps, under General Sir William Birdwood, had succeeded in establishing itself on shore about a mile north of Gaba Tepe, about halfway up the western coast of Gallipoli. It was a marvellous achievement for troops who had had little more than six months' training, but in physique and courage Australians and New Zealanders are unsurpassed by any soldiers in the world, and the conditions under which they were called on to fight made initiative and endurance of greater value than rigid discipline. In their first success they pressed on halfway across the Peninsula; but the ground that they occupied was too great in extent to be held by two divisions, and they were forced to fall back to the coast.

There they held an irregular semicircle drawn at a radius of about a mile from the little cove, christened in their honour *Anzac*. In parts, the Turkish lines were close to the beach, and the Australians clung to the crest with nothing but a precipice between them and the sea: elsewhere a narrow salient pointed inland into a tangle of hills and gullies, meeting with the usual fate of salients in being bombarded from both flanks. As a matter of fact, the whole Anzac position was a salient, and even the beach was regularly swept by the enemy's artillery and pestered by snipers posted on the hills to the northward. However, small as the area gained was, it provided a foothold from which Sir Ian Hamilton could launch his next attack.

The plan adopted for this was as follows:—He proposed to send to Anzac as many reinforcements as space and water would permit,

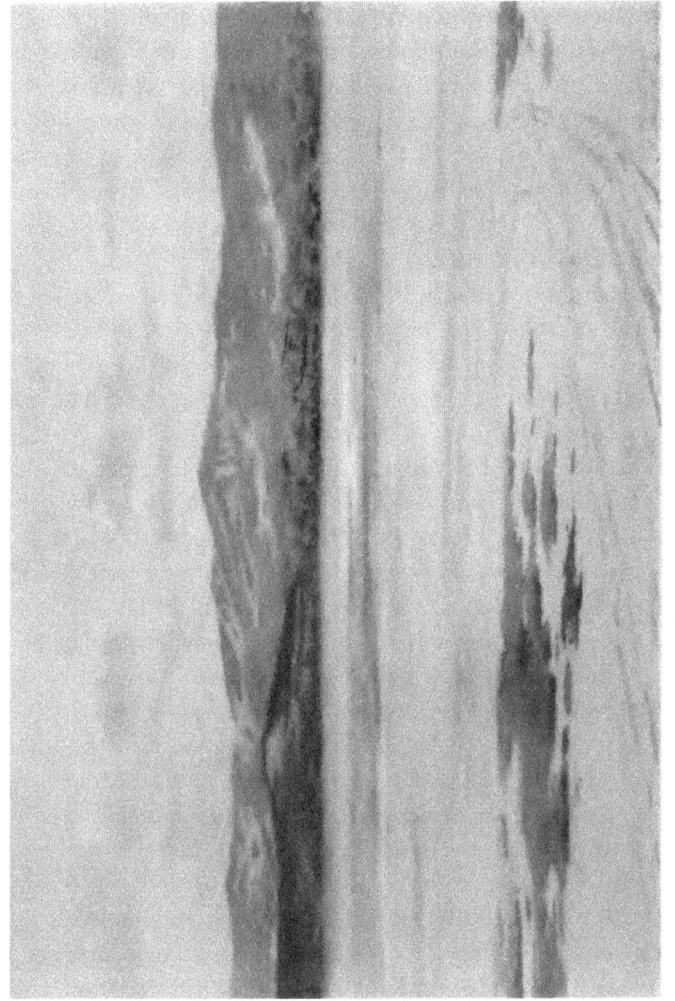

Sari Bair from Suvla

smuggling them in under cover of darkness. This done, he would take advantage of the absence of moonlight on the night of the 7th of August to break out northward from Anzac and seize the backbone of the Peninsula—the high ridge of Sari Bair. This hill ran north-east from Anzac for about four miles, and from its highest point commanded Maidos, the Narrows, and the whole of the lines of communication by which the Turks on Achi Baba were supplied. At the same time, the remainder of the reinforcements for whom there was not room at Anzac, were to effect a landing at Suvla Bay about six miles up the coast, advance in a south-easterly direction across the plain, and establish themselves on the northern end of the Sari Bair ridge, thus protecting the flank of the Anzac force. While the Turks were known to be in strength opposite Anzac, and to have reserves at Maidos, it was believed that Suvla Bay was weakly guarded.

Sir Ian Hamilton was able to dispose of the following troops to execute this operation. He had at Anzac the two Divisions of the Australian and New Zealand Army Corps, and reinforced them by the 29th Indian Infantry Brigade from Cape Helles. The reinforcements he received, and was still receiving, from England, consisted of the 10th, 11th and 13th New Army Divisions, together with the infantry of the 53rd (Welsh) and 54th (East Anglian) Territorial Divisions. The last of these Territorials were not due to reach Mudros till August 10th—three days after the commencement of operations. The whole of these reinforcements on August 1st were either still at sea, or divided between the islands of Imbros (16 miles from Gallipoli), Lemnos (60 miles) and Mitylene (120 miles away).

The commander-in-chief decided to reinforce the two divisions already serving at Anzac under Sir William Birdwood, by the Indian Brigade, the 13th Division and the 29th Brigade of the 10th Division. All these troops had to be conveyed to Anzac, and hidden there before the commencement of operations. To the landing at Suvla Bay he allotted the 11th Division supported by the 10th Division (less one brigade). The 53rd and 54th (Territorial) Divisions were retained as general reserve. The control of the operations at Anzac was entrusted to Sir W. Birdwood, who placed Major-General Sir A. Godley in charge of the attack on Sari Bair. The troops allocated to this operation were, the Australian and N.W Zealand Division, two brigades of the 13th Division, and the Indian Brigade. The Anzac position was to be held, and the feint attack on the Lone Pine position executed by the 1st Australian Division. The 29th Brigade (10th Division) and 38th Brigade (13th Division) were held in reserve. At Suvla, Sir F. Stopford was in command, and it was decided that the 11th Division which was concentrated at Imbros should execute the first landing, and that the 30th and 31st Brigades of the 10th Division should arrive from Mudros and Mitylene at dawn in support.

It will be seen how great a part in these operations was to be played by newly-formed units which had had no experience of war. The Australians, New Zealanders, and Indians had been in the Peninsula for three months, and though their ranks had been thinned yet those who remained were hardened and acclimatized. The New Army and Territorial Divisions had come straight from England, and though the 13th Division had spent ten days in the trenches at Helles, the remainder as units had never heard a shot fired in anger. It is true that they had many experienced soldiers in their ranks. The general commanding the 10th Division had seen the last warriors of Mahdism lying dead on their sheepskins around the corpse of their *Khalifa*.

One of the brigadiers had witnessed the downfall of Cetewayo's power at Ulundi; another had marched with the Guards Brigade across the desert to Tel-el-Kebir; while the third had played his part in the desperate fighting outside Suakim in 1884. Nearly all the colonels and many of the company commanders had served in the South African War, and so had a number of the senior N.C.O.s. Nevertheless, the men, as a whole, were inexperienced, and the organization of the units had not been tested under the stern conditions which prevailed in the Peninsula. To attempt the landing at Suvla with untried troops, and staffs which had not been tested on service and were not in the habit of working together, was a great adventure; but the prizes of victory were great.

One thing was certain: never did soldiers go forth to battle with sterner and more resolved determination to maintain the honour of their country and their regiment unsullied than the men of the 10th Division. It was the first trial of the New Army in a great battle. We remembered the traditions of our regiments—traditions dearly gained and dearly cherished by generations of Irish soldiers. On the colours of the Royal Irish Fusiliers blazed the glorious name of Barrossa, and the Connaught Rangers cherished the memory of Salamanca and the storming of Ciudad Rodrigo and Badajos. The Royal Irish, the oldest Irish regiment of the line, had fought at Namur and Blenheim, and there was no lack of glory won in more recent fighting for the Dublins round Ladysmith and the Inniskillings at Pieter's Hill had performed deeds never to be forgotten. Each and every regiment had had its name inscribed on the scroll of fame by the men of the past: the 10th Division were resolute that their service battalions should be worthy of those imperishable traditions.

CHAPTER 3

The 29th Brigade at Anzac

*Then lift the flag of the Last Crusade
And fill the ranks of the Last Brigade;
March on to the fields where the world's remade
And the Ancient Dreams come true.*—T. M. Kettle.

On August the 4th, as the division were bemoaning the fact that the first anniversary of the war had arrived without their having heard a shot fired in action, the 29th Brigade received orders to send three officers and approximately 180 men from each battalion to the newly formed Divisional Base Depot. These were intended to remain at Mudros and to act as a first reinforcement when needed. As a rule, the officers and men selected for this duty were those who were in bad health, as it was hoped that a few days' rest might make them better acclimatised. They were, however, highly disgusted at being left behind, not knowing that they would rejoin in less than a week. They marched over to their new camp on the afternoon of the 4th, and those who were left packed up in earnest. That evening, definite orders were received: battalions were to hold themselves in readiness to embark for the Peninsula at 9 a.m. next day, and C.O.'s were permitted to inform company commanders in confidence that the destination was Anzac.

At that time, no one had ever heard of the place, but diligent search on the numerous maps, with which units had been supplied, at last revealed Anzac Cove marked a mile north of Gaba Tepe. "The Australian place," the best informed called it. So the brigade were not destined to make a new landing. That, at any rate, was something to know, and we had to content ourselves with it, for nothing further was divulged. Subalterns and the rank-and-file did not even know what the destination was: all that they were told was that we were to embark.

Before dawn, each of the two chaplains attached to the brigade held a service. The Church of England Chaplain, the Rev. J. W. Crozier, celebrated Holy Communion in the operating tent of the 30th Field Ambulance, while Father O'Connor said Mass in the open air just outside the camp. It had been decided that the chaplains were not to come with the brigade, but were to remain with the Field Ambulance. This decision caused much regret, not only to the chaplains themselves, but to all ranks in the brigade. The Roman Catholics in particular disliked losing Father O'Connor even temporarily, for he was personally loved by the men, and in addition the Irish soldier faces death twice as cheerfully when fortified by the ministrations of his Church. Never were more reverent and solemn worshippers seen than at those two short services at Mudros, as the well remembered words were murmured, and the grey twilight shone faintly on the faces of many who were soon to die.

As the last prayers were uttered, the dawn was breaking, a grey dawn fretted with many clouds. The congregations dispersed and took up the burden of work and war again. A hasty breakfast was swallowed, valises were strapped up and carried by fatigue parties down to the pier, while the men rolled up their blankets and ground sheets and fastened them to their packs. In the deserted lines, officers were endeavouring to prevent improvident soldiers from eating or leaving behind them part of the three days' rations with which they had just been issued, while bands of predatory Greek children, who were on the look-out for anything that they could pick up, were driven away with threats and sometimes with blows. Then between eight and nine o'clock the battalions fell in, ready at last for the great adventure.

It is often difficult for the historian, writing years after the event, to ascertain the exact dress worn by those who took part in the events portrayed in his page, and so it may be well to put on record the outward aspect of the Irish Division when it left for Gallipoli. Officers and men were dressed alike in thin, sand-coloured khaki drill. Shorts were forbidden, and the men wore their trousers tucked into *putties* of the darker khaki shade that is worn in England. Except for the metal shoulder titles, there were not many marks to distinguish the different units, since England had been left at such short notice that there had been little time to procure badges of coloured cloth to sew on the big mushroom-shaped helmets. The Royal Irish Rifles had improvised a green and black patch, however, and the officers of the Hampshires had mounted a claret and yellow one. The colonel of the Leinsters had with infinite ingenuity procured ink, and stencilled an enormous black "L" on the side of each helmet.

The Connaught Rangers had ordered shamrock badges with the device "5 C.R.," but their ambition was their undoing, since these elaborate decorations took so long to make that they did not reach the Peninsula until most of those who were to wear them had been killed or invalided. The 7th Munsters were more fortunate, and went into action with a green shamrock on each arm just below the shoulder. A few Fusilier officers sported a hackle of the regimental colour, but this conspicuous ornament drew too much attention to the wearer to make it safe in Gallipoli. It mattered less what the men wore on their bodies, since it was almost impossible to see it, so heavily were they laden.

They hardly looked like fighting, and would have run a poor chance if they had had to swim. On their backs they had their greatcoats, rolled in their packs, on top of which they carried two blankets and a waterproof sheet. Their haversacks contained three days' rations; in their pouches, and festooned round their necks, were two hundred rounds of ammunition, and in addition to rifle, bayonet, entrenching implement and water-bottle, every man carried either a pick, shovel, or camp-kettle. The signallers and machine-gunners were loaded up with their technical equipment, and the effect of the whole parade, topped as it was by broad-brimmed sun-helmets, suggested strength rather than mobility.

Heavily the columns swung down to the beach, and there waited, for embarkation proved a slow process. The sun was hot, and there was no shade,' so that many of the men emptied their water-bottles before they had been there long, though fortunately it was possible to refill them at a neighbouring well. Many more bought watermelons, and the far-seeing laid in a stock of as many eggs and lemons as they could carry, to take to the Peninsula. The loads that the naval pinnaces could carry were small, and it was only after repeated journeys that at 3.30 p.m. the whole brigade embarked. The infantry were not accompanied by either the Field Company Royal Engineers, or the Field Ambulance, which were usually attached to the brigade. They were to accompany the remainder of the division.

The ships used as ferries between Mudros and the Peninsula were not large, and the men found themselves tightly packed fore and aft, with only just enough room to squat or lie on the decks. The boats had, however, seen plenty of service, and their officers and men were able to supply abundance of good advice. As soon as night fell, no lights of any kind were permitted, and consequently it was necessary for every man to remain close to his kit, or fearful confusion would follow at disembarkation. It was evident that landing was likely to be somewhat of a trial, as even the numbers of changes of station that the brigade had had at home had given them no practice in disembarking in pitch darkness. No food was obtainable on board, but there was plenty of hot water, so that the men were able to make tea in their mess-tins to wash down the bully and biscuit taken from their iron ration.

All ranks had settled down pretty comfortably by the time the boats approached Imbros, and the sun sank in a dark bank of clouds behind the Lemnos hills. A few slept, but most were too excited to do so; for as the ship approached the invisible coast the flashes of the guns became visible, and a broad searchlight beam stabbed the sky from the summit of Achi Baba. A little further up the coast a destroyer had focussed her searchlight on a path down the face of a cliff, and the round circle of light looked for all the world like a magic lantern in a village entertainment at home. On they steamed, leaving all this behind, and most dozed off, only to be awakened by the stoppage of the boat. By straining one's eyes one could see a few more ships anchored close by, but the only other sign of life was a couple of dim lights, which seemed to be high overhead. This was Anzac.

The brigade was soon, however, to discover that the Turks were vigilant, for a sniper, hearing the rattle of the anchor-chain of one of the boats, fired at a venture and wounded a man of the Leinster Regiment in the chest. A Connaught Ranger was also wounded in the hand. Clearly the warnings against lights and noise were justified. However, nothing could be done but to get the men into their equipment and wait. At last the lighters grunted up alongside and disembarkation began. The darkness was intense, and it was impossible to speak above a whisper. Men of all companies were crowded together; N.C.O.'s were quite unrecognisable, and no previous rehearsal had been possible. However, good will triumphed over these obstacles. One by one the men and their burdens were hurried into the lighters, the specialists unloaded their technical equipment, and disembarkation proceeded smoothly, if not quickly.

By the time the last ship began to unload her troops the first traces of the dawn were appearing in the sky, and the sailors on the lighters became very anxious. Not only was it undesirable that the Turks should learn that large reinforcements were being sent to Anzac, but the whole of the harbour was exposed to the fire of the enemy's guns, and if the slow-moving lighters were detected by daylight, they would have to pass through a storm of shrapnel, and would have suffered many casualties. Most of the men did not realise this, and were inclined to be deliberate in their movements, but, bustled by sailors and officers, they got ashore safely. They found themselves in the grey dawn standing on the shores of a little bay. Above them towered broken sandy slopes, at the foot of which stood a narrow strip of beach, covered with sand-bagged dug-outs and piles of forage and rations. They massed under cover of these; officers and company-sergeant-majors hurriedly checked their numbers as far as it was possible to do so, and then they were led away by New Zealand guides to a dangerous position.

A certain amount of cover had already been prepared by Australian and New Zealand digging parties, in what was very rightly known as Shrapnel Gully. Battalions followed the guides up a low ridge of sand-hills, through a short sap, and past a row of water-tanks, on to a path which wound up between two high hills. It was, as we discovered later, wider than most gullies in Gallipoli, and if anything the slopes were gentler; but it was a fair specimen of its kind. On the southern side the formation was regular; to the north a smaller gully running into it formed a sort of bay about two hundred yards in circumference. Both slopes were covered with low prickly scrub, rising at its highest to about four feet; in between were patches of sand and the dug-outs prepared for the brigade. To the south these were arranged regularly in rows, something like the galleries of the model coal-mine in the South Kensington Museum, and these were allotted to the Hampshires. Rifles, and Leinsters. On the northern slope they were arranged irregularly on the side of the small bay, and were occupied by the Connaught Rangers. Brigade headquarters were established in a sand-bagged dugout close to the road that ran down the bottom of the gully.

The men were distributed among their dugouts, and the officers sat down to take stock of the situation. We had arrived, but that was all that we knew. There was any amount of noise, but nothing to look at, and as the noise of firing seemed to come from every point of the compass, including the sea, it hardly enlightened us as to where in particular the fighting was going on. It was impossible to try and see anything, as all ranks had been warned that to go up to the top of any of the hills would probably be fatal. Standing orders, however, had been issued to company commanders, who sat down in their dug-outs to study them. No fires or lights of any kind were allowed after dark, and green wood was never to be used for fires. These were obvious precautions, as light or smoke would be certain to cause heavy shelling.

An order was also issued that every man was to wear a white band six inches wide, on each arm, and a white patch eight inches square, in the middle of his back. The materials for these had been brought with battalions from Mudros, and all ranks set to work at tailoring. It was clear from this that we were likely to take part in a night attack, and this impression was confirmed by the warning soon passed round that men were to rest as much as possible during the day. Absolutely nothing more was known, not even where the remainder of the division were. It was not until a conference of commanding officers was held at brigade headquarters at 4.30 p.m. that it was discovered that the brigade was on its own! We also received orders that the men's packs, great-coats, blankets, and waterproof sheets, together with all the officers' valises, were to be left in our present position, one N.C.O. and eight men per battalion remaining in charge of them. Units were instructed to hold themselves in readiness to move off at 1 a.m. the following morning.

Though we had been told to rest, the heat and the flies made sleep impossible. Just before leaving Mudros, a mail from home had arrived, so there were a few three-week old English papers to look at, and the rest of the time was spent in watching the Australians passing up and down the road at the bottom of the gully. They were the first Australians that we had seen, and one could not help admiring their splendid physique and the practical way in which they had adapted their costume to the conditions prevailing on the Peninsula. Some were stripped to the waist, and few wore more clothing than boots, a slouch hat, a sleeveless shirt, open at the breast, and a pair of the shortest shorts that ever occurred to the imagination of a tailor. As a result of this primitive costume, they were burnt to a rich brown by the Gallipoli sun.

They were splendid men, but quite different in physique from the European, for their sloping shoulders, loose-knit limbs, and long thin legs suggested an apparent reversion to the kangaroo type as the result of climatic conditions. Above all, they seemed absolutely devoid of nerves; three months of constant shelling, which had left its mark even on the veterans of the 29th Division, appeared to have no effect of any kind on the Australians. Clearly, they were very good men to fight side by side with.

About eleven a.m. the Turks began to shell the gully with shrapnel. Most of their shells were badly fused, and burst too high, but one "blind" shell knocked off the head of a Connaught Ranger. A man in the Rifles was also killed, and these catastrophes had the effect of inducing the men who had been watching the bursting shells with great curiosity, to take cover in their dug-outs. In spite of this precaution, each unit had several men wounded, Lieutenant Mayne of the Rifles also being hit. About noon the bombardment slackened for a time, only to be renewed about three in the afternoon and continued till dusk with redoubled intensity. Many men were grazed or bruised by spent bullets or fragments of shell, but refused to report themselves to the doctor.

Though we were unaware of it at the time, we were suffering from Turkish retaliation for the attack on Lone Pine, which was going on half-a-mile away, for the Turks knowing that Shrapnel Gully was about the only spot in the Anzac area where reserves could be sheltered from their view, were systematically searching it with their fire. Had their fusing been more accurate, and had dugouts not been prepared in readiness for the brigade, its losses would have been heavy. As it was, the Turks hardly got value for the shells they expended, and the men were encouraged by the result of their baptism of fire.

It was impossible to cook the men any dinner, and after a few mouthfuls of cold bully and lukewarm water they fell asleep in their dug-outs as soon as it became dark. At 12.30 a.m., on Saturday, the 7th, orders were received to fall in, but the order was easier to give than to execute. "Falling in" presupposes a parade ground of some sort, and on a steep slope covered with bushes and dugouts it was not easy to discover an assembly post. Even when it had been chosen by daylight, it was hard to find it in the pitch darkness, and the men scattered in many little dugouts were slow in coming together. In some cases a company commander thought that he had been left behind by his company, only to discover that it had not yet been awakened. The innate perversity of inanimate objects, too, had full play; watches stopped, electric flashlights refused to flash, and lanyards attached themselves to every bush in the neighbourhood.

Eventually, however, the men were collected, their numbers checked, and the brigade moved off in single file down the road at the bottom of the gully in the direction of the sea. The Leinsters led, followed by the Irish Rifles, Connaught Rangers and Hampshires in the order named. Progress was slow, which was fortunate, as the numerous halts made it possible for men who had been late in waking to join their units. At last, however, the head of the long column reached the bottom of Shrapnel Gully and turned northward, moving up a subsidiary gully in the direction of Russell's Top. At that time, however, we knew nothing of where we were going or what we were to do, though we could see the Great Bear hanging low over the hill tops, and knew that we were going north. The night was very dark, and only the outline of the hills against the star-lit sky, and the faint white line of the path were visible. Here and there an officer came hurrying up. "Are you the South Lancashires? Where are the 13th Division?" It was impossible to answer these queries, for we knew nothing of anybody's whereabouts, and the noise was so terrific that the words would have been inaudible.

From every hill-top came the rattle of musketry, but the dominant note in the symphony came from the guns of the monitors drawn in close to the beach at Anzac. They sounded as if they were only ten yards away, although it must have been a full mile. To this accompaniment the long line traced its way up the gully for about an hour, halting every five minutes. While doing this, three miles to the northward, the assaulting columns were working up the Aghyl and Chailak Deres to the assault of Sari Bair, but we knew nothing of this at the time. At last the order came to turn about and retrace our steps, leaving the 6th Leinster Regiment to act as support to the Australians. The remainder of the brigade slowly returned to Shrapnel Gully.

There throughout the day they waited at the side of the road, never knowing when they might be called on to move. Every staff officer who came near was cross-questioned, but they knew little more than ourselves. Rumours, of course, were manifold, and for some curious reason they all centred round a position known as Prussian Officers' Trench. Twice we heard that it had been taken, and twice that the attack on it had failed. To us it seemed as if the capture of this position was vital to our success, although as a matter of fact, it was purely a subsidiary operation. We knew nothing of the fighting at Lone Pine, we had then never heard the name of Sari Bair, we were completely ignorant that our comrades were at that moment landing at Suvla; all our interest was centred on this one name caught from a passing Australian. They were passing pretty frequently now, some on stretchers, and others limping down unattended from the fight at the head of the gully, but they were not communicative. "Pretty tough up there," was as a rule their only response to the volley of queries that came whenever a man looked strong enough to answer.

The wait lasted all day, varied by shrapnel fire. No doubt the three battalions were retained there, as the position was central and covered from view, while if the Turkish counterattacks on the recently captured Lone Pine position should be successful, their services would be badly needed. At 7 p.m., however, General Cooper was instructed to send a battalion into the Southern section of the Anzac area, to act as reserve to the first Australian brigade. No attack had been launched from this part of the defences, and it was feared that the Turks might retaliate for the attack on Sari Bair by attempting to crush Anzac from the South.

The Connaught Rangers, who were selected for this duty, reached the position allotted to them at 8.10 p.m. They detached one company to Brown's Dip, where they were employed in burying the Turks and Australians who were killed in the Lone Pine fighting. The unpleasantness of the task was increased by the fact that the position was being heavily shelled, and several men were wounded. On the following day (August 8th) the Connaught Rangers were again moved, this time to Victoria Gully, about three-quarters of a mile nearer Anzac Cove. The detached company at Brown's Dip was relieved by another from the same battalion, which carried on the duty of burial party, and also sustained a number of casualties. The rest of the battalion remained in reserve at Victoria Gully throughout the 9th of August in dugouts, which had been hastily constructed, and which they did much to improve.

By this time the battalion were becoming something of connoisseurs in the qualities of dugouts. Dugouts are of two kinds, those you dig for yourself and those you dig for somebody else. In the former case, you collect as many sand bags, pieces of corrugated iron, pit props, and other miscellaneous building materials as your ingenuity or your dishonesty can achieve, and then proceed to dig yourself an eligible residence. The depth dug is usually in inverse proportion to rank: the higher, the deeper, though to go too deep was considered to exhibit a somewhat excessive desire to be safe at all costs. The Australians had a story of an officer whom they did not like, and on whose courage they (probably unjustly) reflected. They declare that he was severely wounded, as the rope broke while he was being lowered into the dugout, and he fell the remaining eighteen feet.

The dugout that is dug for another is not so elaborate. You burrow into the vertical face of the hill until a cavity large enough to contain a man is created, and leave it for the occupant to make the best of. Before he has learnt to do this, he has probably bumped his head several times and filled his hair with earth. At the same time, however small it may be, it is unwise to forsake the burrow constructed for you by the experienced inhabitant and strike out a line for yourself. Two officers who attempted to do this were quickly disillusioned. Their first effort installed them in a cemetery, where a corpse was awaiting burial. Their second reopened a recently filled in latrine, while the third found them in the midst of buried Turks. Then they gave it up.

It is now necessary to return to the doings of the 6th Leinster Regiment, and since this battalion was detached from the 29th Brigade throughout the battle of Sari Bair, it will be simpler to give an account of all its actions in this chapter. Though it played a distinguished part in the fight, yet its deeds were performed in a separate theatre and can be understood without a detailed description of the operations elsewhere. At about 3 a.m. on August 7th, the Leinsters were detached from the 29th Brigade and allotted to the 1st Australian Division in order to act as General Reserve for the Northern sector of the old Anzac Defences.

In framing his plans, Lieut.-General Sir William Birdwood was compelled to take into account the possibility that instead of concentrating their forces at Suvla or on Sari Bair, the enemy might decide to make a desperate attack on Anzac, in the hope of breaking through there and cutting the columns operating on Sari Bair off from the sea. It would, no doubt, have been possible for us to obtain supplies and ammunition from Suvla once the landing there had been effected, but the organisation of new lines of communication must inevitably have taken time, and the position of the force would have been a critical one. Two battalions from the General Reserve were, therefore, placed at the disposal of the 1st Australian Division, and of these the 6th Leinsters was one.

The dispositions adopted were as follows: "B" Company, under Major Stannus, went to Courtney's Ridge, and "C" Company, under Major Colquhoun, to Quinn's Post. The other two companies and battalion headquarters remained at the end of Shrapnel Gully. This disposition was adhered to throughout the 7th and 8th, the detached companies earning the praise of the Australians to whom they were attached by the keenness and alacrity with which they carried out the duties that fell to their lot. Naturally, like everyone else in the Anzac area, they suffered from shrapnel and snipers, but the casualties during this period were not heavy.

At sunset on the 8th, the detached companies were withdrawn to battalion headquarters, and the whole unit was warned to hold itself in readiness to move at five minutes' notice. By this time it was clear to the higher command that little danger was to be apprehended from Turkish attacks on Anzac, while the struggle for the Sari Bair ridge was still in a doubtful state, and the presence of a fresh battalion might make the difference between victory and defeat. Accordingly the men of the Leinsters lay down formed in close column of platoons, girt with all their accoutrements and tried to slumber.

Sleep does not come easily when one is wearing full equipment and another man's boots are within an inch of one's face, while an increasing bombardment rages all round; but at Anzac men were tired enough to welcome any possibility of rest. During the night they were not disturbed by fresh orders, and at dawn there was sufficient time to cook tea and refill water-bottles. At 8 a.m. on the 9th, the battalion marched off making its way northward in single file until Number 1 Post was reached. Here there was a halt and a long wait, during which the battalion crowded up behind such shelter as was afforded by a small knoll. Water-bottles were again replenished, and the provident forethought of Colonel Craske procured a number of petrol tins filled with water, which were carried by the battalion as a reserve. After a midday meal of bully and biscuit had been eaten, the battalion received orders to proceed to the relief of the New Zealand battalions holding Rhododendron Spur. This ridge, which was an outcrop of the main Sari Bair range, had been seized by the New Zealanders at dawn on the 7th, and was still held by them.

On the way there, the Leinsters met with an experience similar to that endured by the 31st Brigade at Suvla on the morning of the 7th, for in order to reach the gully leading where they wanted to go, they were compelled to traverse 400 yards of open country, which was exposed to heavy hostile fire. Not only were snipers hidden in the scrub on the hillsides doing their worst, but the space was also covered by a machine-gun high on the slopes of the Chunuk Bair, and shrapnel was continually bursting over it.

Little spurts of dust continually rising where the bullets had struck made the prospect of crossing this area an unattractive one, but the

Leinsters doubled briskly across, half a platoon at a time, and luckily did not incur severe losses. They then entered a gully which was not much safer than the open space, as every corner was under machine-gun fire, and during half the time the men were bending double to avoid observation, and during the other half racing forward to avoid its consequences. Somewhat exhausted by this, and by the great heat, the Leinsters reached the foot of Rhododendron Ridge at three in the afternoon.

Here they remained till dusk in order to carry out the relief after dark; but while they waited the enemy's shrapnel again found them out and one officer and several men were killed. At nightfall, "A" and "D" Companies relieved the New Zealanders, the two others remaining behind the crest in support. The ridge was joined to the main chain of the Chunuk Bair ridge by a col, and in front of this the shallow trenches, which marked the furthest point gained by our advance, had been dug. They were not deep and had not been well sited, but at any rate they served to indicate the line to be held. On the right of the Leinsters the 8th Royal Welsh Fusiliers held a line extending back to the old Anzac position; while on the left, the 6th Loyal North Lancashire Regiment were in possession of the crest of the Chunuk itself.

Throughout the night the Turkish artillery kept up a continual fire, and at daybreak their counter-attack was launched. The general course of these operations will be described in greater detail in the following chapter. For the present, it suffices to say that a Turkish force, estimated at more than a division, came rolling over the crest of the Chunuk Bair against the three battalions holding it. The main force of the attack fell on the Loyal North Lancashires, and to use Sir Ian Hamilton's words, "overwhelmed them by sheer force of numbers." On their left, three companies of the Wiltshires who had only just arrived on the hill were caught in the open and annihilated. But on the right the Leinsters stood their ground.

At last the moment had arrived to which they had so anxiously looked forward. Turk and Irishman, face to face, and hand to hand, could try which was the better man. Modern warfare is so much a struggle of moles, of burrowing and creeping and hiding that it is with a thrill of joy that the soldier looks on the face of his enemy at close quarters. In spite of the odds, the two companies in the front line succeeded in checking the attack, and at the crucial moment they were reinforced by "B" and "C" Companies from the support line. It is said that the alarm was given to the latter by a New Zealander, who ran down the hill shouting, "Fix your bayonets, boys, they're coming!" and that on hearing this the men seized their weapons and rushed up the hill without waiting to put on their *putties* or jackets. It is certain that Colonel Craske led them into action with a cheer, and that their arrival was most timely. Shouting, they flung themselves into the fray, and drove the Turks back after a desperate struggle at close quarters.

It was impossible that such success could be gained without loss, but the Leinsters were fortunate in escaping more lightly than the English regiments on their left. They had, however, three subalterns killed and several officers wounded in this fight, among them Colonel Craske himself, who received a bullet wound in the arm. He was a gallant soldier, who had won the D.S.O. in South Africa, and his men long remembered the way in which he had led his battalion into action. He carried on for a time, but the wound proved serious, and he was obliged to hand over his command to Major R. G. T. Currey. Another officer of the Leinsters who was wounded in this action was Captain J. C. Parke, who was also hit in the arm. Before the War he was one of the greatest, if not the greatest, lawn tennis players in the British Isles, and had represented the United Kingdom in the Davis Cup. Now, though the injury he had received threatened to incapacitate him for his favourite game, he took misfortune with the same smiling composure with which he had been wont to confront all the chances of life.

But while the Leinsters were collecting and bandaging their wounds, on their left the soil was carpeted with dead. The main Turkish attack, after overwhelming the Wiltshires and Loyal North Lancashires, had pressed onward to try and drive the British off Rhododendron Ridge. As they came over the ridge they were full in view of our fleet, and every gun in the ships as well as the bulk of the artillery at Anzac was turned on to them. They fell by thousands, and as the few survivors struggled on, they were met with the fire of a concentrated battery of New Zealand machine-guns. Line after line fell, and those who had the good fortune to escape hastened to place themselves in safety on the further side of the ridge.

The western slope of the Chunuk became No Man's Land, and Rhododendron Ridge remained in our hands, but the price that both sides had paid was terrible. In a land of dry bushes and stunted oak and holly like Gallipoli, the great shrubs that give the ridge its name must in Spring present a feast of beauty to the eye, but they stand in the midst of a cemetery, and are but the adornments of the grave.

Around them Turk and Briton and Anzac lie side by side in glorious fellowship, in a graveyard bought at a great price and made lovely to the eye by the bounty of Nature. To the soul, the spot is made holy by the memory of what passed there and of the courage and self-sacrifice of those who lie under its sod.

The fact that we had been driven off the Chunuk made a modification of the line necessary in order to join up with the position on Rhododendron Ridge, which now marked the boundary of our gains. The Leinsters rested for a little and began to dig in on the new line in the afternoon. The work proved difficult, since whenever the working parties showed themselves the enemy opened with shrapnel, and in consequence as long as daylight lasted very little headway was made.

After dark, however, a fresh attempt was begun and "B" and "C" Companies of the Leinsters were sent out to dig themselves in. The men had had practically no sleep since the uneasy slumber snatched on the night of the 8th, and had fought a stiff action in the morning, but they worked with a will. Progress was, however, slow, as under cover of darkness the Turks were creeping forward, and soon every bush contained a sniper. For a while work went on by fits and starts, advantage being taken of every lull to make headway with the trench until heavier firing compelled the working parties to take cover.

At the end of two hours the hindrance to the work was found to be greater than could be borne. It seemed not unlikely that the annoyance was caused by a comparatively small number of snipers, so No. 9 Platoon was sent out in front of the line to drive them away, and then act as a covering party. The officer commanding this platoon (Lieutenant Barnwell) soon discovered, however, that the Turks had advanced in considerable force, and that his men were outnumbered. A grim struggle was waged in the darkness, and when the platoon at last extricated itself it left nearly half its strength killed and wounded behind it.

Work on the trench now became quite out of the question, and the Leinsters had to fight hard to hold their ground against the repeated attacks of the enemy. At last matters looked menacing and "A" and "D" Companies who had been in support were called up into the firing line. In this fighting Major Stannus who commanded "B" Company, was wounded. It was stern work, for the night was pitch dark and the tired men could see but little except the flash of the hostile rifles. Again and again a wave of shadowy figures pressed forward in close ranks only to be driven back by rifle-fire at close range and bayonet charges.

At last, as the sky grew pale with the dawn, the Turks massed for a final effort. They came on with determination, and the Leinsters, knowing that there was hardly another formed unit available as reserve in the Anzac area, resolved to meet the attack with a counter-charge. With a ringing yell the line of grey bayonets surged forward against the foe, to prove once again that to attack is not only the best defensive policy but is that best suited to the Irish temperament. The Turks faltered as the charge swept against them, and the Leinsters were at last able to take their revenge for the losses of the night. Fatigue and thirst were forgotten and men after much suffering exulted in the taste of victory at last. The pursuit became almost too eager. At one point Captain D'Arcy Irvine and Lieutenant Willington at the head of "D" Company pressed after the enemy so hotly that they were cut off and have never been heard of again. Probably they were surrounded and killed, and their bones still lie with those of many another brave fellow on the slopes of the Chunuk Bair.

All ranks acquitted themselves well in this charge, but the courage displayed by Captain Lyster who commanded "A" Company was so conspicuous as to earn for him the Military Cross. Rewards of this kind were not very freely bestowed in Gallipoli, and to have gained one in a battalion like the Leinsters, which never failed to hold the position allotted to it, was an indication that the officer who won it was a man of exceptional distinction. In addition to this honour, Colonel Craske received a C.M.G., while the whole battalion were thanked by General Godley for the good service done on this occasion.

The charge achieved its object, since the spirit of the Turks was temporarily broken and their snipers were driven back. As a result the battalion spent a quiet day on the nth. The arrangements for supplying water initiated by Colonel Craske had worked well on the whole, and though the men were often thirsty like everyone else in the Peninsula, they did not suffer so much from thirst as some other units. The petrol tins proved of great assistance, as they enabled a reservoir to be formed for each company or platoon which could be easily controlled. When the whole water supply of the unit is contained in the water-bottles of individual soldiers it becomes impossible for officers and N.C.O.'s to check the improvident use of it, and so in times of dearth a central reservoir becomes a necessity.

On the evening of the 11th, the Leinsters were relieved and marched back in the direction of the beach. They had well earned a rest, since they had been fighting hard for thirty-six hours and had been going for two days without sleep. They had, however, acquitted themselves well and were in good spirits.

Chapter 4

Sari Bair

So desperate a battle cannot be described. The Turks came on again and again, fighting magnificently, calling upon the name of God. Our men stood to it, and maintained, by many a deed of daring, the old traditions of their race. There was no flinching. They died in the ranks where they stood.—General Sir Ian Hamilton.

In order to follow the details of the Battle of Sari Bair, it is necessary to understand something of the configuration of the country north-east of Anzac. At Lone Pine and Quinn's Post the Australians had gained a footing on the southern extremity of the Sari Bair range. Thence it ran, increasing in height as it got further from the sea, for about five miles to the north-east, forming the main watershed of the Gallipoli Peninsula. From its sides started the gullies known as Deres, which were of paramount importance in the course of the fighting. In Spring they were foaming torrents, but in August they were bone-dry and formed the only paths in the wilderness by which it was possible to gain the foot of Sari Bair. The country on each side of them was covered by impassable scrub intersected by invisible precipices, but the sandy beds of the Deres afforded smooth, if not easy going.

In places they ran through deep ravines but, for the most part, their banks were from four to six feet high and lined with prickly scrub and an occasional barren olive tree. They would have been invaluable as roads, had it not been for the fact that long stretches of them were under constant fire from the Turkish machine guns on Sari Bair, and could therefore only be safely used at night. The principal gullies beginning from the North were Asmak Dere, Aghyl Dere, Chailak Dere and Sazli Beit Dere. The last of these ran down to what, on the 6th of August, was the Northern extremity of the Anzac position. Between it and Chailak Dere, a spur left the main ridge of Sari Bair and ran down towards the sea: after it came into Christian hands, this spur was christened Rhododendron Ridge and played an important part in the August fighting.

The portion of the Sari Bair range, which was joined by Rhododendron Ridge, was known as the Chunuk Bair and here the battle was to rage most fiercely. It culminated to the northward in a summit called Hill Q., and thence the range trended eastward to Koja Chemen Tepe, the culminating height of the position and the objective of the Suvla force. Halfway down the slope of the Chunuk Bair facing the Gulf of Saros, was a patch of cultivation known as The Farm. The whole of the seaward face of the Chunuk Bair was covered with prickly scrub about four feet high and cut by narrow ravines running down to the Aghyl Dere which starts just below The Farm.

On the night of August 6th General Godley had launched his attack northward from Anzac. By 1.30 a.m. on the 7th the mouths of the Chailak Dere and Aghyl Dere had been seized and a strong lodgement made on Damakjelik Bair, a detached hill between the Asm ah and Aghyl Deres. This lodgment protected the left flank of the assault on the Chunuk Bair which was then launched.

By dawn the left assaulting column had forced its way up the Aghyl Dere, and the Indian Infantry Brigade had occupied The Farm, while on the extreme left the 4th Australian Brigade had reached the Asmak Dere, and were advancing towards Koja Chemen Tepe. The advance of the New Zealanders up the Chailak Dere had been slower, but soon after 6 a.m. they had stormed the Turkish trenches on Rhododendron Ridge, and established themselves at the point where that ridge joins the Chunuk Bair. At the same time they got into touch with the Indian Brigade on their left. Preparations were made for an assault on the main Chunuk Ridge, but the troops were terribly exhausted by their night marches in an impossible country, and the arrival of Turkish reinforcements made further advance by daylight impossible. It was decided to allow the troops to rest, and attack again just before dawn on the 8th.

For this attack the New Zealanders, Australians and Indians who had taken part in the first day's fighting were reinforced by six battalions of the 13th Division. On the right the assault from Rhododendron Ridge on the Chunuk Bair was successful, and a firm footing on the crest was gained; but the centre attack was unable to advance much further than The Farm, and the attempt on Koja Chemen Tepe was unsuccessful. The general resolved to attack again under cover of darkness, and called up the two battalions of the 29th Brigade, which had not already been allotted any duty, to take part in it.

The Hampshires and Royal Irish Rifles had moved at 1 a.m. on the 8th from their bivouacs in Shrapnel Gully, to Rest Gully. This gully was situated near the southern end of the great sap which ran northward from Anzac Beach towards what was known as No. 2 Post. The cove of Anzac itself, between the headlands of Hell Spit and Ari Burnu, though often swept by Turkish fire, was concealed from the enemy's view by overhanging cliffs. To the northward, however, the beach was commanded throughout its length by the heights of the Chunuk Bair, and men moved on it by daylight at their peril. In order to facilitate movement by day, Australians and New Zealanders working by night had dug a sap wide and deep enough to hold a mule, which ran northward parallel with the sea for nearly a mile. This had acquired the name of "The Anzac Sap."

About 10 a.m. on the 8th, the Hampshires and Rifles fell in, and followed brigade headquarters along this sap in single file, until they reached its northern end at No. 2 Post. At this point General Godley had established his headquarters, and here the two battalions collected and waited for the greater part of the day. Late in the afternoon they again moved northwards, and entered the area which had just been won from the enemy. Here they came under fire from hostile snipers, but worse was to come. They had been ordered to move up the Chailak Dere, but the Turks were well aware that this was one of the few paths by which reinforcements could approach the Chunuk Bair, and were shelling its entrance persistently.

In small parties the men dashed through the barrage, and in most cases got off without heavy losses. Lieutenant Graham Martyr's platoon of the Irish Rifles, however, was unlucky, and was almost annihilated. Having passed this dangerous spot, the whole long procession moved on in Indian file up the deep bed of the Dere. Progress was slow, since the gully was half choked already with supplies and reinforcements going up to the hills, as well as with the wounded coming down. As dusk fell the two battalions bivouacked on the slopes leading down to the Gully. They did not however have much time for rest, since at 9.15 p.m. they were aroused to take part in the assault on the Chunuk Bair.

For this, three columns were being organized, the Rifles and Hampshires being allotted to the centre column, which was under the command of Brigadier-General A. H. Baldwin, who had previously commanded the 38th Brigade. Besides the two 10th Division battalions, General Baldwin had also the 6th East Lancashires and 5th Wiltshires, which belonged to the 13th Division. The column which was to move on the right of the centre column was commanded by Major-General F. E. Johnston, and consisted for the most part of New Zealanders. It was intended to operate from and extend the territory already gained on the Chunuk Bair. To the left a column under Major-General H.V. Cox, consisting of the 4th Australian Brigade, the Indian Brigade, and four battalions of the 13th Division, was to attack Hill Q. at the northern end of the Chunuk Bair.

General Baldwin's column was entrusted with the task of moving up the Chailak Dere and attacking Hill Q. from the south-west, with its flanks protected by the columns on the right and left. The intention of the commander-in-chief had been that this centre column should start from the Chailak Dere and deploy behind the line already occupied by the New Zealanders, moving thence at dawn along the crest of the Chunuk Bair to assault Hill Q. Unfortunately, however, this complicated manoeuvre miscarried, as the guides allotted to the column missed their way, with the result that the troops, after alternately marching and halting all through the night, found themselves at dawn on the 9th in the Aghyl Dere at the foot of the Chunuk. The column on the left had been more fortunate, and its head succeeded in reaching its objective, occupying the col which connects Hill Q. with the Chunuk Bair. Hardly however had the Gurkhas and South Lancashires gazed on the town of Maidos and the Dardanelles crowded with transports bringing up reinforcements for the enemy, when they were shelled off the position, which was promptly reoccupied by the Turks.

Meanwhile General Baldwin's column was closing up and getting into formation for the attack. The men went forward with splendid spirit, but the task they were called on to perform was beyond human power. Not only did the enemy's shrapnel fire redouble its force, but the whole of the left flank was enfiladed by hostile machine-guns, which almost wiped out the East Lancashires. In this advance many of the officers of the Rifles were wounded. To climb the Chunuk in broad daylight in the face of an enemy well supplied with machine-guns and possessing observation posts from which he could direct the fire of his still unsubdued artillery, was a harder feat than the storming of the breach of a hostile fortress in the Napoleonic wars, since the distance to be covered was so long and so rugged, that it was impossible to maintain the impetus of the charge. An attempt to find easier ground to the left failed, and so the Rifles and Hampshires took up their position behind the crest of a small underfeature which jutted out some three hundred yards from The Farm.

General Baldwin was accompanied to this position by General Cooper and the staff of the 29th Brigade, who, since the whole Brigade had been allotted piecemeal to different commanders, came up to assist in passing orders. At 9 a.m. a company and a half of the Hampshires under Major Pilleau were ordered to move up the slope to the right and try to get in touch with the New Zealanders of General Johnston's column. While doing so they came under heavy shrapnel fire, but succeeded in working their way up to that part of the ridge which was in the hands of the New Zealanders.

The position thus gained was maintained throughout the 9th, the Hampshires holding a line down the seaward slopes of the Chunuk Bair, and then turning almost at right angles towards the north-east along the crest of the under feature above The Farm. The Rifles prolonged this line on the left to a point where it was taken over by the two battalions of the 38th Brigade. This left flank was somewhat in the air, as the flank-guard on the Damakjelik Bair was more than a mile in rear of the line. The only protection to this flank was that afforded by the left column under General Cox, which had succeeded in occupying Hill Q. at dawn and had been driven off it. These had now withdrawn to the line of the Asmak Dere, but they were terribly exhausted. The Australians and Indians had been marching and fighting in a tropical climate for forty-eight hours without relief, while the New Army battalions had lost heavily, especially in officers.

Throughout that day Baldwin's column lay out on the face of the Chunuk Bair. Pinned to their positions by the Turkish shrapnel which hailed on them without respite, they suffered terribly from the scorching rays of the sun. Shade there was none, for the scrub was so prickly that it was impossible to crawl underneath it, while nothing short of direct cover afforded any protection from the sun vertically overhead. Water was terribly scarce; although wells had been discovered in the bed of the Aghyl Dere, it was a task of great difficulty to convey the water up to the troops, since part of the Aghyl Dere was swept by the enemy's fire. The torments of thirst were increased by the fact that the only food available for the men was salt bully beef and hard dry biscuit. It was an effort to swallow more than a few mouthfuls, and to the

GENERAL R. J. COOPER, C.V.O. COMMANDING 29TH BRIGADE

weakness caused by enteritis was added the weakness of inanition.

The casualties did not appear heavy, but they steadily mounted up, and in the course of the day each of the 29th Brigade battalions lost about a fifth of its strength. Night brought relief from the sun, but no rest, for the battalions were ordered to entrench themselves where they stood. The exhausted men were incapable of heavy labour, but a narrow shallow trench was gradually excavated. Night too gave an opportunity to send the wounded away, for after hasty dressing had been applied by battalion medical officers they had, of necessity, been obliged to await a convenient occasion for their removal. The nearest hospital was four miles away on the shore at Anzac, and a terrible burden thus fell on the stretcher-bearers, who had to carry their comrades all this distance. Every man who could limp or hobble down to the beach, walked, but the serious cases were numerous, and the battalion establishment of stretcher-bearers (which had not been fixed with such an abnormal campaign in view) found itself severely taxed. During the night the New Zealand Brigade on the right of the Hampshires, was withdrawn and relieved by part of the Wiltshires and Loyal North Lancashires, and also by the 6th Leinsters.

Dawn came, and with it the Turkish counterattack. Throughout the night their artillery had thundered unceasingly, but before daybreak it redoubled in violence. As the light grew, an enormous mass of the enemy threw itself against the battalions holding the lodgement effected by the New Zealanders on the crest of the Chunuk Bair, while further hordes moving down from the north and Hill Q. attacked Baldwin's column at The Farm. The two battalions on the crest were almost annihilated, and the ground they held was lost. Fortunately, however, as was described in the last chapter, the momentum of the attack was checked by our artillery.

The Turks moving down the crest of the Chunuk were in full view of the fleet, and the fire brought to bear on them was so terrific that their reinforcements were unable to penetrate the barrage. They pressed on against Rhododendron Ridge, but were stopped by the concentrated fire of ten New Zealand machine-guns which were placed in position by a famous Hythe musketry expert. But although for the time the danger was lessened and the Turkish losses were enormous, yet the fact that the two battalions holding the Ridge of the Chunuk had been driven back, left the right flank of the Hampshires dangerously exposed. Although its losses were very heavy, this company and a half which had been sent out to maintain connection with the ridge succeeded in holding its ground.

The remainder of the Hampshires were now up in the firing line on the right of The Farm position, but were losing very heavily. Colonel Bewsher who commanded them had been seriously wounded in the head about 6 a.m., and was resting before making his way down to the beach when a wounded sergeant-major informed him that there appeared to be no officers left unhurt. He, therefore, wounded as he was, returned to the firing line, and discovered that although there were still two captains with the detached company and a half, the remainder of the battalion had not only lost all its officers but all its company sergeant majors and quartermaster sergeants as well. One machine-gun had been put out of action by a shell, but the men were holding their ground manfully.

Meanwhile, on the left, the hostile attack developed with even greater force. Orders had been received to send the 5th Wiltshires to relieve the New Zealanders on the crest of the Chunuk, but one company had been retained as its withdrawal would have left part of the line completely unmanned. A company of the 9th Warwicks had come up to relieve the Wiltshires, but were found to be very weak. There were also on the left in addition to the Royal Irish Rifles, about 50 men, all that remained of the East Lancashires, and a few Ghurkas and Maoris belonging to the left column who had retired down the hill and joined General Baldwin.

Against these few exhausted men, less than a thousand in all, the Turks were free to throw the whole of their reserves, since by this time (dawn, Tuesday) it was clear that the advance from Suvla was not likely to get much further. They came on again and again, covered by a very heavy shrapnel fire, and again and again they were driven back. Our losses, however, were terribly heavy and they could afford to lose ten men to our one, for our last reserves (except for one battalion five miles away) were already up in the firing line. Worst of all were the casualties in officers. The dawn was misty and just as it began to grow light General Baldwin was killed. Almost at the same instant General Cooper fell, severely wounded in the lungs. Colonel Bradford of the Rifles was then the senior officer with the column, but just as he was informed that the command devolved upon him, he, too, fell seriously wounded.

In quick succession. Major Morphy, the second-in-command of the Rifles, received a bad wound in the thigh, and Major Eastwood, their adjutant, was killed. Very shortly afterwards Captain McCleverty, the brigade major, was hit by a bullet which passed through both cheeks and broke his jaw, while Major Wilford of the Rifles, on whom the command of his battalion had devolved and who had exhibited great courage and resource, sustained a severe wound in the head. Colonel Bewsher of the Hampshires, who had been wounded twice but was able to stand, then took over the command of all that was left of General Baldwin's force. The oft-repeated attacks continued, nearly all the junior officers were down, and though our thin line was never actually pierced yet in many places the enemy came so near that they fought with our men at close quarters. In an effort to repulse a rush of this kind on the left about 9 a.m. Captain Gerald Nugent, staff captain of the 29th Brigade, fell, revolver in hand, leading his men forward. His death was a sorrow to the whole brigade, for he was a man in a thousand. The surliest cynic who cultivated a grievance against all staff officers found himself quite unable to resist Nugent's kindness of heart and wonderful charm of manner. The manner of his death was suited to his bright and unselfish life.

About this time Colonel Bewsher came to the conclusion that the position was untenable. On the right the enemy had reoccupied the crest of the Chunuk Bair and were pressing the Hampshires hard, while on the left General Cox's column had retired to the Damakjelik Bair in rear, leaving the Chunuk completely exposed on that flank. There appeared nothing to prevent the Turks from establishing themselves in the Aghyl Dere and so cutting the only line of communication. The casualties, too, had been terrible. Every staff officer on the hill was either killed or wounded. The Hampshires and Rifles had only four officers left between them and the English companies were in just as bad case. The fight had been raging for over four hours, the men were utterly exhausted, and there was no sign of reinforcements. Colonel Bewsher, therefore, ordered a retirement which was carried out in a regular and orderly manner. This little mixed force, drawn from seven different units, comprising in its number men from Winchester and Salisbury, Birmingham, Burnley and Otago, Belfast and Khatmandu, had held a weak position against enormous odds, with little food and less water, for over 24 hours, and when they retired had hit the enemy so hard that they were not pursued.

Even then they were not disposed of, for at the bottom of the hill a staff officer (Captain Street) who was arranging to send up water and ammunition, called to them to come on again and they responded. The Hampshires on the right under their last officer, the Rifles in the centre, and the Wilts and Warwicks on the left, turned their faces again to the Hill of Death and advanced once more. The effort was futile for by this time the Turkish line was strengthened by machine-guns, but it was heroic, a vindication of the power of the spirit of man to soar above hunger and thirst and the imminent fear of death, and place itself on a level with that of the heroes.

Both battalions had suffered terribly. The Hampshires, who had gone into action on the morning of the 9th, with a strength of approximately twenty officers and over 700 men, had at noon on the 10th one combatant officer (Captain Hellyer) and not more than 200 men fit for duty. A few more who had lost their direction in the retirement rejoined in the course of the following day. The Rifles were in nearly as bad a condition. They were commanded by their junior captain, who had only been promoted to that rank at Mudros, and two subalterns were all the combatant officers that he had under him. The men, too, had been driven back in small parties and had been scattered, and it was clear that neither of the battalions was in a position to fight again for some days. Fortunately for their personal well-being, both of their quartermasters had survived the fight. Lieutenant Dowling of the Rifles had toiled unceasingly in drawing and attempting to send up rations, water, and above all, ammunition. The Rifles, too, had obtained devoted service from their doctor. Lieutenant Adam, R.A.M.C., who had worked like a hero in dealing with the hundreds of cases that had passed through his hands.

The Hampshires had found their quartermaster a tower of strength. Not only had Lieutenant Saunders worked magnificently throughout the fight, but in the difficult days of reorganisation, he turned his hand to anything and acted as adjutant and company commander and in any other capacity in which he could be of use. In spite of the misfortunes of his battalion he remained cheerful and imperturbable, and it was refreshing to look at his beaming, bearded face. In recognition for the good work he had done he was awarded the Military Cross. A quartermaster is described as a non-combatant officer, and his services are not always fully recognized, but in Gallipoli he was exposed to fully as much danger as anyone else, while the load of responsibility on his shoulders was far greater. Any negligence on his part meant that his battalion would go hungry and thirsty and lack ammunition at a pinch. Soldiers will agree that no man does more important work and better deserves recognition than a good quartermaster.

Meanwhile, the last battalion of the brigade was hurrying towards the scene of action. At 7 a.m. on the morning of the 10th the Connaught Rangers received orders to prepare to move at once. The detached company, which had been doing fatigue work at Brown's Dip all night, was hastily recalled, and in less than an hour the battalion moved off. It was necessary for them to take a circuitous route to the beach for fear that the Turkish observers on Gaba Tepe should notice that the right of the Anzac position was being weakened. At 9 a.m. Anzac Cove was reached, and the battalion hurried on northwards. As it entered the long sap leading to No. 2 Post, it began to realise the severity of the fighting for the first time, for the sap was full of wounded.

Most of these wounded, too, belonged to the Leinsters, Hampshires, and Irish Rifles, and their number made it clear that the brigade had suffered heavy losses. It was only, however, when checks in the march allowed an opportunity of speaking to the less seriously injured that the full extent of the casualties became clear. The officers of the Rangers heard with growing sorrow that the whole Brigade Staff were either killed or seriously wounded, and that the Rifles and Hampshires had practically ceased to exist. They saw carried past them, with drawn set faces, half masked by dry and clotted blood, men who had worked and played with them at the Curragh and Basingstoke, whose wives and children were their friends. Even in the pale, unwashed, unshaven faces and strained and suffering eyes of the less seriously wounded who paused to speak to them, they read the realisation of the ordeal that lay before them. Behind all was the thought of the friends lying up on the slope of the Chunuk Bair, whose families would never look on them again.

It was an unnerving ordeal for a young regiment, but, fortunately, there was little time for reflection, and the Rangers hurried on. At No. 2 Post there was a short halt, while Colonel Jourdain interviewed General Birdwood and General Godley, who informed him that the Turks had broken through a section of the line, and that his battalion was placed under the command of General Cox to help him to retrieve matters. He was exhorted to move forward as quickly as possible, as the need for reinforcements was urgent. Accordingly, before the rear of the battalion had extricated itself from the sap, the head was in motion again. It must be borne in mind that except for the brief information which the colonel had received from General Birdwood, officers and men alike were completely ignorant of the previous operations. They knew nothing of the extension of the Anzac position northward on the night of the 6th, nor of the repeated attacks on the Chunuk Bair; above all, they were unaware that a landing had taken place at Suvla. It was, however, clear to them that they were in new country, for up to No. 2 Post they had moved by well-trodden paths protected at any point of danger by saps and sandbags. Now they were in open country, with the sea on their left, and on the right a range of low foot hills, which in places sank sufficiently to enable them to see the ridge of the Chunuk high above them.

Here and there accoutrements hurriedly-cut off a wounded man showed that Turkish shrapnel and snipers had to be reckoned with, but there appeared to be a momentary lull in the fighting. Past the mouth of the Chailak Dere the Rangers hurried in single file sweating under the pitiless sun past Bauchop's Hill, and over a low *nek* into the Aghyl Dere. Here, again, their progress grew slower, for the gully was narrow and filled with wounded and mules and resting Ghurkas. It was stiflingly hot, and the smell of the mules and the dust, shut in tightly between the high scrub-fringed banks of the gully, were almost unendurable. The Rangers moved forward for a hundred yards at a time, until at 11.15 a.m. General Cox's headquarters were reached.

The halt there was a brief one for the Rangers were at once directed to place themselves under the orders of Brigadier-General W. de S. Cayley commanding the 39th Brigade, for the purpose of reinforcing his line. Below General Cox's headquarters, the Aghyl Dere forked into two branches, one coming from the Damakjelik Bair, the other, the southern branch, from the foot of the Chunuk. Along this southern branch the Rangers went in single file for about four hundred yards, passing an extemporised dressing station crowded with Ghurkas in slouch hats, and broad, baggy shorts, until they reached a point where a spur ran down from the Damakjelik Bair and gave a certain amount of protection against rifle fire from the Chunuk.

Here, General Cayley had established his headquarters in the narrow protected area; in rear of it were crowded all that remained of three or four English battalions. Above, the crest was lined by Sikhs. Into this zone of safety the Rangers hurried, and after forming up, lay down to rest while their colonel went to General Cayley for orders. The general was established in an observatory of boughs, which gave some shelter from the view of snipers on the Chunuk, and after giving Colonel Jourdain and the officers who accompanied him a very welcome cup of tea, he proceeded to explain the situation.

Although General Baldwin's column had been driven from The

Farm position, yet, apparently, it had not yet been occupied by the Turks. It was believed that they were greatly exhausted and had been much discouraged by the heavy losses inflicted on them by our artillery, and it was considered that it might be possible to reoccupy The Farm position. Accordingly "A" and "B" Companies of the Connaught Rangers were ordered to advance up the Aghyl Dere, climb the slopes of the Chunuk Bair as far as The Farm, and occupy the position, which was reported to have been partly entrenched. The men were much exhausted, since they had marched about seven miles in the noonday heat without regular halts.

They were allowed an hour's rest, and endeavours were made to fill their water-bottles, but very little water was obtainable, as the allowance at Anzac had been reduced to a pint a day per man. Extra ammunition was given out, and sandbags and entrenching tools were carried by the men. About two in the afternoon, "B" Company, who were to keep The Farm on their right hand, led off into the scrub on the left of the gully, "A" Company followed them, and for about two hundred yards were able to work along the bed of the Dere itself, crouching under the high bank to avoid the bullets which whistled overhead.

Although the main body of the enemy had retired behind the main crest of the Chunuk Bair, yet they had pushed forward snipers and machine-guns in sufficient numbers to render the advance of the two companies a decidedly unpleasant proceeding. A sudden turn in the direction of the gully brought the commander of "A" Company, who was at the head of his column, face to face with a long bare stretch of sand running for three hundred yards straight in the direction of the Chunuk Bair, which was filled with corpses and with the equipment that showed where a wounded man had fallen. Instinctively, he ran forward as the bullets began to throw up the sand all round him, and was followed by his signallers and observers and the men of the leading section. For about fifty yards they ran on until they reached a spot where a cross gully, running down from Rhododendron Ridge, afforded some protection from the pitiless machine-gun fire, but in that fifty yards half of the dozen men had fallen. Accordingly, the subaltern of the leading platoon was sent back to warn the remainder of the company, not to attempt to use the Dere, but to work their way through the scrub on its right. He ran the gauntlet successfully and the advance continued slowly.

Unfortunately, it had been impossible to give the men any definite objective, as from below The Farm was invisible, and many of them lost their way in the thick undergrowth, but about a platoon and a half of each company found its way through the bushes fringing the Aghyl Dere and commenced the ascent of the Chunuk Bair. Once they began to climb they were comparatively free from the attentions of the snipers and machine-guns, since the lower slopes of the hill were dead ground, but the climb itself was almost intolerable. The ascent was extremely steep, and covered in scrub, in which lurked enormous boulders.

The sun was still tropical, and the men, most of whom carried picks or shovels, as well as their weapons, were heavily laden. Often a man was obliged to lay down his rifle to haul himself up a rock, and found it an almost intolerable burden to have to take it up again. It was only by halting and resting every ten minutes that it was possible to make any progress. The officers, who did not know that they might not find the whole position in the hands of the Turks, did their utmost to retain in the men a sufficient reserve of energy to enable them to charge if it proved necessary. As The Farm came in sight three hundred yards ahead, an irregular extension was formed on the hillside, and the two companies got into touch again. "B" on the left, "A" on the right, pressed forward to reach their objective. It was unoccupied.

Unoccupied by the Turks, indeed, yet there were many relics of the struggle that had been waged there at dawn. A narrow ditch hardly a foot deep showed where an attempt had been made to entrench the position, while scattered round it were sandbags and entrenching tools, rifles and bandoliers of ammunition in a confusion so unnatural that it seemed horrible. Normally, such things are carefully stored and arranged, and even more carefully accounted for, and to see them thrown broadcast about a bare hillside was desolate indeed. Among them lay the men who had used them; some groaning for water, while others, under the influence of the scorching sunshine, had already begun to give forth the unspeakably foul sweet odour of corruption that in those August days tainted half the hills and valleys of Gallipoli. The sight was depressing enough, but at least the enemy were not there, and the men would be able to rest before they had to fight.

As the senior officer on the position was congratulating himself on this, a concealed machine-gun opened on the right about two hundred yards away. The right flank of "A" Company was in full view of it, and both Captain Massy, who commanded there, and a subaltern with him were wounded. Captain Massy, however, remained calm, and after binding up his comrade's wounds as neatly as a man with a bullet-hole through his right arm was able to, he withdrew his men to join the remainder of the company on the left. These were screened from the direct view of the hostile machine-gunners by bushes, but the gun was firing at every sound, which made movement, and still more digging, impossible. Gradually, however, sandbags were filled, and a traverse made of them, which protected the men as long as they lay still. A few picked shots were detailed to fire at intervals into the bushes where the invisible machine-gun appeared to be, and the knowledge that they were retaliating encouraged them greatly. Further comfort was given by the capture of a Turkish sniper, who had been found lurking in the bushes behind us. None of the men had ever seen a Turk before, and the general curiosity as to his appearance served to distract the men's minds from their immediate prospects.

These, as they presented themselves to the officer who found himself temporarily in command, were by no means cheerful. The trench which the men were supposed to hold would require at least six hours' work before it would give decent protection from shrapnel. It was also badly sited and only gave a field of fire of a few yards. The men available for work on it were few in number and very weary. There was sufficient food and plenty of ammunition, but water was very scarce, for those who possessed sufficient self-control to refrain from drinking during the weary climb, had been unable to resist the entreaties of the wounded, and had allowed them to empty their water-bottles.

The only road by which supplies of any kind could be obtained was the Aghyl Dere, which was swept by the enemy's fire. In addition, it was also known that very few reinforcements were obtainable. Finally, both flanks of the position were "in the air," the right being already dominated by a hostile machine-gun, which was placed so as to enfilade the line. It was clear that if, after dark, the Turks were to attack, the detachment would be in a hopeless position, and were bound to be either captured or destroyed. However, orders had been given that the line was to be held, and there was nothing to be done but obey them. The men were, therefore, instructed to rest until darkness made it possible for them to improve their position, and all ranks lay down and awaited the enemy's attack.

Before it developed, however, General Cayley sent orders that the detachment was to withdraw at dusk, bringing with it all the wounded who were lying on the face of the hill. Major Money, of "B" Company, who had now taken over the command, at once detailed a party under Lieutenant Blake to cover the withdrawal, and as it was within an hour of sunset, began to collect the wounded at once. These for the most part belonged to the East Lancashire and Wiltshire Regiments, with a few of the Royal Irish Rifles. They had lain out from dawn to dusk under the burning rays of the Mediterranean sun without food, water, or attention, and suffering agonies.

By the time they had been collected, the sun was setting, and the pilgrimage of pain began. There were no stretchers, nor were even waterproof sheets available, so that each wounded man had to be carried by his shoulders and legs. The mountain was pathless, and in the growing darkness the bearers made many a false step, which must have caused torture to the sufferers. Some shrieked with pain, others showered blessings on the heads of the men who were saving them from an agonizing death by thirst, and in the growing dusk, the load of misery was slowly carried to the foot of the hill. To the credit of the Turkish machine-gunners it must be said that they made no attempt to fire as soon as they perceived that wounded were being removed.

On this, as on other occasions in Gallipoli, we were glad to be able to respect the chivalry of our foes. An attempt was made to bring down some of the rifles and equipment that were scattered over the face of the Chunuk Bair, but there were hardly enough men to carry them, and some had to be abandoned. It was after 7 p.m. before the covering party withdrew, being the last British troops to occupy the Chunuk Bair. Among them was Captain Massy, who, ignoring his wound, had insisted on remaining till all the wounded had been removed. For his gallantry on this occasion he was awarded the Military Cross.

It was dark before the Aghyl Dere was reached, and the Rangers were glad to find that the two remaining companies of their battalion had been employed in entrenching a line on each side of the gully and making sand-bag traverses on each side of it. All the wounded who had fallen in the earlier fighting had been dressed and removed. This was a feat requiring extraordinary courage and endurance on the part of the battalion stretcher-bearers. They had been obliged to go into the exposed section of the Agyhl Dere under a storm of bullets, in order to bring out the wounded, and yet they not only did so, but often dressed the man's wounds under fire before they removed him. Then after the medical officer had treated him they had to bear their heavy burden all the way to the beach, returning only to plunge into the fire-swept zone again and rescue another comrade.

There were no men in the force who did their duty more strenuously and fearlessly than the stretcher-bearers of the 5th Connaught

Rangers on the 10th of August, 1915, and officers who had grumbled at having to allot some of their best and strongest men for non-combatant duties realised how well it was that they had done so. Nor must the part played by the medical officer be forgotten. Lieutenant J. I. O'Sullivan, Royal Army Medical Corps, found himself confronted by the debris of two brigades, but he rose to the occasion magnificently. Unpacking his panniers under a bush just behind the line, he not only worked on till long after dark without a rest, but remained cheerful and encouraging through it all. Only those who passed through his hands know what they owe to him.

So at sunset on August 10th ended the Battle of Sari Bair, which had begun on the night of the 6th. It had been hard fighting, and Mr. Ashmead Bartlett, the newspaper correspondent, has described it as the hardest battle in which British soldiers have been engaged since Inkerman. Those who took part in it, however, prefer to think of General Godley's restrained but deeply significant testimony:—

> I do not believe that any troops in the world could have accomplished more. All ranks vied with one another in the performance of gallant deeds, and more than worthily upheld the best traditions of the British Army.
>
> *Note.*—*Since this chapter was written, Brigadier-General Cooper has been awarded a C.B., and Colonel Bewsher of the Hampshires, and Major Wilford, Indian Army (attached Royal Irish Rifles) have received the D.S.O. for their services in this action.*

CHAPTER 5

Suvla Bay and Chocolate Hill

Death is nothing; but to live vanquished and without glory is to die every day.—Napoleon.

If you sail up the western coast of the Gallipoli Peninsula, soon after passing Anzac Cove, you will notice that the hills which have fringed the shore all the way from Cape Helles begin to run further inland, and that a gradually widening strip of level ground becomes visible between the cliffs and the sea. The coast line, too, which has hitherto pointed north and south, turns in a north-westerly direction, and thus increases the extent of plain until it culminates at the end of four miles in a cape known as Nibrunesi Point. Two miles north of Nibrunesi is another promontory called Suvla Point, and these are the two extremities of a semi-circular bay, which had no name on the original maps issued to the army, but which was soon to be well known as Suvla Bay. It is a name which has brought sorrow to many homes, and which will be perpetually associated with failure, but there are many glorious memories associated with it.

There are old and historic regiments that think more proudly of Maiwand and Chillianwallah than of victories gained with less stern fighting; and it may well be, that in the future the four Fusilier regiments from Ireland and the Royal Irish Regiment will be glad to remember that their service battalions fought at Suvla. A year later, at Salonica, when the gates of the Supply Depot were christened after great battles of the war, the name of Suvla was thought not unworthy to be associated with those of Ypres and Verdun. Greater glory no man could ask for, and none of the few survivors of the 10th Division could pass that gate without a throb of pride.

Suvla was well suited to a landing, since the beach shelved gently and offered a long slope of sand on which lighters could run ashore. West of Nibrunesi Point an isolated hill, known as Lala Baba, rose to a height of a hundred and fifty feet close to the shore, while behind this was the curious feature known as the Salt Lake. In August, this was dry and presented a surface of white sticky mud nearly a mile across gleaming brightly in the sun. Northeast of the Salt Lake the ground rose gently till it culminated in Tekke Tepe, nine hundred feet high and four miles inland. South of Tekke Tepe and about three miles east of the Salt Lake, was the village of Anafarta Sagir in a cultivated valley. South of this again was a lower ridge known as Scimitar Hill, and then another valley containing the village of Biyuk Anafarta. South of Biyuk Anafarta the ground rose steeply to form the main chain of the Sari Bair. Between the two Anafartas and the Salt Lake was a cultivated plain, studded with little cornfields and isolated olive trees, but from this plain, nearly two miles inland, rose two isolated hills, about two hundred feet high, known as Yilghin Burnu (or Green Hill) and Chocolate Hill.

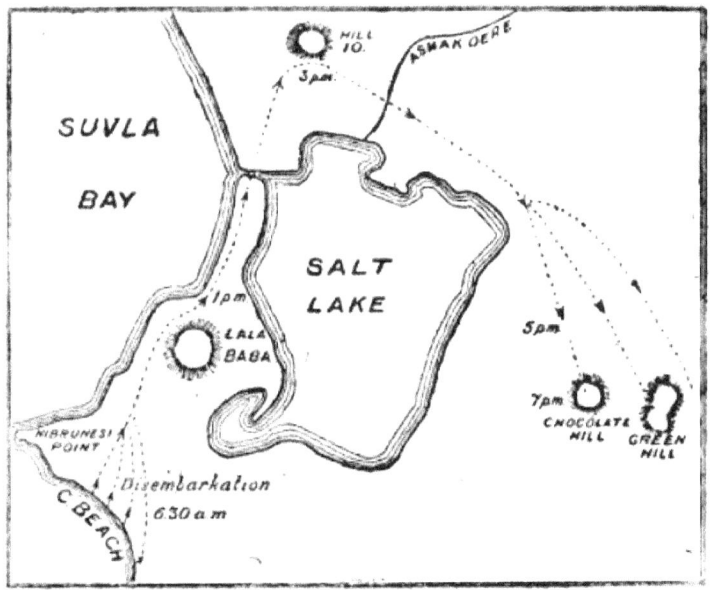

The landscape was finally framed by a high crest running inland in a north-easterly direction from Suvla Point, falling steeply in cliffs to the Gulf of Saros on the north, but presenting a gentler slope to the southern plain. This ridge reached a height of 400 feet near the sea and was there called the Karakol Dagh, while further inland, where it

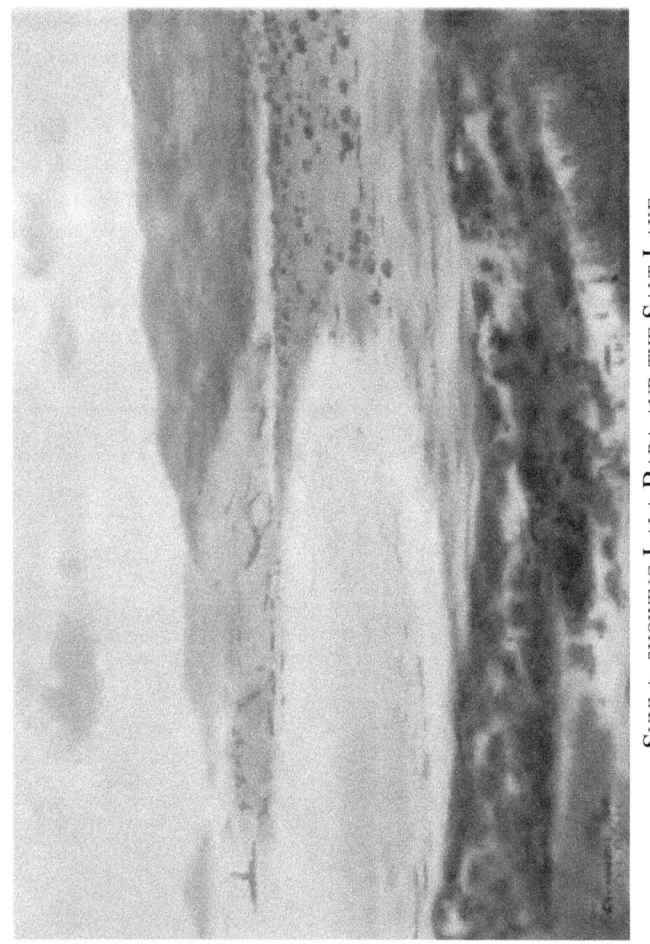
Suvla, showing Lala Baba and the Salt Lake

maintained an average height of 600 feet, it was known as the Kiretch Tepe Sirt. From its crest could be seen the whole of the plain enclosed by Tekke Tepe, Sari Bair and Damakjelik Bair, on which the battle was destined to be fought.

The commander-in-chief had planned that the transports conveying the 11th Division from Imbros were to leave as soon as night fell on the 6th, and effect their landing under cover of darkness. The 10th Division, having a longer voyage (Mudros being 60 and Mitylene 120 miles away) were intended to reinforce them on the following day. It was believed that the Turks would be taken by surprise, and that little or no resistance was to be anticipated. Three landing places had been arranged for; one known as Beach A in Suvla Bay itself, the others, Beach B and Beach C, on the shore south of Nibrunesi Point. The three brigades of the 11th Division landed simultaneously, and met with slight resistance from a Turkish picket entrenched on Lala Baba. The hill was, however, taken with the bayonet, and the whole of the beaches made good, while the 11th Manchester Regiment drove the enemy's outposts on the Karakol Dagh back on to the Kiretch Tepe Sirt. By the time this much had been gained, day dawned and the first portion of the 10th Division began to appear on the scene.

This consisted of the 31st Brigade and the two battalions of Royal Dublin Fusiliers, which had been waiting at Mitylene, the whole force being under the command of Brigadier-General F. F. Hill. Early in the afternoon of the 6th, the battalions had left the transports, on which they had spent nearly a month, and transferred themselves to trawlers and channel steamers. At sunset they weighed anchor and steamed northward, all, except a few on board, being completely ignorant of their destination. The lights on the shore told them that they had passed Achi Baba, and as they steamed by Anzac, the noise of battle at Lone Fine and on Sari Bair reached them from afar. Just as the pale morning light began to make it possible to distinguish the difference between sea and land, the ships anchored off Nibrunesi Point.

In the original plan of operations it was designed that the 11th Division should form the right wing and the 10th the left of the advance, and with this scheme in view it had been arranged to land the 10th on Beach A, inside Suvla Bay. The landing at Beach A during the night had, however, been considerably delayed owing to the fact that many of the lighters had run aground in the shallow waters of the bay, and the naval authorities had, therefore, decided to land General Hill's force on Beach C below Nibrunesi Point. At the same time, General

Hill was directed to reinforce the 11th Division, placing himself under the orders of Major-General Hammersley, who commanded that unit.

The process of disembarkation began about 5.30 a.m., the first two lighters taking to the shore a company of the 6th Inniskillings and a company of the 5th Royal Irish Fusiliers, as well as General Hill and his staff.

It was at once clear to all that the Turks had not been completely taken by surprise. The scrub which covered the slopes of all the surrounding hills, combined with the scattered olive groves to make it impossible to detect the numbers of the enemy, but it was obvious that they were well supplied with artillery. Their shrapnel was bursting fiercely over the men of the 11th Division as they moved forward, and as soon as the lighters reached the beaches, an effective barrage was at once established there. Even the troops awaiting disembarkation were under fire, and suffered the painful experience of having to lie down, closely packed together, and unable to retaliate. The lighters were obvious and easy targets, and in one boat alone the 7th Dublins lost an officer and seventeen men. On the whole, however, the force was lucky, and the casualties on landing were not heavy. Little could be done to keep down the hostile artillery fire, since the enemy's guns were well concealed, and but few of our batteries had landed. Two mountain guns on Lala Baba kept up a constant fire, and the warships cooperated, though lack of facilities for observation rendered their fire comparatively ineffective.

General Hill reached the landing place two hundred yards south of Nibrunesi Point about 6.30 a.m. Leaving orders for units as they landed to rendezvous on the seaward side of Lala Baba, he went in search of General Hammersley in order to ascertain his wishes. At this time the Turkish detachments, which had been watching the beaches, were retiring slowly across the wooded plain which stretches between the Salt Lake and Anafarta Saghir, pursued by the 11th Division. This pursuit, however, was considerably impeded by the fact that two small eminences, each about a hundred-and-sixty feet high, about half-a-mile from the south-eastern corner of the Salt Lake, were still in the enemy's hands. These positions were afterwards known as Chocolate Hill and Green Hill respectively, the Turkish name for the range being Yilghin Burnu. As long as the Turks held these knolls, they were in a position to bring enfilade artillery fire to bear on the advance across the Anafarta plain; and accordingly General Hill was directed to co-operate with two battalions of the 11th Division in their capture. This order had unfortunately the result of making any future junction with the portion of the division under Sir Bryan Mahon's command impossible, since that was directed to guard the left flank of the advance, while General Hill's force was to move to the extreme right. Owing to this detachment of a brigade and a half, the work of the staff tended to become more difficult.

By the time that General Hill rejoined his force with these orders, he found that the 6th Inniskillings and 5th Royal Irish Fusiliers had reached the rendezvous under Lala Baba. Two companies of the 7th Dublins under Major Lonsdale, the second-in-command, had also arrived there, and the remainder of the battalion, followed by the 6th Dublins and 6th Royal Irish Fusiliers, were coming up. The latter unit had been put ashore some way down the beach, and had had to march a considerable distance in order to reach Lala Baba.

The process of disembarkation and assembly had naturally taken a considerable time, and it was not till close on noon that the advance began. In order to reach the northern shores of the Salt Lake, and get in touch with the 11th Division, the units of General Hill's force had to pass over a narrow neck of land between the Salt Lake and the sea, on which the hostile artillery had carefully registered. Every minute it was swept by bursts of shrapnel, and the only way in which it crossed was by a section at a time rushing over it and trusting to luck. It was a trying ordeal for young troops engaged in their first action, but they faced it cheerfully. The 7th Dublins in particular were much encouraged by the example of their colonel. As an old soldier, he knew that there were times when an officer must be prepared to run what would otherwise appear unnecessary risks; so while everyone else was dashing swiftly across the neck, or keeping close under cover, it is recorded that Colonel Downing—a man of unusual height and girth—stood in the centre of the bullet-swept zone, quietly twirling his stick. The sight of his fearlessness must have been an inspiration to his men.

As soon as each battalion had crossed the neck, it formed up on the low ground north of the Salt Lake, under the slight amount of cover afforded by a low eminence known as Hill 10. When all had got across, the advance eastward began. The crossing of the neck had occupied a good deal of time, and it was close on 3 p.m. For more than four hours the sun had been directly overhead, a blinding glare was reflected from the shining surface of the Salt Lake, and the heat was almost overpowering. Few of the men had slept during the night, since excitement and the discomfort caused by their closely packed quarters on board the fleet sweepers had combined to keep them awake. Except for a cup of tea about 3 a.m., and a mouthful hastily swallowed before moving off, they were fasting, and already many of the more improvident had emptied their water-bottles. In addition, these young soldiers who had never seen war before, had been since four in the morning exposed to shrapnel fire, with but little chance either of taking cover or of retaliating. They had seen their comrades fall stricken at their sides without the consolation of knowing that the enemy was suffering to an equal extent. However, the prospect of action was encouraging, and it was with confident faces that they turned towards the foe. Their one desire was to come to close quarters with the enemy on their immediate front, but he was invisible.

From the low ground across which they were moving little could be seen but the masses of scrub backed by the semicircle of hills, and only broken by the minarets of Anafarta. The three leading battalions (6th Inniskilling Fusiliers, 5th Royal Irish Fusiliers and 7th Dublins) crossed the dry bed of the Azmak Dere, and began to turn southward towards Chocolate Hill. Up to this point the left flank of the movement had been protected by the troops of the 11th Division, who were advancing in the direction of Anafarta, but every yard gained to the southward tended to throw this flank more and more into the air. Though invisible, the enemy was making his presence felt. Round white balls of shrapnel were continually forming overhead, and out of the dense bushes rifle bullets came whizzing past the men's heads. Now and then a Turkish sniper was caught, sometimes festooned in boughs to enable him to escape notice; but the casualties caused by snipers were not so serious on the first day as they became later. The heaviest losses were caused by the artillery, for near the sea the scrub was thinner, and the long lines of men slowly advancing were plainly visible to the enemy's observers on the surrounding hills. Occasionally too, a Taube buzzed overhead, making its observations with comparative impunity, since except on the ships, there were no anti-aircraft guns.

Still the men pressed on, driving the Turks through the scrub before them. It was unpleasant work, particularly for officers, since little or nothing was known, either of the country or of the strength of dispositions of the enemy, and at any moment a platoon might have found itself confronted by a heavy counter-attack launched from the depths of the scrub, or enfiladed by hidden machine guns. Also, it proved a good deal harder to keep in touch with other units than it had in training days at the Curragh or in the Phoenix Park. The danger of pushing on too fast and finding oneself isolated was no imaginary one, but was alarmingly illustrated by the disaster which befell the 1st/5th Norfolks four days later. Nor did the tropical heat, which wore out and exhausted the men, help to quicken the movement. All these considerations combined with the pressure exercised by the enemy on the left flank of the Royal Irish Fusiliers tended to make the advance slow.

The dispositions of the force for the attack were as follows :—

On the right "A" and "B" Companies of the 6th Royal Inniskilling Fusiliers were in the firing line, supported by "C" and "D" Companies of the same unit; and by the 6th Royal Irish Fusiliers who had been brought up from the reserve. The 5th Royal Irish Fusiliers were on the left, having "A" and "B" Companies in the firing line and "C" and "D" in support. Owing to the fact that the left flank was exposed, this battalion was gradually being compelled to face in a south-easterly direction, with the result that a gap began to appear between it and the 6th Inniskillings. This gap was filled by "A" Company of the 7th Royal Dublin Fusiliers, closely supported by "D" Company ("The Pals"') of the same unit. The 6th Royal Dublin Fusiliers, who had been the last to come ashore, were still in reserve, and the 5th Inniskillings had not yet landed.

Steadfastly the fusiliers went forward, moving on a line parallel to that which they had taken in the morning, but in the opposite direction. As they passed the Salt Lake, the Inniskillings, who were on exposed ground, suffered severely, as many of the men stuck in the swamp. Landmines, too, which exploded on contact, were encountered and caused losses, while the shrapnel burst overhead unceasingly. Nothing, however, could have been more encouraging to the men than the demeanour of their leader. Wherever the danger was greatest General Hill was to be found, calm and collected, trying to save the men as much as possible. His fearlessness, his complete disregard of personal danger, set an inspiring example, and officers and men alike went forward more cheerfully, thanks to the lead given them by their general.

As the advance continued high explosive shells were mingled with the shrapnel, and though they did not claim so many victims, they were infinitely more trying to the strained nerves of the weary men in the ranks. By 5 p.m. they had come within 300 yards of the hill, and

Brigadier-General F. F. Hill, C.B., C.M.G.
Commanding 31st Brigade

were under a heavy rifle fire. By this time the men were very weary. They had had a long voyage of 120 miles under most uncomfortable conditions, they had been under unceasing artillery fire for more than twelve hours, they had marched more than five miles burdened by rifle and ammunition through the noon of a tropical day, and it was no wonder that they were exhausted. Chocolate Hill, too, was a formidable proposition: though only a hundred and sixty feet high, it rose steeply from the plain, and it was now obvious that it had been carefully prepared as a defensive position, for its sides were seamed by trenches. Though it was impossible to ascertain how strongly those trenches were held, yet it was clearly imperative that the men should have a rest before making the assault.

While the fleet and the batteries that had now been landed bombarded the position, the men of General Hill's force lay down in their ranks on the sun-baked ground, firing a shot from time to time, but with abundant leisure to look about them. On their right they could see the white houses and tiled roofs of Anafarta Saghir, while to the left they gazed across the shining white surface of the Salt Lake, past Lala Baba, to the bay crowded with warships and transports and hurrying launches, and to the calm and splendid peak of Samothrace. Many of "D" Company ("The Pals") of the 7th Dublins were men who had taken degrees at Trinity or the National University, and they may well have recalled past studies and thrilled to remember that the word "Samothrace" had always been associated with victory. Most of all, however, they watched the hill in front of them and wondered what fate might have in store for them there.

At last the bombardment ceased and the lines rose. General Hill had ordered that at all costs the position was to be taken before dark, and reinforced by two battalions of the 11th Division at 7 p.m. the charge began. On one flank the Inniskillings and on the other the Irish Fusiliers pressed forward. "A" Company of the 7th Dublins, led by Major Harrison, a splendid soldier, closely supported by "The Pals" under Captain Poole Hickman (a barrister who had served in the ranks of the company which he now commanded) made for the centre of the hill. The gleaming line of bayonets recked little of the Turkish fire, but rushed onward up the slopes. The Turk, on the defensive always, stands his ground well, and in more than one place the bayonets crossed; but the rush of the Irish charge was not to be denied. Fatigue and thirst were forgotten as the fusiliers, exulting in the force of their attack, dashed over trench and communication trench until the crest of the hill was gained.

As they reached it, the sun sank behind Samothrace, and the impending darkness made further pursuit fruitless. There was much work to be done in the short Southern twilight, for the hill was a maze of trenches and dugouts, with paths leading everywhere and nowhere, so that it was hard to find one's way. Outposts were hastily detailed and pushed forward over the crest, and the battalions which were much mixed, after a hurried reorganisation, bivouacked on and around the hill that they had taken. Their work, however, was by no means at an end, for it was necessary to make arrangements for bringing up food and water, to replenish ammunition, to bury the dead, and to collect the wounded. This last was by no means a pleasant task, since they were scattered all over the area across which the attack had taken place, and in the darkness it was easy for an unconscious man lying under a bush to escape notice. Here, as everywhere, however, the stretcher-bearers worked magnificently, and the doctors who had marched with their units all day, settled down to a night of strenuous labour. It is impossible to exaggerate the devotion to duty displayed by the regimental medical officers: they utterly ignored their own fatigue in order to ease the sufferings of their comrades.

While they were working, the task of replenishing supplies was going forward, though it proved to be one of considerable difficulty. The heaviest share of the burden fell on quartermasters of units and on the staff at the beach, who were left to regulate this matter. The night was pitch dark, and lighters were discharging their loads at various points along two miles of beach, so that it was by no means easy to find the stores required, or when they were found to entrust them to the representative of the unit that required them. Fortunately, however, a considerable surplus of rations and ammunition had been brought on the fleet sweepers from Mitylene, and this was divided among quartermasters. It was then necessary to have it sent up to Chocolate Hill, and since no animals or transport of any kind were available, this task became one of considerable difficulty. However, the men of the 6th Dublins, who had been in reserve during the day, were employed on this service, and their fatigue parties toiled throughout the night transporting the heavy boxes over the two-and-a-half miles of broken ground that intervened between the beach and the hill.

The crux of the whole situation was water. The single water-bottle that each man had brought ashore had long been empty, and all were parched with thirst. Though some water lighters had run aground in the bay, others had reached the shore, but there were no vessels of any kind in which the priceless fluid could be carried up to the firing line. In view of the facts that the position had only been captured at dusk, and had barely been consolidated, and that it was reasonable to expect that the enemy would counter-attack, it was felt that it was impossible to send men down to the beach to fill their water-bottles, and yet there appeared no method by which the water could be conveyed to the position. Petrol cans and biscuit-tins were not forthcoming, and though Lieutenant Byrne, the quartermaster of the 6th Dublins, tried the experiment of sending up water in empty small-arm ammunition boxes, it was not wholly successful.

At last the camp-kettles belonging to units came ashore, and by utilizing these, a scanty supply of water was sent up into the firing line. This work of organising the supply of water, food and ammunition occupied the whole of the night of the 7th, and it was not till late on the 8th that it was complete. The main responsibility for it so far as General Hill's force was concerned, rested on Capt. T. J. D. Atkinson, the staff captain of the 31st Brigade. He received invaluable assistance from Lieutenant and Quartermaster R. Byrne of the 6th Dublins, who on this, as on many other occasions, displayed such conspicuous ability and energy as to gain him the Military Cross.

Meanwhile, units began to take stock of their losses. Judged by the scale of later fighting in the Peninsula the casualties were not very heavy, though at first sight they appeared formidable enough. However, having regard to the fact that the troops had been under constant shell fire for twelve hours and at the end of it had taken an entrenched position by assault, the force could consider itself fortunate in not having suffered more severely. The bulk of the wounds were caused by shrapnel, which tended to confirm the impression that the hostile infantry who held Chocolate Hill were not very numerous. Had they been in equal strength to our men and been well supplied with machine guns, the losses sustained in the attack must inevitably have been far greater. Nevertheless, the capture of the Chocolate Hill-Green Hill position was a highly creditable performance for young troops who were receiving their baptism of fire. When it is remembered that they had been on the move throughout the greater part of the day in a temperature of well over 100°, the dash and determination exhibited by all the Irish regiments engaged augured well for their future.

Unfortunately, several senior officers had fallen. The 7th Dublins lost Major Tippett, who had served for years in the old Dublin City

Militia, and had left the security of a political agent's post in an English country constituency to die in his old regiment. Lieutenant Julian of the same battalion, who died of his wounds, was a young officer of great promise, whose death was deeply mourned. The 5th Royal Irish Fusiliers, who had suffered severely from the enemy on their left flank, lost Major Garstin killed; and their adjutant and nearly a dozen more officers wounded. In traversing the open ground by the Salt Lake and in the assault on the hill, the 6th Inniskillings had also sustained many casualties. Colonel Cliffe (destined to die later in France) was wounded, and so was Major Musgrave, his second-in-command; while half-a-dozen more officers were *hors de combat*. One of these was the quartermaster, Lieutenant Dooley, who was struck by shrapnel while superintending the unloading of ammunition from a lighter on the beach.

While Chocolate Hill was being attacked, the remainder of the division was hotly engaged to the northward.

When Sir Bryan Mahon arrived from Mudros with the 6th and 7th Royal Munster Fusiliers and the 5th Royal Irish Regiment, he found that the force under General Hill had already landed, and was in action. Nothing remained of the division which he had raised and trained for nearly a year, but the three battalions which he had brought with him and the 5th Royal Inniskilling Fusiliers, which had not begun to disembark. It was an extraordinary position for an officer who was a lieutenant-general of three years' standing, and had commanded a division for more than six years, to find himself entering into an action with only four battalions under his command, the whole of the rest of his command having been diverted elsewhere. However, he made the best of the situation and proceeded so far as the force at his disposal would permit, to carry out the task which had been allotted to the division, namely advancing on the left of the 11th Division and securing the Kiretch Tepe Sirt.

Beach "A" had been found unsuitable for use, as the water near it was so shallow that the lighters ran aground at a considerable distance from the shore. The navy had by this time found a better landing place on the north shore of Suvla Bay, slightly to the east of an isolated peak called Ghazi Baba, which rises from the shore. To this new landing place the two Munster battalions of the 30th Brigade with Brigadier-General L. L. Nicol and their Brigade Headquarters and the Divisional Pioneer Battalion were directed. It proved by no means ideal, since many of the lighters ran aground a considerable distance

Brigadier-General L. L. Nicol, C.B.,
Commanding 30th Brigade

from the shore, and officers and men had to plunge into the water, which was waist deep, and wade to the land. Fortunately, wet clothes were soon dried by the Gallipoli sun, but the stranded boats afforded excellent targets to the Turkish artillery. On reaching the shore a little before noon, the 6th Munsters who landed first found that the enemy had sown the beach with land mines which exploded on contact. Several men were injured by these, while the adjutant of the 6th Munsters was knocked down, but not hurt.

The orders given to the two battalions of Munsters and the Royal Irish who acted as support, were to climb the Kiretch Tepe Sirt Ridge at its western end and push forward along the crest as fast as possible. A certain amount of ground had been made good in the course of the night by the 11th Manchester Regiment, but it was desirable that the whole ridge should be secured as quickly as possible in order to safeguard the left flank of the advance across the Anafarta plain. The Munsters accordingly struggled up the steep bushy slope under the burning rays of the midday sun, and deployed for advance about 1.30 p.m. The 6th Munsters were on the left and the 7th on the right. They then pushed forward, but it was at once obvious that the country was one which offered many advantages to an enemy who wished to fight a delaying action.

Although from a distance the Kiretch Tepe Sirt appeared to be a long whale-backed hill six hundred feet high, yet its sides were seamed with gullies and tiny peaks almost invisible from below, which detached themselves from the main contour of the crest line. Moreover, it was covered with dense oak and holly scrub, which entirely concealed the numbers of the enemy and made it impossible to ascertain whether a unit was being opposed by a handful of snipers or a battalion. As they pushed through this dense thicket, the Munsters passed many indications of this fight waged by the 11th Manchesters, and soon the sight of fly-infested corpses ceased to cause a shudder. Soon they came in contact with the battalion itself, or rather what was left of it, since it had suffered heavily. Its colonel was wounded, his second-in-command killed, and nearly half its strength were out of action.

Those who remained were exhausted and very thirsty, and were unable to advance further. The Turks were holding a rocky mound which commanded the crest of the ridge for about six hundred yards to the west of it. From this point of vantage they were pouring a considerable volume of rifle fire on any troops who attempted to advance. Having taken in the situation, the Munsters went forward to attack the position, and had succeeded in getting within about a hundred yards of it when darkness fell.

In this engagement, fought in an unknown country against an enemy who knew every track and gully, and was able to leave snipers in the bushes behind him as he retired, the Munsters suffered severely, but were ready to advance again at dawn. A night attack was considered impracticable, since the country was absolutely unknown to the troops and very intricate. On the following day (the 8th) the Turkish position was attacked and finally stormed. The party of the 6th Munsters who took the culminating point, were led by the second-in-command of their battalion. Major Jephson, and the knoll was christened after him, Jephson's Post. Further advance proved impossible, the enemy being in possession of a strongly entrenched position, extending right across the ridge, and steps were taken to dig in on the line held.

In this brisk engagement the two battalions of Munsters, supported by the Royal Irish Regiment, and on the 8th by the 5th Royal Inniskilling Fusiliers, had had to contend with an enemy possibly weaker in numbers, but possessing an intimate knowledge of the country and favoured by the lie of the ground. It was believed at Headquarters that the Turkish force on the Kiretch Tepe Sirt consisted of close on 700 *gendarmeries*, who had been for months patrolling the Suvla district, and had the advantage of having already prepared entrenchments on the ridge. Against such a foe it was no mean achievement for a newly landed force to have advanced over two miles in a puzzling and intricate country and to have expelled the enemy from a well-fortified position, the whole being accomplished within twenty-four hours of landing.

Naturally, there were numerous casualties. The 7th Munsters suffered most severely, having Captain Cullinan, Lieutenant Harper, Lieutenant Travers and 2nd-Lieutenant Bennett killed, and Major Hendricks, Captain Cooper-Key, Captain Henn and half-a-dozen subalterns wounded. In the 6th Munsters, Lieutenant J. B. Lee, a Dublin barrister, was killed on the 7th, and Major Conway, a Regular officer of the Munster Fusiliers, fell in the assault on Jephson's Post on the 6th. Several subalterns were wounded, and there were numerous casualties among the rank and file. It was, however, fortunate that the enemy had no machine guns, and that the thick scrub made it hard to direct their artillery fire with accuracy, or the losses would have been far heavier.

For a week the battalions held the line that they had captured, being reinforced by the 5th Inniskillings, who took over the trenches on the northern slope of the ridge looking down on to the Gulf of Saros. This flank was guarded by a destroyer, which did invaluable service by giving notice of enemy movements, by searchlight work at night, and by rendering artillery support when necessary.

The period spent in these trenches was by no means an enjoyable one, for water was very short and had to be fetched from a considerable distance away. Shade there was none, since the sun pierced vertically downwards, and the prickly scrub gave but little cover from above. The trenches had been hastily constructed In a sandy soil that crumbled and fell in at the first opportunity and required constant work at them. By day the Turkish snipers made this impossible, so the men lay, too hot and thirsty and tormented by flies to sleep, and by night they were stirred up to work again. To add to the horror of the position, the unburied bodies of those who had fallen in the previous fighting, lying in inaccessible gullies or in the midst of the scrub, began to spread around the foul, sweet, sickly odour of decay. Once smelt, this cannot be forgotten, for it clings to the nostrils, and many a man recalled how true an insight Shakespeare had into the soldier's mind when he made Coriolanus use as his expression of supreme contempt the words:

Whose love I prize
As the dead carcases of unburied men
That do corrupt the air.

This, however, was only an aggravation of the situation; the real trouble was thirst. Men lied to get water, honest men stole it, some even went mad for want of it; but it was cruelly hard to obtain. Owing to some error, an insufficient supply of vessels for carrying it had arrived from Mudros, and it became necessary to send down a platoon from each company with the company's water-bottles to the beach to fill them. It was a long and trying walk in the dark, and even when the beach was reached, water was by no means easy to obtain, since thirsty soldiers had cut holes in the hoses that filled the tanks on shore from the water-boats, and consequently much was wasted.

It had been hoped to utilise the resources of the country, but the Turks had foreseen our difficulties, and when the engineers examined a well near Ghazi Baba, they found it surrounded by a circle of land-mines. Other wells further inland were well watched by snipers. Nor even when sufficient water was obtainable, was it easy to convey it back to the battalion. Some water-bottles leaked; others had been only half filled, or carelessly corked, while occasionally a thirsty soldier took advantage of the darkness to refresh himself from one of the bottles which he was carrying. As a result, when the bottles were distributed, there were bitter complaints from the men who found themselves presented with only a few spoonfuls of water as a supply for twenty-four hours. Tea-making, too, became difficult, since it was almost out of the question to obtain the water required in equal quantities from each man.

It soon became clear that the system of regulating the whole water supply of the unit by the water-bottle of the individual soldier was not a sound one, since the improvident consumed their day's supply at once, and the fool who lost his water-bottle was in a hopeless position. Commanding officers and company commanders first began by pooling all water-bottles, and issuing their contents in mess-tins from time to time; while gradually they collected petrol and biscuit tins in which to store a reserve fund. Thanks to these measures, and to the experience gained by the men, matters gradually improved.

Two events that occurred during this period gave some fillip to the spirits of the men on the ridge. The first of these was the arrival of a mail which brought not only letters and papers, but also parcels, and some of these parcels contained cake. Cake was a priceless boon in Gallipoli. Home-made and home-packed ones sometimes met with disaster and arrived in the form of crumbs, but those made by an expert, and sealed in an air-tight tin arrived safely, and were more welcome than anyone unacquainted with the ration biscuit can imagine. The ration biscuit takes various forms, some of which are small and palatable, but the type most frequently met with in Gallipoli was large and square, possessing the appearance of a dog biscuit and the consistency of a rock. It was no doubt of excellent nutritive quality, but, unfortunately, no ordinary pair of teeth was able to cope with it. Some spread jam upon it, and then licked the surface, thereby absorbing a few crumbs; others soaked it in tea (when there was any); while a few pounded it between two stones, and found that the result did not make bad porridge. After a week of this regimen, it is easily imagined how glad men were to put their teeth into something soft again.

The second encouragement was the arrival of the first reinforcements from Mudros. The worn and jaded men who had spent a week on the ridge, and had lost the glamour and excitement caused by the first experience of action, were surprised to find how glad their comrades were to rejoin them. The tawny scrub and fresher air of Gallipoli seemed delightful to them after Mudros, and their pleasure was so infectious that many of the older hands came to the conclusion that the Peninsula was not such a bad place after all.

During the first two or three days spent in holding the ridge position, the attention of officers was given more to the details of water supply than to the movements of the enemy. The latter had, however, been reinforced, and were becoming more aggressive. The Kiretch Tepe Sirt was of considerable tactical value to them, as if they were able to regain their ground, they would be able to enfilade our troops on the Anafarta plain, as well as being able to watch all movements on the beaches. Not only therefore did they push forward snipers, who picked off individual officers and men—among them Lieutenant Burrows, machine-gun officer of the 6th Munsters; but more organised attempts at lodgements were made, and patrol fights were not uncommon. One of these may be described as typical. The 6th Munsters, who were holding Jephson's Post, discovered that the Turks were digging in close to their immediate front, and Colonel Worship gave orders that a party under Captain Oldnall were to attack them at dawn and drive them out. Lieutenant Waller, R.E., accompanied the party in charge of the bombers.

Just before daylight the attack was made, and after a strenuous struggle, in which Captain Oldnall was seriously and Lieutenant Gaffney mortally, wounded, the post was seized. Lieutenant Waller displayed the most conspicuous courage in going out three times under very heavy fire to rescue Lieutenant Gaffney and two other wounded men. It is the custom of the corps of Royal Engineers to disregard all danger in the performance of their duty, and sapper officers have many splendid achievements to their credit. But no sapper officer can ever have shown greater courage and self-sacrifice than Lieutenant Waller did on this occasion. His action was worthy of the best traditions of his corps.

The post captured turned out to be the end of a Turkish communication trench leading down to the south-east end of the ridge. It was blocked with sand-bags, and the portion nearest the Munsters' trench retained as an advanced post. The garrison holding this were somewhat surprised when later in the afternoon an enormous Turk came wandering up the trench alone with an armful of bombs, but he was promptly made prisoner by Lieutenant J. L. Fashom, of the Munsters, who disputed with Lieutenant Burke, of the Connaught Rangers, the claim to be the smallest officer in the 10th Division.

Incidents like this enlivened the general monotony, but on the whole the time spent in these trenches was a dreary, thirsty one, and all ranks were pleased when it became evident that the remainder of the division was beginning to rejoin them, and that there was some prospect of an advance.

CHAPTER 6

Kiretch Tepe Sirt. August 15th-16th, 1915

If you can force your heart and nerve and sinew
To serve your turn long after they are gone.
And so hold on when there is nothing in you.
Except the will that says to them 'Hold on.'
—Kipling.

Before dealing with the Battle of Kiretch Tepe Sirt, it is necessary to give some account of the doings of General Hill's force after the capture of Chocolate Hill on the 7th. Dawn on the 8th found them bivouacking on the position they had taken on the previous evening and during the day, a defensive trench system, including both Chocolate Hill and Green Hill (Hill 50), 500 yards to the eastward of it. By this time the line taken up by our troops ran from the sea at Beach "B" to the two hills held by the 31st Brigade and thence northward across the Anafarta Plain at an average distance of three miles from the sea.

Throughout the 8th no advance was made from this line, since the corps commander was of opinion that the troops were very exhausted, and that there was insufficient artillery support at his disposal to justify him in making an attack on an enemy of unknown strength possessing the advantages of a superior position and knowledge of the ground. Unquestionably there was a considerable amount to be said in favour of this contention. On the previous day the enemy's barrage fire had taken a heavy toll of casualties, and but little effective reply had been made to it.

This was in part due to difficulties of observation, but also to the fact that up to the 8th, only three batteries had been landed, two of which, being mountain batteries, possessed only guns of small calibre. There were also the guns of the ships, but it was not always easy to communicate with the fleet in time to achieve the desired object, and it must also be borne in mind that space in a warship is limited, and that once its magazine is empty it cannot quickly be replenished. Added to these considerations the fact that the men were suffering terribly from want of water, that no transport of any kind was available, and that in consequence every unit found itself compelled to detach about a quarter of its men for the purpose of carrying up rations and ammunition, made it not unnatural for a commander to exercise caution.

On the whole, the 8th was a quiet day for the troops, though the sun shone as fiercely as ever and there was plenty of work to be done in burying the dead and getting up supplies. There was not much shelling, but hostile snipers were ubiquitous and much in evidence. These crawled up through the scrub or climbed trees in such manner that they commanded the greater part of our line, and made it dangerous to move about.

On Monday, the 9th, the corps commander had decided to attack the high ground behind Anafarta Saghir with the 11th Division and part of the newly-landed 53rd (Territorial) Division. For the purpose of this attack. General Hill was ordered to place two battalions under the orders of the general officer commanding the 32nd Brigade (11th Division). The 6th Royal Irish Fusiliers and the 6th Royal Dublin Fusiliers, neither of which had sustained very heavy losses in the previous fighting, were detailed for this duty and co-operated in the attack. The objective allotted to them was a height known as Hill 70, the culminating ridge of a spur which ran out to the north-east of Chocolate Hill between the hill and Anafarta Saghir about a mile and a half south-west of that village.

As soon as the advance began, it became evident, both from the increase in the volume of musketry and from the growing intensity of the hostile artillery fire, that the Turks had been heavily reinforced, but in spite of their losses, the fusiliers effected a lodgement on the ridge. For a time they clung to it though the enemy were delivering repeated counter-attacks, and a series of bush fires caused by their shells made the position almost untenable, and threatened the wounded with the most terrible of deaths. Further to the left, however, the 32nd Brigade found that they were unable to hold the ground that they had won in their first advance, and were compelled by attacks on their flanks to withdraw to their original alignment.

The fusiliers, who had suffered heavily under the violent Turkish attacks, conformed to their movements and returned to their first position. Captain Johnston, the Adjutant of the 6th Royal Irish Fusiliers, was killed and so was Lieutenant MacDermot of the same regiment, which also lost eight officers wounded: the Dublins also lost heavily. In the course of this action, a curious incident is said to have occurred. The medical officer of the 6th Dublins had followed his battalion in its forward movement, and had established his advanced dressing station under a tree in the newly-captured territory. After a time he noticed that several of the wounded, who were brought back by the stretcher bearers, were hit a second time as they lay waiting to have their wounds attended to. A search was made for snipers in the surrounding bushes without result, but eventually a Turk was discovered perched in the tree itself.

While these operations were in progress, the remainder of General Hill's force had been employed in support. While fulfilling this role, they suffered both from the ubiquitous snipers and from the enemy's shrapnel fire, which had become far heavier than it was two days earlier. The casualties, however, were not very heavy, except in the two attacking battalions. Another sphere of usefulness was also found for portions of the supporting units.

The prolonged fire fight waged by the 11th Division had exhausted their ammunition, and officers and men from General Hill's force were detailed to carry up fresh supplies. It is not particularly pleasant work, carrying up thousands of rounds of ball cartridge in a tropical country through bushes infested with snipers, but the men did it splendidly. Lieutenant J. F. Hunter, of the 6th Inniskilling Fusiliers, was afterwards awarded the Military Cross for the courage and disregard of danger exhibited by him on this occasion. Often, too, the ammunition carriers when they had delivered their loads attached themselves to the nearest unit and joined the firing line. Captain Tobin and a party of the 7th Dublins fought side by side with an English regiment in this manner throughout the day. There was little wrong with the morale of the troops when men voluntarily thrust themselves into the positions of greatest danger.

On the following day, August 10th, the day on which the struggle on Sari Bair reached its height, another unsuccessful attack was made on the Anafarta ridge, but in this General Hill's force took no part. They were now, and for the rest of the week occupied in holding the line that they had captured on the 7th through Green Hill. This position was heavily shelled by the enemy and some units lost heavily.

Throughout this period, however, the troops suffered most for want of water. Though by this time a certain number of petrol cans and other receptacles for carrying water had been obtained yet these were quite insufficient to satisfy the men's consuming thirst. It is hard to find words to convey the true state of affairs. No doubt it would be too much to say that at home thirst is unknown, but at any rate the passionate craving for water felt in Gallipoli is seldom experienced. When the water came up, the most careful supervision was needed in order to see that the much-needed liquid was used to fill the water-bottles and not consumed at once. When the bottles were filled, or rather had received their share, since there was not water enough to fill them, it was necessary to watch them vigilantly in order to make the supply last as long as possible.

Some men became hardly responsible for their actions; the heat was intense, the biscuit was dry and the bully beef very salty while many men were suffering from dysentery or enteritis and were parched with fever though they were unwilling to report sick in the face of the enemy. In such times surface civilization vanishes, and man becomes a primitive savage. A few men crept away to look for water by themselves, others stole bottles from their neighbours and emptied them, but on the whole the discipline of the force stood the strain remarkably well. It was a severe trial for young unacclimatized soldiers who had less than a year's service, but the months of training had not been in vain. The men knew and trusted their officers, and felt that they would do their best for them. Perhaps the officer's position was hardest of all. Thirsty himself, rationing himself by spoonfuls in order to make the contents of his water-bottle last longer, he was compelled to watch his men suffering from pangs which he could not relieve, and at the same time to try and keep their spirits up by laughing and joking with them. There had always been friendship between the officers and men of the 10th Division, but a bond not easily to be broken was cemented in those scorching suffering days.

By this time it had become evident to the higher command that no further progress could be made at Suvla without reinforcements, and steps were taken to obtain them from Egypt and from the Cape Helles area. In the meanwhile it was decided that the 10th Division should be reunited, and accordingly, one by one, the battalions of General Hill's force were relieved from their posts on Chocolate Hill and Green Hill and marched down to the beach to rest.

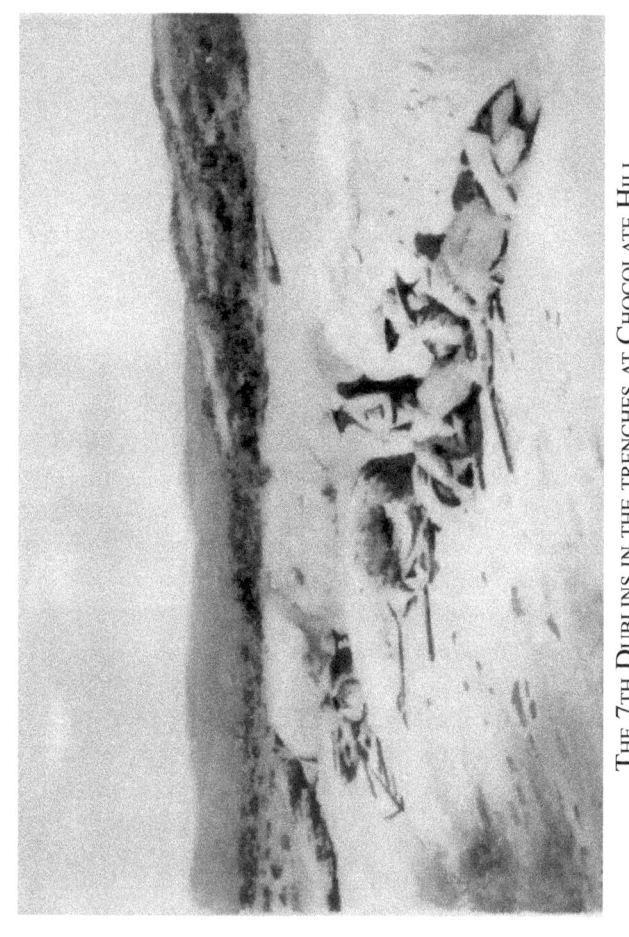

THE 7TH DUBLINS IN THE TRENCHES AT CHOCOLATE HILL

The battalions as they tramped back to the shore again were very different in appearance from those that had marched up from it less than a week before. Officers and men alike were dirty and unshaven, for water had been precious, and the sweat dried on the face, and the five days' growth of stubble told plainly of the hardships they had been through. Even more clearly did the eyes tell it, and the worn cheeks and leanness of limb. Clothes and boots had not been taken off since landing, and both were soiled with sweat and blood. There were many gaps in the ranks: death, wounds and sickness had taken their toll, and nearly every man had to mourn for a lost comrade, yet for all the sorrow and the weariness there was something in the men's bearing that was not there before. When they landed they were full of high hopes and eager to justify splendid traditions, but they were untried. Now they had proved themselves, and faced the future filled with confidence gained from their own deeds. The move began on the 10th and was completed when the 7th Dublins marched down on the 13th.

On the beach, though the comfort of the rest-camp was nothing to boast of, men were at least able to wash and shave, though the amount of fresh water available for this purpose was limited, and the man who got a mugful was lucky. Even so, most hurried to remove the long stubble that covered their chins, for a five days' old beard is not only unsightly, but uncomfortable, pricking and tickling the skin at every movement, and harbouring any quantity of dust and sand. Fortunately too, though fresh water was scarce, the sea was at hand, and it was possible to bathe. Some poet should sing of the delight of bathing in Gallipoli. Not even Mr. Masefield has done it justice. In the water one could for the first time be cool and free from care, though not from danger. By day the water sparkled in the sunshine: at night the form of the swimmer was outlined in phosphorescence and great bubbles of glowing light broke round him as he moved, and by day and night alike the bather could free himself from the burden of responsibility which weighed him down on shore. As Antaeus renewed his strength whenever he touched the earth, so the island people gained fresh stores of endurance from a dip in the sea. In the water, too, all men were equal, and rank could be laid aside.

After resting for a day or so on the beach, and receiving the first reinforcement which had just arrived from Mudros, the 10th Division (less 29th Brigade) concentrated on the Kiretch Tepe Sirt, General Hill's force once more coming under the command of Divisional Headquarters. As General Birdwood had reported that Anzac was not yet in a position to co-operate in an attack on Ismail Oglu Tepe, it was decided to occupy the Turks by attacking along the crest of the Kiretch Tepe Sirt, and thus rendering it impossible for them to bring an enfilade fire to bear against our operations on the Anafarta plain. This attack was to be made on August 15th, and the 10th Division was ordered to undertake it. They were to be assisted on their left by the guns of two destroyers in the Gulf of Saros, and on their right by the 162nd Brigade of the 54th Territorial Division. Artillery support was also, of course, arranged for. The task before the division was one of considerable difficulty since the enemy occupied a strongly entrenched position, and was known to have received large reinforcements. However, waiting would only make him stronger, and everyone was pleased at the prospect of action.

The 15th of August was not only a Sunday, but also the day known in Ireland as "Lady Day in Harvest," a great Church festival, and the chaplains had endeavoured to arrange services for their battalions. These had to be hurried through or attended only by the few who could be spared, but nevertheless Canon McLean was able to administer Holy Communion to some of the officers and men of the Dublins, and Father Murphy visited each battalion of the 30th Brigade and gave the men absolution. Then at peace with God they turned their faces again towards the enemy.

The dispositions adopted for the attack were as follows: The 30th Brigade (Dublins and Munsters) were to form the left wing of the advance, with the extreme left of the 7th Munsters resting on the Gulf of Saros. They thus covered the whole of the northern and part of the southern slope of the Kiretch Tepe Sirt. To their right two battalions of the 31st Brigade were to advance through the southern foothills of the Kiretch Tepe Sirt and across the open plain to attack a spur known as Kidney Hill, which jutted out southward from the main chain of the ridge. The 5th and 6th Royal Irish Fusiliers and the 7th Royal Dublin Fusiliers were in reserve.

Soon after noon the attack commenced, and it was at once evident that the Turks were holding their position in strength, the volume of fire which they were bringing to bear on our men being infinitely greater than that which had greeted us at the first landing. A captured Turkish officer afterwards declared that they had in their firing line six fresh battalions, each possessing twelve machine-guns. The rattle of these seventy-two guns was painfully prominent, and made it clear that the advance would be a costly one. The actual crest of the hill was a bare rocky ridge covered with great scattered boulders running for about a mile-and-a-half at a height of six hundred feet above sea level. Part of the ridge rose about fifty feet higher than this, and from this central portion three small eminences stood out. The central one of these was known as the "Pimple," and was marked by a cairn of stones.

The division had gained a footing on the western end of the ridge on August 8th by capturing the position afterwards known as Jephson's Post, and now the Turkish trenches ran across the hill between that point and the "Pimple." On the northern face the slope fell steeply away from the crest, so steeply as to be almost precipitous until it reached a height of three hundred feet above sea-level, from which contour the descent to the sea was more gradual though the ground was intersected by numerous gullies. On the southern face the hill also fell away rapidly for about three hundred feet, after which the descent became more easy, and various knolls and foot-hills detached themselves from the main range. Both slopes of the hill were covered with thick dry scrub, which had in a few places been set on fire either by matches or shells, and consequently had become blackened. This prickly scrub was a great impediment to movement of any kind and rendered all operations painfully slow.

For more than two hours after the commencement of the action, but little ground was gained. The enemy's rifle and machine-gun fire was well sustained, and efficiently supported by artillery, and it was considered rash to advance until a fire fight had done somewhat to silence the Turks. During this stage of the action, Major Jephson, of the 6th Munsters, was mortally wounded on the peak that, a week earlier, had received his name, and several other casualties occurred among officers and men. At last, General Nicol, seeing that the Turkish fire showed no signs of slackening, and that darkness would soon make further operations impossible, directed that an attempt to advance should be made along the northern slope of the ridge. The order was at once complied with. Two companies of the 6th Munsters and two of the 6th Dublins pressed forward accordingly, and succeeded, thanks to a piece of dead ground, in traversing about half of the five hundred yards that lay between Jephson's Post and the Turkish line of defence.

There for a while they rested, and then about 6 p.m. with the setting sun at their backs they charged the Turkish positions. Crags and scrub and cliff were as nothing to them, nor did they regard the hostile fire but rushed on with gleaming bayonets in the force of an irresistible attack. Few of the Turks stayed to meet them, and those that did were in no mood to receive the charge, but held up their hands and surrendered. Then as the Dublins and Munsters, Major Tynte of the 6th Munsters at their head, gained the enemy's position, they gave a rousing cheer. It was taken up by the troops in support and by all who watched the magnificent charge until from the Gulf of Saros to the Salt Lake the air resounded with the shouts of victory. There had not been much cause for cheering at Suvla, and the sight of the dashing attack and the sound of the Irish triumph cry, thrilled the hearts of many who had previously been despondent, and awakened hope once more in their breasts. Most surprising of all was its effect on the Turks. They had been heavily bombarded by the destroyers, they had seen a position that they believed impregnable taken with the bayonet, and now with the magic of the cries of the *infidels* ringing in their ears, they abandoned their trenches and retired in haste.

The Dublins and Munsters pursued and drove them before them until the whole of the northern slope of the Kiretch Tepe Sirt as far as and even beyond the "Pimple" was cleared. The men were disappointed that more of the enemy did not stay to face them. One soldier was heard to cry to a stout Turk who fled before him: "I don't want to stick ye behind. Turn round now and I'll stick ye in the belly dacent." Then, as night was falling and nearly a mile of ground had been gained, a halt was called so that the captured position might be consolidated.

On the right, meanwhile, the attack had unfortunately been less successful. The main attack on Kidney Hill had been entrusted to the 5th Inniskilling Fusiliers, who, owing to the fact that they had not disembarked till evening of the 7th, had sustained fewer casualties than the rest of the division; it was to be supported by the 6th Battalion of the same regiment. The Inniskillings had probably the most difficult task of any unit before them.

On the seaward side of the Kiretch Tepe Sirt the guns of the destroyers were of tremendous assistance to the attack, but they were unable to fire over the ridge. The remainder of our artillery, especially the mountain batteries, did their best to keep down the enemy's fire, but they were shooting at a venture since the exact position of the enemy's trenches was not accurately known. In consequence of this comparatively little had been done to prevent the Turks on Kidney Hill from bringing their full rifle and machine-gun fire to bear on our advance. The nature of the ground, too, lent little help to the attackers. Though the scrub was thick and prickly enough to break up the advancing lines into small groups, and to render it impossible for an officer to influence any more than the four or five men who happened to be in sight of him, yet on the plain it grew in scattered clumps. Between these clumps were patches of sand or withered grass, on which the enemy were able to concentrate their rifle and machine-gun fire. Added to this, the fact that from the surrounding hills the Turkish gunners could see every detail of the advance over the plain (khaki drill shows up clearly in the Gallipoli scrub) and could spray it with shrapnel and high explosive, made the operation three times as difficult. Nor was there any distraction elsewhere in the Suvla area. The hostile artillery was able to concentrate its whole force on the Inniskillings.

At noon the battalion began its advance, "A" and "D" Companies leading. There lay before them a gradual ascent dotted with scrub for about two hundred yards, and then half-a-mile of flat ground, from which Kidney Hill rose abruptly.

The Turkish trenches were invisible and consequently there was little attempt to subdue the enemy by a fire fight. The platoons went straight forward, racing over the exposed patches, losing officers and men at every step. The fire grew hotter and hotter and men fell more and more quickly, but still the front line pressed only to be swept out of existence. The distance was too far to cover in a single rush, and no troops in the world could cross the five hundred yards in front of the enemy's trenches at a walk and live. The supports came up and another attempt was made, but again the lines melted away. The task was one impossible of achievement, for it is now known that against modern weapons in the hands of an undemoralised enemy, a frontal attack by daylight on an entrenched position a thousand yards away is certain to fail.

Yet even when they had failed, the 5th Inniskillings did not fall back. Nearly all the officers were down, but little groups of men still clustered in the bushes waiting for orders. They could not advance; they would not retire until they were told to. Lieutenant G. B. Lyndon, of the 6th Inniskillings, went out after sunset and collected many of these little parties and brought them in. For this he received the Military Cross. Invaluable service, too, was done by the stretcher-bearers of the battalions and field ambulances, who here, as everywhere, showed themselves fearless and tireless in the performance of their duties.

The casualty list was a terribly heavy one. Colonel Vanrenen, of the 5th Inniskillings, was killed, and so were Captain Robinson, Captain Vernon, Lieutenant McCormack, Lieutenant Nelis, and Lieutenant

The Anafarta Plain

Grubb of the same unit. Both its majors were wounded, together with two captains and nearly a dozen subalterns. The losses among the rank and file were in proportion, and the whole organisation of the regiment was temporarily shattered. The 6th Inniskillings, who were in support, had been heavily shelled, but had been lucky in escaping severe loss.

The result of the failure of the right attack was that while we held the northern slope of the Kiretch Tepe Sirt up to and even beyond the Pimple, yet on the Southern face of the hill we had been unable to advance our line much beyond the trenches which we held when operations on the 15th began. As a consequence, the line held by the division somewhat resembled a Z. The upper horizontal was represented by a line of trench running from the Gulf of Saros to the most advanced point on the crest of the ridge that was reached by the charge of the 6th Munsters and 6th Dublins. This trench was exposed to fire not only from the hills which continued the line of the Kiretch Tepe Sirt eastward, but also from a spur known as 103, which ran northwards into the sea.

The diagonal joining the two horizontals of the Z was represented by a line running along the northern or seaward slope of Kiretch Tepe Sirt just below the crest. The crest itself, since it was liable to be swept by shrapnel and machine-gun fire, and since its rocky nature made it difficult to entrench, was not held except at the lower horizontal, which represented the trench running past Jephson's Post, from which the attack had begun. The position thus created was clearly far harder to hold than if it had been merely a trench running across the ridge from North to South, and would obviously require far more men. The two battalions from the Reserve were, therefore, called up without delay.

The 7th Dublins had begun to move forward already, and were advancing under circumstances of some difficulty. The enemy's artillery were shelling the line behind our position with considerable vigour, and in addition snipers were more than usually active. One of these pests, who was ensconced in a bush, succeeded in shooting Colonel Downing in the foot, and though the colonel promptly retaliated with his revolver, and insisted that the wound was trivial, he found himself unable to walk and was compelled to leave his beloved battalion. Major Harrison took over command of the Unit.

After the reserves came up, the dispositions made for the defence of the line running just below the crest of the Kiretch Tepe Sirt were as follows :—The extreme end to the eastward was held by the 6th Royal Irish Fusiliers; next to them came the 6th Munsters, and beyond them "D," "A" and "C" Companies of the 7th Dublins. "B" Company of the last-named regiment had been sent down the hill on the seaward side to dig a trench covering Hill 103. The 6th Dublins, who had sustained heavy losses in the charge, were withdrawn to rest. These dispositions were adopted just before nightfall.

The soil of the ridge was too stony to admit of much entrenching, and in most cases the men lay down on their arms just behind the crest on the seaward side, though in one or two spots stone *sangars* were constructed. They were given but little time to work before they were attacked. The knowledge that no advance had been made on any part of the plain below made it possible for the enemy to employ a large proportion of his reserves in the recovery of the ground lost on the Kiretch Tepe Sirt, while the fact that the Southern slope of the hill was still in his possession enabled him to push men along it to attack any portion of our long, thinly-held line at close quarters.

The first of the hostile counter-attacks began about 10 p.m., when a wave of Turks who had crept along the landward slope and up to the crest in silence, burst over it with a yell and fell upon the British line. Fortunately, our men were not taken by surprise; a roar of musketry at close range received the enemy, and when it came to bayonet work our morale proved more than sufficient to dispose of the foe. After a stiff fight, the attackers disappeared over the crest leaving a good proportion of their numbers behind them on the ground. Listening posts were then sent out to the further side of the ridge in order to preclude the possibility of a surprise attack succeeding, and the remainder of the tired men lay down again, rifle in hand to secure as much rest as possible.

Little sleep was allowed them. Before the first light of the early summer dawn began to appear in the sky, the listening posts were driven in, and a fresh Turkish attack was made. On this occasion the assault was led by bomb-throwers, and although those who crossed the crest and came to close quarters were disposed of by the Irish with rifle and bayonet, yet a considerable force of the enemy, well-furnished with grenades, succeeded in establishing themselves on the southern slope of the Kiretch Tepe Sirt. From this position they proceeded to bomb the whole length of our line incessantly, throwing the grenades over the crest of the ridge so that they burst in the midst of our ranks with deadly effect. Had the fusiliers been in possession of enough bombs they could have retaliated in kind, but the few that they had were quickly used, and no more were forthcoming. Even if they had been, the contest would scarcely have been a fair one, since the grenade employed by the Turks in Gallipoli was infinitely superior to that issued to the British. The latter was an extemporised production, consisting of a detonator inserted in a jam tin and furnished with a fuse, which had to be lighted with a match.

The Turkish bomb, which was shaped like a cricket-ball, was both more accurately fused and easier to throw. However, could they have been obtained, the Dublins and Munsters and Irish Fusiliers would have been glad even of jam-tins, since they would have enabled them to make some reply to the enemy. Rifles and bayonets were useless against an invisible foe, on the other side of a rocky ridge. The two forces were, to use a homely comparison, in the position of men sitting in the gutters of a house and fighting across the roof. Under these circumstances grenades were obviously the most effective weapon, and the side that lacked them suffered from an appalling handicap.

As day broke, officers were able to take stock of the situation, though the sight that met their eyes was not encouraging. On every side men had fallen, and the strain on the survivors was appalling, for the rain of bombs still continued. Here and there individual officers organised attempts to drive the enemy back at the point of the bayonet, but without success. A description of one of these efforts will serve to make clear the fate with which they met. Major Harrison, of the 7th Dublins, finding that his line was becoming dangerously thin, determined to try the effect of a charge. He selected for this purpose a party of "D" Company, "The Pals," under the command of Captain Poole Hickman.

The men were only too delighted at the prospect of action, and charged fearlessly up the hill. As they appeared on the crest, however, they were met by a storm of concentrated rifle and machine-gun fire. Captain Poole Hickman fell mortally wounded, but Major Harrison rushed forward bareheaded and took his place, leading his men on till they reached the Turkish line. There he was struck by a grenade thrown at close quarters, and of all the gallant spirits who had followed him so pluckily only four made their way back over the crest to their battalions. Similar charges made elsewhere met with similar results; in some cases a whole platoon disappeared and was never seen again. Among the officers who were lost in this way were Captain Grant, 6th Munsters, and Lieutenant Crichton, 7th Dublins. It was obvious that to cross the crest by daylight meant death, since the Turks had been able to install machine-guns in positions that enfiladed it.

Since advance was impossible, the troops were compelled to remain on their position, exposed to a perpetual fire of grenades, to which they had no means of replying. The sun rose higher in the sky and reached the zenith and still the bombing went on without intermission, and the men of the 10th Division continued to suffer and endure. The faces of dead comrades, lying at their sides, stiffened and grew rigid, and the flies gathered in clouds to feast on their blood, while from the ridge in front came the groans of the wounded, whom it was impossible to succour. The men lying behind the crest knew that at any moment a similar fate might come to any of them, and they might fall a shattered corpse, or be carried back moaning, but still they held on. The unceasing noise of the bursting grenades, the smell of death, the sight of suffering, wore their nerves to tatters, but worst of all was the feeling that they were helpless, unable to strike a blow to ward off death and revenge their comrades.

It is by no means easy to realise what the men felt during this ordeal. Perhaps the strongest emotion was not the sense of duty, the prompting of pride, or even the fear of imminent death, but blind, helpless rage. In a charge or an advance a soldier rarely feels anger. His whole soul is concentrated on reaching a definite objective, and though he is prepared to kill anyone who stands in his way, he does so without passion. The exultation born from rapid movement, the thrill produced by the sense of achievement, banish all personal feelings. But lying on the ridge under the pitiless bombing, watching the mangled bodies of the dead, men had time to think, and the fruit of their thoughts and of their impotence was black and bitter hatred of the enemy. They were ready to run any risk in order to do something to hurt him.

Some tried to catch the Turkish bombs as they were falling and throw them back into the enemy's lines before they exploded. Five times Private Wilkin, of the 7th Dublins, performed this feat, but at the sixth attempt he was blown to pieces. Elsewhere men, sooner than lie impotent, took up stones and hurled them at the foe. Everywhere the few remaining officers moved about among their men, calming the over-eager, encouraging the weary, giving an example of calmness and leadership, of which the land that bore them may well be proud. In doing this they made themselves a mark for the inevitable snipers, who by now had ensconced themselves in coigns of vantage on the crest of the ridge, and many died there. Thus fell Capt. Tobin, of the 7th Dublins, a man greatly beloved. Here, too, fell Lieut. Fitzgibbon and Lieut. Weatherill, of the same regiment. Fitzgibbon, a son of the Nationalist M.P. for South Mayo, who, in the black days of Ireland's past had had many a dispute with the forces of the law, and had now sent his son to die gloriously in the king's uniform; Weatherill, a boy who had made himself conspicuous in a very gallant battalion for courage. Here, too, many other heroic souls laid down their lives, but still the line held on.

The sun reached the west and began to sink; the ranks were thin, the men were weary, and many mangled bodies lay along the fatal ridge. The 6th Royal Irish Fusiliers, exposed both in front and in flank, had been practically annihilated. Their 5th Battalion came up to reinforce them and shared their fate. Three officers of this regiment. Captains Panton and Kidd, and 2nd-Lieut. Heuston, earned the Military Cross by the inspiring example they gave on this occasion. The last-named was reported as "wounded and missing," and was probably killed in this fight. Nearly all the officers of the Irish Fusiliers had fallen, and the other regiments were in nearly as bad a case; but still the line held on. Tired and hungry and thirsty as they were, unable to strike a blow in their own defence, yet still the men of the 10th Division were resolved not to retire a step until the order to do so came. They were but young soldiers, who had had less than a year's training, and had received their baptism of fire only a week earlier; but they were determined that however stern the ordeal they would not disgrace their regiments.

In old days, in the thick of a hard-contested struggle, men rallied round the colours—the visible symbol of the regimental honour. There were no colours to rally round on the slope of the Kiretch Tepe Sirt, but the regimental name was a talisman that held the battered ranks to their ground. Their regiments had in the past won great glory, but neither the men of the 87th who cleared the pine woods of Barrosa with the cry of "Faugh a Ballagh!" nor the Dublins and Munsters who leapt from the bows of the *River Clyd*e into certain death, need blush to own comradeship with their newly-raised Service Battalions, who died on the Kiretch Tepe Sirt.

Darkness at last fell, and the sorely-tried men hoped for relief. This was indeed at hand, though it did not take the form of fresh troops. None were available, so the units of the division who had suffered heavily in the charge of the previous day, and who had had less than twenty-four hours' rest, were called up again. The 6th Dublins, and with them the 5th Royal Irish (Pioneers), took over the line of the ridge from the battalions who had held it so stoutly. Nor were their sufferings less, for throughout the night the bombing continued, and our men were still unable to make any effective retaliation. Many officers and men fell, but the remainder set their teeth and held their ground, until at last they received the order to withdraw from the untenable position.

Not a man moved until he received the order, and then slowly, deliberately, almost reluctantly, they retired. Bullets fell thickly among them, and took a heavy toll, one of those killed being 2nd-Lieut. W. Nesbitt, a young officer of the 6th Dublins, who, though junior in rank, had made a tremendous impression by his character, and had earned the name of "the Soul of the Battalion." Before he was hit, the 6th Dublins had had Major Preston and their Adjutant, Capt. Richards, killed, and in the course of these operations three subalterns, 2nd-Lieut. Clery, 2nd-Lieut. Stanton, and 2nd-Lieut. McGarry, were reported missing. Probably they died in some unseen struggle, and their bones now lie in a nameless, but honoured grave on the field where their regiment won such fame.

Gradually the shattered units withdrew to their original line, but when the roll was called there were many names unanswered. The charge on the 15th had cost many lives, the holding of the captured position very many more, and yet all the effort and all the suffering seemed to have been futile. The 10th Division had been shattered, the work of a year had been destroyed in a week, and nothing material had been gained. Yet all was not in vain. It is no new thing for the sons of Ireland to perish in a forlorn hope and a fruitless struggle; they go forth to battle only to fall, yet there springs from their graves a glorious memory for the example of future generations. Kiretch Tepe Sirt was a little-known fight in an unlucky campaign, but if the young soldiers of the 10th Division who died there added a single leaf to Ireland's crown of cypress and laurel, their death was not in vain.

Chapter 7

Kaba Kuyu and Hill 60

Oh, bad the march, the weary march, beneath these alien skies.
But good the night, the friendly night, that soothes our tired eyes;
And bad the war, the weary war, that keeps us waiting here.
But good the hour, the friendly hour, that brings the battle near.
—Emily Lawless.

After the close of the battle of Sari Bair, the 29th Brigade of the 10th Division was in urgent need of re-organisation. The Brigade Staff had ceased to exist, and the Hampshires and Rifles were in almost as bad a case, since almost every officer was killed or wounded. The Leinsters, though they had sustained serious losses, had still a fair number of senior officers left, and the Connaught Rangers had suffered less severely, having up to the 11th only lost five officers. The latter unit was therefore retained in the front line, while the other battalions were withdrawn to refit.

Throughout the 11th the Rangers held the line, which had been entrenched by two of their companies on the 10th, between the foot of Rhododendron Ridge and the north-eastern extremity of the Damakjelik Bair. This line, based on two natural ravines, was a strong one, but General Cayley considered that it was too far in rear, and accordingly after sunset on the 11th the battalion advanced to an underfeature at the foot of the Chunuk Bair, and commenced to dig in there. The advance was by no means an easy one, since it had been impossible to make a detailed reconnaissance of the ground over which it had to take place, as by day it was exposed to the enemy's fire from the Chunuk. In consequence of this the left flank unexpectedly found themselves descending a slope so steep that it was almost a precipice. Fortunately, there were bushes at the bottom to break the fall of those whose feet slipped, and if the bushes happened to be prickly ones, well, it was no good complaining about trifles in Gallipoli.

The position when reached was not an ideal one. Though protected to a certain extent from bullets from the Chunuk, it did not afford a very good field of fire, and lack of shelter from the sun, shortage of water, and the smell proceeding from a gully full of corpses, combined to make the position of those holding it unpleasant. The greatest disadvantage, however, was the fact that the only avenue of approach to the trench line was the Aghyl Dere, which was swept by a hostile machine-gun. Supplies and ammunition had to be carried up under cover of darkness, and everyone who went up or down by daylight was obliged to run the gauntlet for about three hundred yards. Several casualties were caused while doing this, among the sufferers being the senior captain of the Rangers, Captain Hog, who received the wound from which he died in this manner. He was a man of forty-five years of age, who had served in the 1st Battalion of the Rangers in South Africa, and had rejoined from the Reserve of Officers at the beginning of the war. Though double the age of some of his comrades, he had set them a magnificent example by the way in which he accepted hardships, and the loyalty with which he submitted to the commands of men younger than himself.

The hardships were by this time considerable, since officers and men alike were reduced to bully beef and biscuits. It had been impossible to bring any mess stores to the Peninsula, and though each officer had stuffed a tin of sardines, or some potted meat into his haversack, these did not last long, and the rather reduced ration of a tin of bully beef and four biscuits *per diem* was all that was obtainable by anyone. Cooking was practically impossible, though occasionally one got a cup of tea, and men ate at odd moments, seldom sitting down to a regular meal. It was noticeable that on the whole the single men stood this discomfort better than those who were married. In part, no doubt, this was due to the fact that they were younger, but some of the oldest men proved to be the toughest.

One old sergeant, who had marched to Kandahar with Lord Roberts in 1879, went through the whole Gallipoli campaign with the division, and also through the operations in Serbia in December without once going sick. The married men were more used to being looked after, to having their comfort considered, and to decent cooking, and to regular meals, and the semi-barbaric existence upset them. Those who stood it best were the tinkers, members of that strange nomad tribe who in Ireland take the place of the English gipsies. It was no new thing for them to eat sparingly, and sleep under the stars, and their previous life made it easy for them to adapt themselves to circumstances.

For three days the Rangers held this position, and during this period the re-organisation of the brigade proceeded. The only battalion commander left unhurt was Lieutenant-Colonel Jourdain, of the Connaught Rangers, who took over command as a temporary measure, but on the 13th he was succeeded by Lieutenant-Colonel G. K. Agnew, M.V.O., D.S.O., Royal Scots Fusiliers. Captain R.V. Pollok, 15th Hussars, was appointed Brigade Major, and on August 20th, Captain R. J. H. Shaw, 5th Connaught Rangers, took up the post of Staff Captain. The officers and men of the first reinforcement who had been left at Mudros rejoined their units on the 11th, and were very welcome. In two cases officers arriving with this draft found themselves in command of their battalions, since Major Morley, of the Hampshires, and Captain R. de R. Rose, of the Rifles, were senior to any of the few surviving officers of their units. The task before them was by no means a light one, for the whole company organisation had been destroyed, and nearly all the officers and senior N.C.O.s were *hors de combat*. However, they buckled to it with a will, and every suitable man received temporary promotion.

On August 13th, the Connaught Rangers were withdrawn from the line they were holding and given four days' rest, which was, of course, broken by numerous demands for fatigues. It is the universal experience of soldiers that in this war one never works so hard as when one is supposed to be resting. On the 17th they relieved the 6th South Lancashire and 6th East Lancashire Regiments in trenches, which they held for three days, and considerably strengthened. On the 20th they were withdrawn from these trenches, and ordered to hold themselves in readiness to join General Cox's Brigade and take part in an attack on the following day.

This attack had been planned in order to co-operate with the movements at Suvla. Reinforcements in the shape of the 29th Division from Cape Helles, and the 2nd Mounted Division (without their horses) from Egypt, had arrived there, and an attack on Ismail Oglu Tepe had been planned. This steep, thickly-wooded hill acted as buttress to Koja Chemen Tepe, and as it overlooked the whole of the Suvla Plain, afforded a valuable observation post to the enemy's artillery. With it in our hands we should not only be able to interrupt

The Anafarta Plain from the south

communication between the two Anafartas, but would have gained a valuable *point d'appui* for any further attack.

Communication between the Anzac and Suvla forces had been obtained on the 13th at Susuk Kuyu, north of the Asmak Dere, but it hung by a narrow thread. It was therefore decided that simultaneously with the attack on Ismail Oglu Tepe, General Birdwood should attack the Turkish trenches north of him, and endeavour to win enough ground to safeguard inter-communication. The execution of this operation was entrusted to Major-General Cox, who was allotted the whole of his own Indian Brigade, two battalions of New Zealand Mounted Rifles, the 4th South Wales Borderers from the 11th Division, and the 5th Connaught Rangers and 10th Hampshires from the 29th Brigade. All these units had suffered heavily in the fighting a fortnight before, and the Indian Brigade in particular was terribly handicapped by the fact that it had lost almost all its British officers.

The objective of this attack was contained in the salient enclosed by the sea on the west, and the Damakjelik Bair on the south. A thin line of outposts close to the sea connected Anzac and Suvla, but the low ground which they held was commanded by a hill known as Kaiajik Aghala, or Hill 60. At the point where this eminence began to rise in a gentle slope from the plain, about four hundred yards north of the Damakjelik, stood two wells called Kaba Kuyu. These wells were extremely valuable to the Turks, since they, too, were short of water, and it was against them that the first stages of the attack were to be directed. There was, indeed, no object for which any man in the rank and file would more willingly fight in Gallipoli in August than a well. At the same time the wells, which the Turks were known to have entrenched, were not the sole objective.

The capture of Hill 60 was extremely desirable, since not only did it menace inter-communication between Suvla and Anzac, but with it in our hands we should be in a position to enfilade a considerable portion of the Turkish forces, which were opposing the attack from Suvla. General Cox disposed of his forces as follows. On the extreme left the 5th Ghurkas were to sweep across the low ground near the sea and get in touch with the right flank of the Suvla force. In the centre, the 5th Connaught Rangers were to deploy in a gully of the Damakjelik Bair, known as South Wales Borderers' Gully, and charge across three hundred yards of open ground to capture the wells. On the right, the two battalions of New Zealanders, under Brigadier-General Russell, forming up behind the trenches on Damakjelik Bair were to make an attack on Hill 60 direct. Still further to the right a feint attack, intended to draw off the Turkish reserves, was to be executed by the 10th Hampshire Regiment. The remainder of the force was in reserve.

The Connaught Rangers reached South Wales Borderers' Gully after dark on the 20th and bivouacked there for the night. As the attack was not to be launched till 3 p.m. on the 21st, they had a long wait before them, but there was plenty to be done. Officers spent the morning in visiting the trenches held by the South Wales Borderers on Damakjelik Bair and inspecting their objective through a periscope, for the enemy snipers were too active to permit of any direct observation. The Turks had constructed a trench in front of the wells to guard them, which was connected with their main position by a communication trench improvised from a deep water course which ran eastward. To the northward a sunken road led from the wells in the direction of Anafarta. No barbed wire appeared to have been erected, but it was obvious that the crest of Hill 60 was strongly entrenched and held.

After this reconnaissance, orders were issued for the attack, and while they were being prepared, officers and men alike were receiving the consolations of religion. For the Church of England men, the Rev. J. W. Crozier celebrated Holy Communion; and Father O'Connor gave absolution to his flock. The bullets of snipers were whistling overhead, and ploughed furrows through the ground as the men knelt in prayer and listened to the message of peace and comfort delivered by the tall khaki-clad figure. In a few hours they were to plunge into a hand-to-hand struggle with the old enemy of Christendom, and their pulses throbbed with the spirit of Tancred and Godfrey de Bouillon, as they fitted themselves to take their places in the last of the Crusades.

Nor was encouragement from their generals lacking. Two hours before the advance was due to begin, Major-General Godley visited the gully and addressed as many of the men as could be collected. His speech was not a long one, but he told them what he expected them to do. One regiment had already failed to capture the wells; now the Rangers were to do it with the cold steel. The men were not permitted to cheer, but their faces showed their feelings. General Godley, himself an Irishman, showed an intimate knowledge of the Irish character by delivering this address. The knowledge that the credit of their regiment was at stake and that the eyes of their leaders were on them, was sufficient to nerve every man to do his utmost. As a matter of fact, the spirit of the men was excellent; though dysentery and enteric were raging not a man reported sick that morning for fear of missing the fight.

At 2 p.m. the men paraded and worked slowly forward to the old Turkish trench running across the mouth of the gully from which the attack was to be launched. There was only sufficient frontage for a platoon at a time to extend, so the advance was to be made by successive waves of platoons, "C" Company leading, followed by "D," whilst "A" and "B" Companies were kept in support. Though every precaution was taken to avoid making dust and so attracting the attention of the Turks, yet bullets were continually falling among the men, and two officers were wounded before the hour to advance arrived. This was prefaced by a violent bombardment of the enemy's position, conducted not only by the batteries at Anzac, but also by the monitors in the Gulf of Saros, which were in a position that enabled them to enfilade the enemy's line. The noise and dust were terrific, but most of the Turks were well under cover and did not suffer seriously.

Meanwhile, the men waited. A hundred years earlier an officer of the Connaught Rangers had described the appearance and feeling of his battalion as they stood awaiting the signal that was to call them to the assault of the great breach of Ciudad Rodrigo, and his description might have been fitted to their descendants in Gallipoli. Here and there a man murmured a prayer or put up a hand to grasp his rosary, but for the most part they waited silent and motionless till the order to advance was given.

At last, at 3.40, the bombardment ceased, the word came, and the leading platoon dashed forward with a yell like hounds breaking covert. They were met with a roar of rifle fire, coming not only from the trench attacked, but also from Hill 60, and from snipers concealed in the scattered bushes. Not a man stopped to return it; all dashed on with levelled bayonets across the four hundred yards of open country, each man striving to be the first into the enemy's trench. That honour fell to the platoon commander, Second-Lieutenant T. W. G. Johnson, who had gained Amateur International Colours for Ireland at Association Football, and was a bad man to beat across country. Rifle and bayonet in hand, he made such good use of his lead that before his platoon caught him up he had bayoneted six Turks and shot two more. For these and other gallant deeds he was awarded the Military Cross.

The Turks stood their ground well, but succumbed to superior numbers, for soon the supporting platoons came up, while "D" Company moving more to the left was prolonging the line in that direction. The whole of the trenches guarding the wells, together with the wells themselves, were now in the hands of the Rangers, while the communication trench leading to Hill 60 was cleared and blocked, and the two companies in support were moved forward.

Meanwhile the New Zealanders' attack on Hill 60 was not making quite such satisfactory progress. The hill was both fortified with care and held in strength by the enemy, and though General Russell had succeeded in making a lodgement at its foot, he was unable to get further. The Rangers had been ordered, after seizing the wells, to do their utmost to assist his attack, and accordingly "A" Company was detailed to advance and attack the western slopes of the hill. By this time companies had become very mixed, and the charge was composed of a crowd of men belonging to all the companies, mad with the lust for battle. Their officers did little to restrain them, for their Irish blood was aflame, and they were as eager as the men. The line surged up the bare exposed glacis, only to encounter tremendously heavy rifle and machine-gun fire from the crest. At the same moment the enemy's guns opened, displaying marvellous accuracy in ranging, and the attack was annihilated.

In spite of this the men went on as long as they were able to stand, and fell still facing the foe. From the wells below their bodies could be seen, lying in ordered ranks on the hillside, with their bayonets pointing to the front.

It was clear that further advance was impossible, and it only remained for the survivors to consolidate the captured position, which was now being heavily shelled. At 5.15 p.m. the 5th Ghurkas, who had been unable to advance earlier in the afternoon, came up and took over the left flank, including the sunken road running towards Anafarta. The Rangers were then concentrated near the wells, which they protected by a sandbag barricade, while steps were taken to get in touch with General Russell's New Zealanders, who were digging themselves in at the foot of Hill 60, a little further to the east. A portion of the gap between them and the Rangers was bridged by the captured Turkish communication trench, and a sap to cover the remainder was begun at once.

Contrary to anticipation, the enemy did not launch a counter-attack to endeavour to recapture the wells, but their artillery was taking a heavy toll of the conquerors, and officers and men were falling fast. The adjutant of the Rangers, Captain Maling, an officer to whose judgment and courage the battalion owed an incalculable debt, was severely wounded here, and the sergeant-major, who had joined in the charge, had already been carried off with a wound in his leg. "D" Company had only one officer left, and its sergeant-major and quartermaster-sergeant had fallen, while "C" Company had had all its officers hit, two of them fatally. Nevertheless, the men worked hard to put their position in a good state of defence, and before nightfall their object was achieved. At 7 p.m. communication with the New Zealanders was obtained, and two platoons under Lieutenant Blake effected a junction with them.

All through the afternoon the devoted stretcher-bearers were transporting their burdens to the dressing-station in South Wales Borderers' Gully, where the doctor and the priest waited to render devoted service. The labour imposed upon them may be imagined from the fact that over a hundred and fifty cases passed through this dressing-station alone. Now, nightfall made it possible to get up supplies and ammunition. By this time the lesson of the battle of Sari Bair had been learnt, and everything had been carefully pre-arranged. The staff of the 29th Brigade were indefatigable in getting up food and water, and though the Brigade-Major, Captain Pollok, was wounded by a stray shot, his place was well filled by the staff-captain. By daylight the whole position was in a thoroughly defensible state, being well-stocked with food, water and ammunition.

During the night, however, the New Zealanders had had a bad time, and in this the two platoons of Connaught Rangers which had joined them shared. Their position at the foot of Hill 60 was near enough to the Turkish trenches at the top to enable the enemy to throw down bombs, and this they did all night. At intervals, too, they charged down with the bayonet in large numbers only to be repulsed. Heavy casualties were caused in this fight, and among the killed was Lieutenant Blake. His place was taken by Sergeant Nealon, an old soldier, who had taken his discharge long before the war and started business in Ballina.

When war broke out he was among the first to re-enlist, and so inspiring was his example that Ballina disputes with Belfast the credit for having the largest number of recruits in proportion to population of any town in Ireland. No man ever looked less martial, but his stout, comfortable figure concealed the spirit of a hero. When his officer fell he took over the command, led back a mixed group of Rangers and New Zealanders to a sector of trench that had been abandoned owing to the violent bombing that it was suffering, and held it until he was relieved. Another N.C.O. of the Rangers who distinguished himself here was Sergeant John O'Connell, an Irish American, who went out under heavy fire to bring in a wounded New Zealander who was endeavouring to get back under cover. For this and for unvarying courage he was awarded the D.C.M.

On the morning of the 22nd, the newly-landed 18th Australian Battalion arrived on the scene, and attacked the crest of the hill, in company with the New Zealanders. For a time one trench was captured, but the captors were unable to maintain themselves in it, and were driven out by bombing. The Rangers did not take part in this attack, and on the evening of the 22nd were relieved, and returned to their bivouac in South Wales Borderers' Gully.

This engagement has been described in greater detail than its intrinsic importance perhaps deserves, because hitherto the capture of Kaba Kuyu Wells has not been officially attributed to an Irish regiment at all.

The Rangers had not to complain of any lack of immediate recognition, since on the day following their withdrawal Lieutenant-General Sir W. Birdwood, accompanied by Sir A. Godley and General Cox, visited their bivouac. He congratulated them on their gallantry, and promised them four days' rest, after which he intended to call on them for another attack. Sir A. Godley and General Cox were also warm in their congratulations.

Nor was the applause of their comrades lacking, since the Australians and New Zealanders were loud in their praises of the dash and courage of the battalion. This memory long continued with them. More than three months later, Mr. John Redmond, M.P., was showing a party of Australian convalescents over the House of Commons, and asked them if they had seen anything of the 10th (Irish) Division. They replied that they had, and in their opinion the charge made by the Connaught Rangers at Kaba Kuyu was the finest thing they had seen in the war. This praise was worth having, since no men on earth are better able to appreciate courage and are less prone to be imposed upon than the Australians. They have no use for paper reputations; they judge only by what they have seen with their own eyes. Tried by this exacting standard, the Rangers were none the less able to abide it.

While the attack on Kaba Kuyu and Hill 60 was being executed the 10th Hampshires were carrying out their feint. They achieved their object in distracting the enemy's attention, but, unfortunately, incurred heavy losses. Major Morley, the commanding officer, was wounded, and Captain Hellyer, the only officer of the battalion who had come through the stiff fighting on Sari Bair on the 10th unhurt, was killed. The casualties among the rank and file amounted to close on a hundred and fifty. Nor had the Connaught Rangers come off lightly, having lost twelve officers and over two hundred and fifty men. It is interesting to note how much more severely units suffer in modern war than a hundred years ago. Under Wellington in Spain and Portugal, the Connaught Rangers played a distinguished part in many great battles and sieges. At Busaco, in company with half a battalion of the 45th Foot, they charged and routed the eleven battalions of Merle's French Division. They attacked the great breach at Ciudad Rodrigo, and stormed the Castle of Badajoz. At Salamanca, in company with the other two battalions of Wallace's Brigade, they crossed bayonets with Thomieres' Division and drove eight battalions off the field in disorder. All these were famous engagements, and in them the 88th deservedly won great glory, yet in none of them were their losses as heavy as those incurred by their newly-formed service battalion in the little-known engagement at Kaba Kuyu. See table following (the Peninsular figures are taken from Oman's *Peninsular War,* Volumes III and V.):—

* The exact figures are:—

	Killed		Wounded		Missing	
	Officers.	Other ranks.	Officers.	Other ranks.	Officers.	Other ranks.
Busaco	1	30	8	94	—	—
Ciudad Rodrigo	—	7	4	23	—	—
Badajoz	3	28	7	106	—	—
Salamanca	2	11	4	110	—	8
Kaba Kuyu	3	43	9	159	—	47 Nearly all killed.

Elsewhere the issue of the fighting had not been propitious to our arms, since in spite of the never-failing courage of the 29th Division and the magnificent gallantry displayed by the Yeomen, the attacks made from Suvla had failed. The losses were terribly heavy, a very brave Irish Brigadier-General, the Earl of Longford, K.P., having fallen in the forefront of the battle. In consequence of these heavy casualties it was impossible to conduct further offensive operations at Suvla until reinforcements should arrive. It was, however, eminently desirable to effect the capture of Hill 60, since it constituted a perpetual menace to the Suvla-Anzac line of communication. So long as the Turks were able to maintain their position on its crest, not only were they able to enfilade the trenches at Suvla, but also they possessed the power of massing troops behind it and launching them suddenly against our line. They were fully aware of the advantage which this gave them, and had made the defence of the hill extremely strong.

It was determined to make an assault on this position at 5 p.m. on August the 27th. Brigadier-General Russell was placed in command of the assaulting parties, which consisted of 350 Australians who formed the right attack, 300 New Zealanders and 100 Australians, who composed the attack on the centre, and 250 Connaught Rangers, who formed the left attack. By this time units at Anzac were so reduced by casualties and sickness that instead of merely detailing units the numbers required were also specified. At the time the orders were issued the Rangers could only muster seven officers, three hundred men, and of these more than half the officers, and a large proportion of the men were suffering from dysentery or enteritis.

The Australians were to attack the trenches running to the base of the hill in a south-easterly direction. The New Zealanders had as their objective the summit of Hill 60 itself, while the Rangers were given as their objective the system of trenches running from the crest northwards towards Anafarta. At 3 p.m. the assaulting parties of the Rangers filed down the sap, which had been dug to connect Kaba Kuyu with South Wales Borderers' Gully, and into the trenches round the well which they had captured a week earlier. They were narrow and were manned by the Indian Brigade so that progress was slow, but by 4 p.m. the storming party of fifty men had reached the point from which the left assault was to commence.

At four the bombardment began. Ships, howitzers, mountain-guns, all combined to create a babel which if less intense than that of the previous week, was nevertheless sufficiently formidable. The trenches were so close to one another that our troops waiting to advance were covered with dust from the high explosives, but no injury was done. At last, at five, the bombardment ceased and the stormers, led by Lieutenant S. H. Lewis, went over the top. They were into the Turkish trenches almost before the enemy were aware of their coming and forced their way along them with bayonet and bomb. The supporting parties, however, were not so fortunate. The range to the parapet from whence they started was accurately known to the enemy, and from every part of the trench which was not actually under assault violent machine-gun and rifle fire opened. Man after man as he climbed over the parapet fell back into the trench dead, yet the next man calmly stepped forward to take his place. One old soldier, a company cook. Private Glavey, of Athlone, as his turn came, said: "I have three sons fighting in France and one of them has got the D.C.M. Let's see if the old father can't get it now," and advanced to meet the common fate.

Now, too, the enemy's artillery opened, and as, unmenaced elsewhere, they were able to concentrate all their forces on the defence of Hill 60, their fire was terrific. Incessant salvoes of shrapnel burst overhead, while the parapet of the trench from which the advance was taking place was blown in by high explosive. Yet, still, the men went on over the parapet and gradually a few succeeded in struggling through the barrage, and in reinforcing their comrades in the captured trench. There a stern struggle was taking place, but by dint of hard hand-to-hand bayonet fighting the Turks were driven out, and at six p.m. the Rangers had carried the whole of their objective.

The Australians on the right had encountered concentrated machine-gun fire and had been unable to make any progress, but the New Zealanders had carried the trenches on the southern side of the crest and a few of them had worked along and joined up with the Rangers. When night fell the whole of the southern face of the hill was in British hands, but the Turks were not disposed to acquiesce in this decision. As there was no indication of any attack elsewhere, they were free to use the bulk of their reserves at Hill 60, and wave after wave of assailants hurled itself on the position. There was a half moon which enabled the outlines of the charges to be seen as the mass of Turks surged forward preluding their onset with a shower of bombs. The Rangers suffered particularly badly in this respect, since parallel to the trench they held ran two newly-dug Turkish communication trenches which were within bombing distance. There were not enough men available to assault these trenches or to hold them if they were taken, for the losses in the attack had been heavy. It was true that the remainder of the Connaught Rangers had been sent up as a reinforcement, but this only amounted to forty-four men, most of whom were weakened by dysentery.

Again and again, the Turks attacked, mad with fanaticism, shrieking at the top of their voices and calling on *Allah*. The Irish, however, were not impressed. As one Connaught Ranger put it, "they came on shouting and calling for a man named Allen, and there was no man of that name in the trench at all." Still, however, the merciless bombing continued and the trenches slowly became encumbered with dead. It was a soldiers' battle: every officer but one on the Rangers' position was wounded, and in any case the trench was so blocked with debris from the bombardment and Turkish and Irish corpses, that it became almost impossible to move from point to point. Lieutenant Lewis who had led the charge, was wounded in two places. He had himself lifted on to the parapet in the hope of being able to make his way down to the dressing-station, but was never seen again.

At last about 10.30 p.m., after the fight had lasted five hours, a crowd of Turks succeeded in entering the Rangers' trench near its northern extremity. This northern end was held by a small party of men who died where they stood. The remainder of the trench was, however, blocked and further progress by the enemy arrested. Still the fight raged and bombs and ammunition were running short, while the losses became so heavy that it was growing harder and harder to procure. Major Money, who was in command of the advanced position, sent for reinforcements, but found that they were unobtainable. Fresh Turkish attacks kept coming on, and for every assailant that was struck down, two more sprang up in his place.

It was clear that soon the defenders would be swept away by force of numbers, and they were compelled at midnight to fall back to the southern end of the captured trench. This point they blocked with a sandbag barricade and held until at last they were relieved at 8.30 a.m. on the 28th. Five hours earlier the 9th Australian Light Horse had attempted to recover the trench from which the Rangers had been driven, but found that the Turks were too strong. It was not until the 29th that a combined attack launched from the position which the New Zealanders had taken and had been able to hold, finally established our line on the northern slopes of Hill 60.

The Turkish losses were enormous and were nearly all inflicted in fighting at close quarters. The captures from them included three machineguns, three trench mortars and 60,000 rounds of small arm ammunition, while Sir Ian Hamilton estimated that 5,000 Turks had been killed and wounded. When it is remembered that the total strength of our attacking columns was under a thousand, and that the reinforcements received in the course of the fight barely reached that figure, it will be realised that each of our men must have disposed of at least two of his opponents. Unfortunately, our losses were by no means small: of 250 Connaught Rangers who charged over the parapet on the 27th, less than a hundred returned unwounded.

The battalion had, however, no reason on this occasion to complain of lack of official recognition, since Sir Ian Hamilton in his official despatch paid an eloquent tribute to the deeds of the Connaught Rangers. His words may be quoted:

> On the left the 250 men of the 6th Connaught Rangers excited the admiration of all beholders by the swiftness and cohesion of their charge. In five minutes they had carried their objective, the northern Turkish communications, when they at once set to and began a lively bomb fight along the trenches against strong parties which came hurrying up from the enemy supports and afterwards from their reserves. At midnight fresh troops were to have strengthened our grip on the hill, but before that hour the Irishmen had been out-bombed.

That the battalion acquitted itself so well was in the main due to the manner in which it had been trained by its commanding officer, Lieut.-Colonel Jourdain. He thoroughly understood the men with whom he had to deal, and had instilled into all ranks a rigid but sympathetic discipline which proved invaluable in time of trial. He was unwearied in working for the comfort of his men, and was repaid not only by their respect and affection, but by a well-earned C.M.G.

CHAPTER 8

Routine

Scars given and taken without spite or shame, for the Turk be it said is always at his best at that game.—G. K. Chesterton.

Before continuing to describe the doings of the 30th and 31st Brigades after their withdrawal from the Kiretch Tepe Sirt, a word must be said about the units which were attached to them, the Pioneer Battalion, the Royal Engineers and the Field Ambulances. Details of the movements of these units are hard to obtain, but it would not be fair to overlook them.

The Pioneer Battalion, the 5th Royal Irish Regiment, was trained as an infantry unit but also received instruction in engineering work, especially in road-making. The majority of its men were miners or artificers and its function was to do the odd jobs of the division and also to provide a guard for Divisional Headquarters. On the Peninsula, however, these duties soon fell into abeyance, since it was called on to fill up gaps in the line, and did so eagerly. It was an exceptionally fine battalion, formed by Lord Granard, whose ancestor, Sir Arthur Forbes, had first raised the 18th (Royal Irish) two hundred and thirty years before, and possessed an unusually large proportion of Regular officers. Fighting under difficult conditions, usually by detached companies, it did well wherever it was engaged, losing Lieutenants Costello and MacAndrew killed, and Major Fulda, Captain Morel, and half a dozen subalterns wounded.

The Engineers at Suvla, as everywhere, fully justified the splendid reputation of their corps. Few braver actions were noted in the Division than Lieutenant Waller's rescue of three wounded men on the Kiretch Tepe Sirt, and throughout the campaign the Sappers defied danger and did their duty.

The 30th Field Ambulance, which disembarked at Suvla without its bearer section on the afternoon of the 7th, was, for the first ten days of the campaign, working single-handed. Then the 31st and 32nd arrived and the pressure became less, but all the ambulances were working under great difficulties. There was little room for them, they had been unable to bring all their stores with them, and, as will be told later, medical comforts were conspicuous by their absence. In spite of these handicaps, they had to deal, not only with a very large number of wounded, but with a never ceasing flow of sick. The doctors, however, did admirable work and everyone was loud in praise of the ambulance stretcher-bearers who used regularly to go out under heavy fire across the plain to bring in the wounded.

After the close of the fighting on August 17th, what was left of the 30th and 31st Brigades was withdrawn to the rest camp on the beach at Suvla. The fighting had reduced their strength terribly and nearly three-quarters of the officers and half the men who had landed ten days earlier, had fallen or been invalided. Worst of all, was the fact that, owing to so many senior N.C.O.'s having been hit, the internal organisation of units had been practically destroyed. An extemporized company quartermaster-sergeant, who possesses no previous knowledge of his work, will rarely be successful in promoting the comfort and efficiency of his men, however hard he may try. Matters were made even more serious by the continued sickness, which became worse and worse when units were withdrawn from the front line. Many who had been able to force their will power to keep them going on, while actually opposed to the enemy, now succumbed, and among them an officer, whose departure inflicted a serious loss on the division as a whole and on the 31st Brigade in particular.

On August 22nd, General Hill, who had been in bad health ever since landing in Gallipoli, was invalided, suffering from acute dysentery. His departure was deeply regretted by his brigade, who had learnt to admire his coolness and courage, and to appreciate his constant attention to their comfort. Though the staff captain of the brigade, Captain T. J. D. Atkinson, had been wounded on the 16th, fortunately the Brigade-Major, Captain Cooke Collis, still remained, and as the command was taken over by Colonel King-King the General Staff Officer (1) of the division, officers and men did not feel that they had to deal with a stranger.

It was marvellous how many men who were in bad health, resisted the temptation to go sick and be sent on board the white hospital

Brigadier-General J. G. King-King, D.S.O.

ships, where there was shade and ice and plenty to drink. No man was invalided who was not sick, but there were very few people doing duty in Gallipoli who did not from time to time possess a temperature, and none whose stomachs were not periodically out of order. The doctors did their utmost to retain men with their units, but all medical comforts were difficult to obtain, even condensed milk being precious, and to feed men sickening for dysentery on tinned meat, is to ask for trouble. Rice was a great stand-by, though the men did not much appreciate it unless it was boiled in milk.

It was therefore inevitable that men reporting sick should be sent to the field ambulances, and since these were little better off than the regimental M.O.'s so far as provision for special diet was concerned, and since their resources were overtaxed, it followed that it was almost invariably necessary to send invalids away overseas. Though all ranks belonging to them showed the utmost devotion to duty, and worked till they were worn out, a field ambulance at Suvla was not a place in which a quick recovery could be made. True, it had tents, and it is hard to appreciate the amount of solid comfort offered by a tent to one who has spent weeks in the open under a tropical sun. There were also a certain number of beds, and it was very pleasant to find doctors and orderlies taking an interest in you, and doing their best to make you comfortable.

There were, however, discomforts which they were powerless to remove. One was the swarm of flies which made sleep by day impossible, and another was the shortage of water. The worst, however, was the enemy fire: for although the Turk respected the Red Cross flag, yet the hospitals were close to the beach, and not far from some of our batteries, which naturally drew the enemy's artillery. The sound of the shells rushing through the air, and the shock of their explosion were plainly heard and felt by the patients in hospital, and threw an additional strain on nerves that were already worn out. It could not be helped; there was no room on the peninsula to put hospitals at a distance from fighting troops, but it was very hard on the sick and wounded.

Gradually, however, things grew better. Medical comforts began to be forthcoming; fresh bread was baked at Imbros and sent across, milk was less scarce, and a few eggs were issued not only to hospitals, but in some cases to medical officers of battalions. They also obtained a compound known as tinned fowl, which appeared to consist entirely of bones. Fly whisks and veils were provided by the British Red Cross, an organisation to which the soldier owes more than he will ever be able to say. By the flexibility of its management, and its freedom from red tape, it has done wonders to secure the speedier recovery of our wounded.

The rest-camp to which the residue of the nine battalions came, was somewhat of a jest. It was situated on the beach, and consisted of a collection of shallow dug-outs burrowed into the yielding sand. As it was close to some of the extemporized piers at which the lighters bearing the rations and ammunition were unloaded, and was in the neighbourhood of the A.S.C. and Ordnance Depots, it naturally attracted a good share of the shells which the Turks directed at those points, and casualties were by no means infrequent. However, the men were able to take off the clothes which they had worn for nearly a fortnight, and wash. Some shaved, but others thought it waste of time and also of the more precious water. Bathing was possible, for the sea was close by, and the delight of plunging into the warm sparkling sea was hardly diminished by the thought that a Turkish shell might possibly find you out as you did so.

The period in the rest-camp gave an opportunity of writing home, and describing, as far as the censorship permitted, the events of the previous week. It was clear that the first attempt at Suvla had not been successful, but reinforcements were arriving nightly, a new General (Major-General H. B. de Lisle) had taken over command of the 9th Corps, and everyone was hoping for eventual success. In this they were much assisted by rumour, which produced scores of encouraging "shaves." Occasionally one heard that General Botha with a large force of Boers, had landed at Helles, but the favourite and apparently best-authenticated report, was that an army of 150,000 Italians had landed at Bulair and were taking the Turks in reverse. It did not seem to occur to any of those who circulated this report that their guns must have been heard at Suvla if they were really doing so. By this time, however, most sensible people had discovered that nothing is ever so thoroughly well-authenticated as a thoroughly baseless rumour, and believed nothing that they were told. At any rate the *"canards"* gave a subject for conversation, and helped to pass the time.

On August 21st, General de Lisle proposed to take the offensive again, having been reinforced from Egypt and Helles. Although the Turks had by now brought up ample reinforcements, and carefully entrenched their whole line, it was thought that it might be possible to capture Ismail Oglu Tepe, a wooded hill, which buttressed the Khoja

Chemen Tepe. This attack General de Lisle entrusted to the 11th and 29th Divisions, the latter being on the left. The 53rd and 54th Territorial Divisions were to hold the remainder of the line northwards to the Gulf of Saros, including the trenches on the Kir etch Tepe Sirt. The newly-landed 2nd Mounted Division (Yeomanry) and the two brigades of the 10th Division, which had suffered so heavily in the previous fighting as to be almost unfit for further aggressive action, were placed in Corps Reserve. At the same time the co-operation of the Anzac troops, which took the form of the attack on Kaba Kuyu and Hill 60, and was described in the previous chapter, was arranged for.

The 10th Division was disposed as follows:—The 31st Brigade, which was allotted as reserve to the 29th Division, formed up behind Hill 10 on the northern shores of the Salt Lake. There was very little cover, and the 6th Inniskilling Fusiliers, who found themselves in rear of one of our batteries, suffered severely from the shell fire with which the Turks retaliated on it. The 30th Brigade were at Lala Baba at the south-western angle of the lake. At 3 p.m. the attack was launched, and the front line of Turkish trenches were occupied. Atmospheric conditions, however, were unfavourable, and further progress was only made with great difficulty, the 11th Division, which had been much weakened by previous fighting, finding it almost impossible to get on. The reserves were then called up, and the Yeomen went forward across the bare shell-swept plain.

The long extended lines suffered heavily as they moved forward to a position in rear of Chocolate Hill, but though they were young troops who had never been in action before, there was no wavering, and the formation was preserved throughout. About the same time the 30th Brigade received orders to advance and occupy the Turkish trenches, which had been captured at the commencement of operations. As they moved forward to do this they, too, came under a heavy fire of shrapnel and sustained numerous casualties, among them being Lieut.-Col. Worship, of the 6th Munster Fusiliers, who was wounded in the foot. The most active part in these operations, however, so far as the 10th Division was concerned, was taken by the stretcher-bearers of the three Field Ambulances, who had just arrived.

Again and again they went out over the shell-swept plain, picking up the wounded of the 11th and 29th Divisions, and bringing them back to the hospitals on the beach. The work was not only hot and heavy, but dangerous, since although the Turk proved a fair fighter on

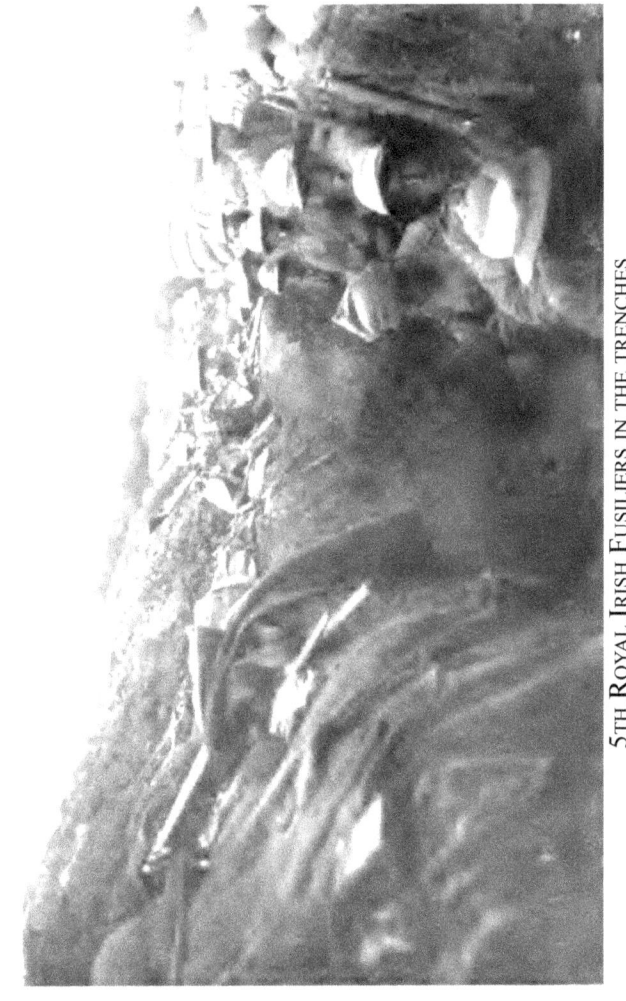
5TH ROYAL IRISH FUSILIERS IN THE TRENCHES

the whole and respected the Red Cross, yet his shrapnel could not discriminate between fighters and non-combatants. Good and plucky work done on this occasion earned the D.C.M. for Staff-Sergeant Hughes and Corporal Fitch, of the 30th Field Ambulance.

On the following day, the two brigades moved southward, and took over the front line trenches, the two Inniskilling battalions being just north of Chocolate Hill, with the Royal Irish Fusiliers on their right, and the 30th Brigade prolonging the line to the southward. At the same time, Divisional Headquarters were transferred from the Kiretch Tepe Sirt to Lala Baba. While the division was holding this southern sector, it very nearly came in touch with part of its detached Brigade operating to the north of Anzac; and the 6th Dublin Fusiliers from their trenches were able to watch the charge of the 5th Connaught Rangers on August 27th. The 29th Brigade, however, remained under the orders of the Anzac Command.

After the fight of the 27th-28th of August, described in the last chapter, this brigade also became incapable of further aggressive action. Every battalion had lost about three-quarters of its strength, while the casualties in the commissioned ranks had been exceptionally heavy. Sickness was bad here, as elsewhere, and early in September three out of the four units composing the brigade had only two officers apiece left. The 6th Leinsters were in better case; but even with them, sickness was taking its toll—Major Currey, the CO., being one of the victims. He was succeeded by Major Colquhoun. The battalion remained with the New Zealand and Australian Division, doing duty in the trenches at "Russell's Top" until August 26th, when it withdrew to Anzac and joined the Royal Irish Rifles in "Reserve Gully."

The Rifles and Hampshires, which suffered terribly in the Sari Bair fighting, were retained behind the Aghyl Dere line for about a week after the 10th August. Then the Rifles returned to Anzac, where it took up its quarters in Reserve Gully. After the feint attack on August 21st, in which they suffered so heavily, the 10th Hampshires were also withdrawn to the beach, bivouacking near No. 2 Post. The brigade was completed by the arrival of the 5th Connaught Rangers, who, after the assault on Hill 60 on the 27th August, remained in reserve for a week and then moved back to a bivouac on Bauchop's Hill.

Though two companies of the Royal Irish Rifles were lent to General Walker, of the Australians, and did duty for him for three weeks, the bulk of the brigade were employed on fatigue duties. These included road-making, unloading ration boats, and guarding Turkish prisoners. The work was hard, the sun still hot, and the enemy's shells did not spare the fatigue parties, but casualties were not heavy.

During this period the 29th Brigade received a new commander. Colonel Agnew returned to Mudros on September 9th, and on the 22nd September Brigadier-General R. S. Vandeleur, C.M.G., who had come from the Seaforth Highlanders in France, took over command. Major T. G. Anderson, R.F.A., had previously been appointed Brigade-Major.

While in many respects fighting in Gallipoli was more unpleasant than in France or Flanders, yet its trench warfare had certain advantages over that engaged in there. Though the heat by day and the cold by night were trying, yet there was but little rain, and it was easy to keep the trenches dry. Except on the Kiretch Tepe Sirt and close to the sea, the soil was firm, so that the sides of trenches did not require much revetment, and repairs were not constantly called for. Above all, the character of the enemy gave the defender an easier time.

The Turk is inflexibly stubborn in defence, and when stirred up to make a mass attack, he appears fearless of death: but he is not an enterprising foe. Except at one or two points—notably at Apex and at Quinn's Post in the Anzac area, where the opposing trench lines were close together, and trench mortars and bomb-throwers raged perpetually—he was content to leave the enemy to the attention of his snipers. These, of course, were persistent and ingenious, and any point in a trench which could be overlooked, either from a tree or from high ground in the enemy's lines, required to be specially defended. Otherwise, however, the Turk was not much disposed to institute aggressive enterprises, and his bombardments, though intensely annoying, and causing a good many casualties, were not to be compared in intensity with those employed by the Germans in Flanders.

Trench-life, however much its details may be mitigated, is none the less painfully monotonous, and in the Peninsula there were none of the distractions sometimes experienced on the Western Front. There were only two breaks in the tedium: the arrival of the mail and a visit from a chaplain. The latter should perhaps have precedence, both out of respect for his cloth and because it happened more frequently. Walking about at Anzac and Suvla was neither pleasant nor safe; but the chaplains were quite indefatigable, and would walk any distance and brave any danger in order to visit the units to which they were attached. By dint of untiring endeavour, the Church of England and Roman Catholic chaplains used, as a rule, to hold a service for each of the battalions in their charge on Sunday, and one during the week as well. Sometimes these services took place right up in the firing line, the celebrant moving along the trench to each communicant in turn. It was in this manner Canon McLean celebrated Holy Communion for the 6th and 7th Dublins an hour before the advance on the 15th of August. Often, too, the priests were able to give absolution to their flock before they went into action. Besides doing this, the Roman Catholic chaplains heard confessions regularly, and all denominations were indefatigable in ministering to the sick.

Apart, however, from the spiritual side of the question, the mere presence of the "*padre*" himself was stimulating. The division had been exceptionally fortunate in its chaplains. The robust cheerfulness of Father Murphy, the recondite knowledge of Father Stafford, Father O'Farrell's boyish keenness, and the straightforward charm that made Father O'Connor such a good sportsman and such a good friend, were coupled with a fearlessness and devotion to duty common to all, that made them beloved by their own flock and liked and respected by those of other creeds. There was but little colour in Gallipoli; grey olives, bleached scrub and parched sand combined to make a picture in monotone, and, even to the Protestant eye it was grateful to see, as the one gleam of colour in a dreary landscape, the shining golden chasuble of the priest as he celebrated Mass. Few who beheld those services will ever forget them; the circle of kneeling worshippers, the robed figure in the centre, the long shadows cast by the newly-risen sun, and the drone of the shells passing through the air overhead, made an ineffaceable impression on the mind.

Nor were the Protestant chaplains behind their Roman Catholic colleagues in zeal and cheerfulness. The Reverend S. Hutchinson in the 31st Brigade, and the Reverend J. W. Crozier (a son of the Primate of All Ireland) in the 29th, worked untiringly and devotedly for the good of the men who belonged to the Church of England. Nor should the Reverend F. J. Roche, who was Church of England Chaplain to the divisional troops, be forgotten. Originally, he was sent to Cairo with the artillery of the division; but he had seen service in South Africa in the Imperial Yeomanry, and was mad to get into the firing line once more. By dint of many entreaties and much ingenuity, he finally succeeded in reaching Suvla on August 29th, and laboured unceasingly with the Pioneers and Royal Engineers. He was a man of exceptionally high character, and all who knew him were grieved when two days before the division left the Peninsula he was invalided with dysentery. Unfortunately, the attack was a severe one, and after rallying slightly he died in hospital at Alexandria. The Presbyterian and Methodist chaplains, too, did excellent work, though since their flock was so widely scattered they had less opportunity of becoming personally known to those outside it.

The jewel of the Protestant chaplains, however, was Canon McLean. Although he must have been nearly sixty years of age, and was probably the oldest man in the division, he had the heart of a boy and the courage of a lion. No dangers or hardships were too great for him to endure, and his one regret was that his cloth did not permit him to lead his brigade in a charge. He had, too, the more valuable form of courage—the power of patient endurance, for though seriously ill with dysentery, he absolutely refused to go sick and leave his men. There were many brave fellows in the division, but none gained a greater reputation for courage than Canon McLean.

The second great alleviation of the monotony of trench life was the arrival of the mail. In France, this happens daily, and is taken as a matter of course; but in Gallipoli it rarely arrived more often than once a week, and great joy was felt in the battalions when Brigade headquarters telephoned that a mail was coming up. Expectation grew, until at last the Indian *drabis* led up their grunting mules, and deposited the mail-bags at the door of the headquarters dugout. Orderly sergeants of the companies were at once summoned, and the slow process of sorting began—a process made even slower by the fact that in many cases the writers had not indicated anything more than the name of the addressee, and that it took a considerable time in an Irish regiment to ascertain which Private Kelly was meant.

"The postmark's Glasgow. Is either of your Kelly's a Scotsman, Sergeant McGrath?" the adjutant would say.

"They are not, sorr. One's a Mayo man and the other's from Dublin. Try 'B' Company, sorr."

The orderly sergeant of "B" also disclaims any Scotch Kelly, but is reminded by the signalling sergeant of a Glasgow man of that name who went sick from Mudros. Repeated *ad infinitum* this process takes time, and it was long before the officer who had undertaken the sorting could turn to his own correspondence. Then followed the painful task of returning the letters that could not be delivered. These were sent back from companies to the orderly-room and were there sorted into three piles:—

     Dead,   Missing,   Hospital.

The officer then endorsed each, writing the word in an indelible pencil, always dreading that by some accident this might be the first intimation of the casualty that the sender of the letter had received. The "Hospital" letters, of course, were not returned to the writer, but were sent in pursuit of the addressee round Mudros, Malta, and Alexandria, usually returning to the battalion after he had rejoined it.

Nor did one's own mail consist entirely of personal letters, for the officers who survived found themselves in September receiving many letters from the relatives of their comrades who had fallen begging for details of how they died. These letters were not easy to answer, since details were often lacking, and the writer was always afraid of inadvertently opening the wound again; but it was a labour of love to reply to them. More amusing semi-official letters were also received, such as the demands of railway companies for sums of three-and-sixpence due by men who had travelled without tickets four months earlier. As even supposing the men in question had not been killed or wounded, they had certainly received no pay for more than a month, and were unlikely to receive any for an indefinite period, so the prospect that the company officer would be able to recover the debts before being killed or wounded himself did not seem large.

With the mail came newspapers and sometimes parcels. The latter were specially welcome, since they served to fill up the nakedness of the officers' mess, and as a rule they arrived safely when sent by parcels post. Complaints of non-arrival of parcels were indeed frequent, but in most cases this was caused either by inaccurate addressing, or by careless packing. Very seldom was a parcels mail-bag opened for sorting at the battalion without the bottom being found to be filled with broken cigarettes, crumbs of crushed cake, and a mass of cardboard, brown paper and string. It must be remembered that the mails had to stand a good deal of rough handling. The bags were sent by ship to Alexandria, then thrown on to a lorry and jolted over the stony streets to the Base Post Office, there sorted, sent on shipboard again, conveyed to Mudros, transhipped to Suvla, Anzac, or Helles, thrown overboard on to a lighter, dumped on the beach, and finally carried up to their destination on the back of a pack mule. It was not astonishing that a parcel was occasionally crushed, or even that a bag sometimes fell into the sea. Under normal conditions, however, parcels usually arrived safely.

The arrival of parcels meant a welcome addition to mess stores, for although the A.S.C. had recovered from the natural confusion caused by the operations at the beginning of August, and rations were regular and plentiful, yet the diet became painfully dull. It must be remembered that in Gallipoli, unlike the Western Front, there was absolutely no possibility of using the resources of the country. In France, it is often possible to buy eggs, butter, and perhaps a chicken, not to speak of wine or beer; but on the Peninsula there was literally nothing obtainable. From Suvla the distant houses of the Anafarta's mocked the eye with the sight of human habitations; but Anzac was literally a desert. The map, it is true, marked a spot as "Fisherman's Hut," but both fishermen and their nets had departed, and the huts had fallen into ruin. Nor did Nature supply anything—except where the trampled stubble told of a ruined cornfield, all was barren, dry scrub, and prickly holly and bare, thankless sand. With such destitution all round, it was no wonder that the post was eagerly looked for.

The most welcome gift of all was tinned fruit, since these and the syrup that came with them quenched thirst. Lemonade tablets, too, were welcome, and sauces and curry-powders to disguise the taste of the eternal bully-beef, were much appreciated. Some things failed to stand the climate; chocolate usually arrived in a liquid condition, while a parcel of butter became a greasy rag. (It must be borne in mind while reading this description of life in Gallipoli that the Expeditionary Force Canteens were not established there till after the 10th Division had left the Peninsula. They did a great deal to fill the want, though it was almost impossible to keep them properly stocked.)

Although life in September was distinctly less trying than it was in August, yet it had its disadvantages. Among them was the fact that wherever a battalion occupied an old Turkish bivouac, it found that the enemy had left behind a peculiarly ferocious breed of flea. There were other minor annoyances in washing; but the main disadvantage of Gallipoli unquestionably was the uncertainty of life. The whole Peninsula was exposed to shell fire, and much of it to snipers as well, and though some places were less dangerous than others, it was impossible ever to feel that one was safe. Every day almost one heard of a fresh casualty. Now an orderly was hit as he brought a message; now a cook fell as he bent over his fire; another day the storeman looking after kits on the beach was killed; or a shell made havoc among a party drawing rations or water.

Drawing rations was one of the most dangerous occupations on the Peninsula, especially at Anzac, and was usually performed at the double. The beaches, where the supply depots were situated, were among the enemy's favourite targets, as they knew that there were always people moving there, and they shelled them persistently. In France, the A.S.C. are said to have safe and "cushy" jobs; but this was certainly not the case in Gallipoli. Their work, in addition to being dangerous, was not exciting, which made things worse; for though Death is the same wherever he comes, it is easier to encounter him in a charge than when cutting up bacon. The memory of the courage of their representatives at Suvla and Anzac should always be a proud one with the A.S.C. But though the beaches were particularly nasty spots, there was no escaping from Death anywhere. If one took a walk one was almost certain to pass a festering and fly-blown mule, or a heap of equipment that showed where a man had been wounded. At one point a barricade of sandbags suggested that it was wise to keep in close to them, at another a deep sap had been dug to allow secure passage through an area commanded by the Chunuk Bair.

The blind impartiality of shrapnel spared no one: the doctor of one battalion sent a man to hospital who was suffering from bronchitis, and was surprised to discover afterwards that when admitted he was suffering from a wound in the right arm which he had acquired on the way down. Even if one remained in one's own bivouac or trench, there was no assurance of safety. It was always possible that a sudden shell might catch one outside one's dugout and finish one. Several fell in this way, among them one of the finest officers in the division, Major N. C. K. Money of the Connaught Rangers. He was a magnificent soldier, always cool and resourceful, and had made his mark on every occasion on which his battalion was engaged. After coming untouched through three stiff fights, and being awarded the D.S.O. for his courage and capacity, he was mortally wounded in bivouac by an unexpected burst of shrapnel. It was a miserable end for one who had done so much, and was destined, had he lived, to do so much more.

After a few weeks on the Peninsula one grew into a fatalistic mood. Most of one's friends had already been knocked out, and it seemed impossible that in the long run anyone could escape. Sooner or later the shrapnel was bound to get you, unless dysentery or enteric got you first. If you were unlucky, you would be killed; if lucky, you would get a wound that would send you either home, or at any rate to Malta or Alexandria, or some other civilized place. Only one thing seemed out of the question, and that was that one should see the end of the campaign. Certainly very few of us did.

CHAPTER 9

Last Days

It is better not to begin than never to finish.
—Serbian Proverb.

At the beginning of September a portion of the Divisional Artillery arrived in the Peninsula. The three brigades (54th, 55th and 56th) which sailed from England with the division, had been landed at Alexandria and sent into camp near Cairo. Rumour had assured the remainder of the division that they were ultimately destined for Aden, but in this as in almost every other instance, rumour lied. After about three weeks in Egypt, where a certain number of horses died as the result of eating sand which caused colic, the 55th and 56th Brigades were transferred to Mudros and thence without their horses to the Peninsula. The 55th Brigade went to Cape Helles, where it took up a position near the Great Gully with its sixteen guns crowded closely together, and suffered a good deal in that congested area from the enemy's shell-fire. This brigade was definitely removed from the division and had no further dealings with it.

The 56th Brigade, on the other hand, came to the Suvla area, though it did not actually rejoin the division. Gun positions were not very easy to discover, but the "A" and "B" Batteries of the brigade came into action below Lala Baba. "C" Battery was out on the plain in a low-lying spot, which was flooded out by the November blizzard, while "D" Battery moved southward into the Anzac area. Here they took up a position on the Damakjelik Bair near the South Wales Borderers' Gully facing northward, which enabled them to enfilade the Turkish trenches on Scimitar Hill, and did excellent work. The whole brigade remained in its positions when the rest of the division left the Peninsula, and did not depart till the final evacuation of Suvla and

Anzac. They consequently definitely severed their connection with the 10th Division.

Throughout September the days passed with monotonous regularity. The routine of trench work, and the telling off and supervision of fatigue parties did not do much to occupy the imagination, and plenty of time was spent gazing out over the sea to Imbros and Samothrace and wondering what was going to happen next. There did not seem much prospect of an advance but it was never easy for junior officers and men to tell what was brewing.

It was somewhat trying to the nerves to know that one was never certain that one would not be required at a moment's notice. Even when nominally resting behind the line units were frequently obliged to stand to in consequence of an alarm of some kind. By this time, blankets and officers' valises had been retrieved, but one felt that one was tempting Providence if one undressed or even took off one's boots at night, for one was always liable to be roused suddenly. The Turks, during this period, were not in at all an aggressive mood, but they too, were subject to nerves, and used occasionally to open fire all along the line for no particular reason. Except for these spasms of nervousness, however, they confined their attention to sniping, intermittent shelling, and where the trenches were very close together, to trench mortar work and bombing.

Two minor distractions were the swallows and the *Peninsula Press*. In August Anzac was a singularly birdless place; in fact except for one cornfield the area had no sign of life of any kind in it. About the middle of September, however, it was invaded by troops of swallows on their way southward, and every gully was full of diving, swooping birds. They brought back many memories of home and of warm Spring evenings and long twilights, and it was a pleasure to watch them circling past the dugouts. They did not seem to mind the shellfire, and there was much discussion as to whether they would winter in Gallipoli, but we did not remain in the Peninsula long enough to make sure.

The other alleviation of the dullness was a half-sheet of news issued by the authority and entitled *The Peninsula Press*. The perusal of this piece of foolscap, which was printed at Army Headquarters and sent to units with more or less regularity, was sufficient to fill one with admiration for the art and mystery of journalism. It was surprising how different the string of *communiqués* and bulletins served up raw without amplification or comment was from the newspaper that one

IMBROS FROM ANZAC

had been accustomed to. For the first time one realised the enormous importance of sub-editing. Nor were the *communiqués* very informing, since for the most part they dealt with Polish towns whose names had never been heard of before by any of us. An atlas was a possession extremely rare in Gallipoli, so we were compelled to take the bulk of the news on trust and hope for the best.

Another minor inconvenience was lack of exercise. In the early days of August there had been no reason to complain on this score, but by the time that we had settled down to routine work in September, many found it hard to keep in condition. Unless you went out with a fatigue party ration-carrying or road-making, your work was confined to a comparatively small area. Walks for the sake of exercise only were discouraged by those in authority, partly because officers were few and could not easily be spared from the possible call of duty that might come at any time, and partly because walking, unless you confined your movements to saps, was not a particularly safe amusement. It was extremely easy to go out for a stroll and come home on a stretcher. Added to this was the possibility, that if you went outside the area in which you were known that you might be taken for a spy. Lurid stories were told of unknown officers who had walked the whole length of Anzac Beach asking questions and then disappeared, and though like most rumours these were probably quite unfounded, yet there was always a chance that some over-zealous and suspicious individual might give you an unpleasant half-hour. All these considerations tended to make walking for pleasure an amusement to be indulged in with moderation.

Fairly soon, however, officers began to work at training again, for early in September steps were taken to fill up the depleted ranks of the division. The first reinforcements had been quickly absorbed on their arrival from Mudros, and by the end of August every unit was much below strength. Since under normal conditions the voyage from England to Mudros usually occupied from ten days to a fortnight it naturally took some time before the gaps in the units were filled. At the end of the first week in September, however, news was received that the first drafts from home had arrived. The men who composed these drafts were for the most part drawn from the reserve battalions of Irish regiments and were excellent material, many of them being men of the old Regular Army who had been wounded in France.

The summer of 1915 in Flanders had been a comparatively quiet one, since there had been a lull in the fighting after the second battle of Ypres. The Regular battalions of the Irish regiments serving there had made comparatively small demands on their Reserve battalions for reinforcements, and consequently large and good drafts were sent out to the 10th Division. This consideration, however, did not apply to the Inniskilling, Munster and Dublin Fusiliers, whose 1st Battalions were serving in Gallipoli with the 29th Division and had sustained terrible losses. Unfortunately, the officers who accompanied the first drafts were not those who had been trained with the units of the division, and had been left behind as surplus to establishment, but were drawn, as a general rule, from Scotch regiments. They were excellent fellows and showed no lack of keenness or courage, but officers who had had some previous knowledge of the units in which they were serving would have been more useful, and in addition, from the sentimental point of view, it was felt that an influx of trews and glengarries tended to remove the Irish character of the division. However, with the later drafts received, a number of Irish officers did arrive.

It was not entirely an easy matter to assimilate these reinforcements. As a rule, a draft is a comparatively small body of men which easily adopts the character of the unit in which it is merged. In Gallipoli, however, units had been so much reduced in strength that in some cases the draft was stronger than the battalion that it joined, while it almost invariably increased the strength of what was left of the original unit by half as much again. As a result after two or three drafts had arrived, the old battalion had been swamped.

For many reasons this was unfortunate. It took a considerable time for the officers and N.C.O.'s even to learn the names of the newcomers, still more to acquire that insight into their characters necessary for the smooth working of a company or platoon. The shortage of good and experienced N.C.O.'s, too, had the result of throwing rather too much influence into the hands of bad characters. In every large body of soldiers there are bound to be men who dislike danger and do their best to avoid it. As a rule these undesirables are known and are unable to do much harm; but among an influx of young soldiers a few men of this stamp, posing as experienced veterans, may do a considerable amount of mischief, till they are discovered and dealt with.

It was unfortunately impossible to adopt the most favourable method of assimilating the new men. To teach men to act together, to recognise and obey the voice of their officer or sergeant there is nothing like drill, and particularly drill in close order. Only from drill can be obtained the surrender of individuality in order to achieve a common purpose which is the foundation of military discipline. It is on the barrack square that a platoon or company first "gets together" and realises its corporate entity; it is "on the square" that an officer first begins to distinguish his men and to discriminate between their characters, and it is "on the square" that men first begin to know their officer. Barrack square drill is not, as it was in the Eighteenth Century, the end-all and be-all of military training, but it is an indispensable foundation for it, and no effective substitute has ever yet been found to take its place.

Unfortunately, in Gallipoli, drill was out of the question. When on the move, men straggled along in single file without thought of step, while the duties of trench-manning, road making, or onion carrying, did not encourage smartness. While off duty the men were scattered round a rabbit warren of dugouts, and any gathering for parade purposes was at once dispersed by hostile shrapnel. All that could be done was to practise bombing in disused Turkish trenches and carry out the usual inspections of rifles, ammunition and iron rations. The severity of the handicap thus imposed upon battalions will be best appreciated by those who have served in France. There units periodically go behind the line to rest, and during the rest-period are able by drill and discipline to learn to know and assimilate their new men.

Among other matters that had to be faced was the training of specialists. Most battalions had lost the bulk of their machine-gunners and signallers and it was extraordinarily rare to find a unit in which both the signalling and machine-gun officer survived. If they did the adjutant probably did not, and one of them had been promoted to fill his place. In any case, fresh officers and men had to be trained for the duty. It proved to be unfortunate that very few of the officers who joined with drafts had had any training in either of these branches. A reserve battalion, if well-organised, should be a kind of military university in which an energetic officer can pick up some knowledge of every branch of infantry work since he can never tell what he may not be required to do when posted to a battalion on active service. The power to command a platoon is only the foundation, not the climax, of a subaltern's training. Fortunately, in addition to the second-lieutenants who accompanied drafts, a certain number of officers and men rejoined from hospital. These had mostly been wounded or gone sick during the fighting at the beginning of August, and they formed a very welcome reinforcement, since they were both experienced and seasoned to the climate.

Unfortunately, as much could not be said for the new drafts, who suffered very badly from dysentery. It was a common experience for a company commander to congratulate himself on having discovered a good sergeant-major or platoon-sergeant only to hear on the following day that he had been invalided. The men who had been wounded in France seemed to be peculiarly liable to dysentery.

While steps were being taken to reorganise the shattered units, rumours began to spread that the division was to leave the Peninsula to rest. By this time most people had begun to discredit all rumours, but it appeared possible that there might be something in this. It was known that both the 29th Division and what was left of the original Australians had been removed to Mudros for a change of ten days or so, and from a military point of view it was eminently desirable to give the division a chance of training its new drafts in a spot free from shell-fire.

It was, however, very uncertain when and where we were to go. The place varied between Mudros and Imbros, while the time suggested was always "next week." Finally, the 29th Brigade received orders on September 28th to prepare to move on the following evening, not to either of the places anticipated but to Suvla. For a moment people thought that an attack was in prospect since a day or two earlier *The Peninsula Press* had announced great victories in France. Since units of the division had been paraded at Mudros in July and ordered to cheer for the impending fall of Bagdad, most people were a little distrustful of official bulletins, but if it really was true, and the German line was broken both at Loos and in Champagne, then, of course, we should push the enemy as hard as possible wherever we could. All these speculations were shattered, however, early on the 29th, by the cancellation of the orders to proceed to Suvla, and the receipt of instructions to embark at Anzac for Mudros on the same evening.

Somehow one was not as glad to be leaving Gallipoli as one had anticipated. To be sure it was all to the good to be out of the shelling for a time and the Turks took steps to intensify the pleasure caused by this prospect by firing on the bivouacs of the 29th Brigade on their last day with unusual vigour. One shell fell immediately outside the guard room of the Connaught Rangers, but fortunately failed to explode. Another burst in the camp of the Royal Irish Rifles and wounded Lieutenant Elliot. This officer was the last survivor except for the quartermaster and doctor, of the officers of the battalion who had landed at Anzac on August 6th, and was unlucky in being hit on the last day. Even the prospect of immunity from bombardment could not however disguise the fact that one was sorry to leave. As the 29th Brigade filed down the long sap to Anzac in the darkness, as the 30th and 31st Brigades retraced their steps past Lala Baba and over the beaches at Suvla, it was impossible to avoid retrospect. We had passed that way less than two months before, but going in the opposite direction full of high hopes. Now we were leaving the Peninsula again, our work unfinished and the Turks still in possession of the Narrows. Nor was it possible to help thinking of the friends lying in narrow graves on the scrub-covered hillside or covered by the debris of filled-in trenches, whom we seemed to be abandoning.

Yet though there was sorrow at departing there was no despondency. We had the memory of strenuous effort and achievement to inspire us, and the bond of friendship among the few officers who survived had been knit closer than it had ever been before. The men, too, felt a new spirit towards their officers, and the hard times they had shared together had cemented the feeling of comradeship which had always existed. They knew now that whatever the danger might be their officers would be the first to face it, and the officers had proved that their men would follow them anywhere. Once that sentiment exists in a battalion it is impossible to break its spirit.

The 29th Brigade reached Mudros at dawn on September 30th and went under canvas in the Mudros East area, which was on the opposite side of the harbour to the bivouac they had previously occupied. The remainder of the division followed them thither in the course of the week. There was unfortunately not many of the original division left.

Though the Divisional Staff had not greatly changed, only one brigadier still held his original command. This was Brigadier-General Nicol, who had won the admiration and affection of the 30th Brigade by his unfailing courage and tenacity. He was not a young man, but in spite of the sickness which afflicted everyone in Gallipoli he resolutely refused to go to hospital, and by his example encouraged many younger officers to "stick it out." Of the original brigade staffs only one brigade-major, Captain Cooke Collis, and one staff captain, Captain Goodland, survived, and sickness and wounds had so thinned the ranks of the commanding officers that only Lieutenant-Colonel Jourdain of the Connaught Rangers, Lieutenant-Colonel Cox of the 6th Royal Dublin Fusiliers, Lieutenant-Colonel Pike of the 5th Royal Irish Fusiliers, and Lieutenant-Colonel Lord Granard of the Royal

Irish Regiment, were still with their units. One Lieutenant-Colonel, Vanrenen, of the 5th Inniskillings, had fallen, and the other eight were wounded or sick. The battalions, too, had suffered terribly, and it was an exceptional unit that possessed more than half-a-dozen of its original officers and 200 of the men who had gone with it to the Peninsula at the beginning of August. Even of these a fair proportion had spent part of the time in hospital and rejoined; those who had seen the campaign through from start to finish were rare.

There was, however, little time to think of these matters. The concentration of the division was not completed till October 3rd and on October 4th its first two battalions sailed for another theatre of war.

Chapter 10

Retrospect

So awakened in their hearts the strongest of all fellowships, the fellowship of the sword.—W. B. Yeats.

What does one recollect most clearly when one looks back at Gallipoli?

A multitude of memories cluster together: dry, sand-floored gullies, thirsty men crowded round a well, Indians grooming their mules, lithe, half-naked Australians, parched, sun-dried scrub, but above and beyond all these one remembers the graves. Not a man came back from the Peninsula without leaving some friend behind there, and it is bitter to think that the last resting-place of those we loved is in the hands of our enemy. Not all the dead of Gallipoli lie in the Peninsula itself. There are crowded cemeteries at Malta and Alexandria, and many a brave body has been lowered over the side of a hospital ship into the Aegean to mingle his bones with those of Argonauts and Crusaders and all the heroes of a bygone age. Nevertheless, when one thinks of Gallipoli one thinks first of graves.

You could not walk far in the Peninsula without seeing them, sometimes thickly crowded together outside a field-ambulance, sometimes a solitary cross marking the spot where a sniper's victim had been buried. Each of these tombs had at its head a little wooden cross bearing the man's name, regiment, and rank, and the date of his death, and in some cases his comrades had done a little more. Here Australian gunners had made a pattern with fuse caps on the earth that covered their friend, and there a lid of a biscuit-tin had been beaten into a plaque, bearing a crucifix. Death had made strange bedfellows: in one little cemetery high up at the Chailak Dere behind Rhododendron Ridge there lay side by side Private John Jones, Royal Welsh Fusiliers

A Faugh-a-Ballagh teases a Turkish Sniper

and Sergeant Rotahiru of the Maoris. From the two ends of the earth Christian and Buddhist and Sikh had come to fight in the same cause, and in death they lay together. It was my lot in the last days of September to endeavour to compile a register of where the men of my battalion had been interred, and as I went from grave to grave writing down the name of one Irishman after another I was irresistibly reminded of Davis's lines:

But on far foreign fields from Dunkirk to Belgrade
Lie the heroes and chiefs of the Irish Brigade.

Now the age-long quarrel with the Turk had carried Irishmen even further afield and the "Wild Geese" who fought on the Danube under Prince Eugene[1] found their successors in those of the 10th Division who lay under the Cross of Christ in the barren waste of Gallipoli.

Not indeed that every grave was marked with a cross. Some had fallen within the enemy's lines and others were hastily buried under the parados of a captured trench without even a stone to mark where they lay. In the heat of battle, it was impossible to delay for forms and ceremonies, and often even the names of the fallen were not noted. Only those who died in hospital were buried with proper rites, but it mattered little where the bodies of the heroes rested. The whole land is one shrine, made sacred by the memory of devotion to duty and self-sacrifice, and no man could wish to lie elsewhere than in the ground he had won from the enemy.

Yet it seemed a pity that it should be knocked to pieces so soon. Much labour spread over many weary months had gone to form it and to make it worthy of the name of Irish, and it was tragic that it should practically be annihilated with so little tangible result achieved. It is not perhaps altogether easy for the civilian to understand how sorrowful it seems unless he realises that a unit trained to arms has a spiritual as well as a material being. A battalion of infantry is not merely a collection of a thousand men armed with rifles; it is, or at any rate, it should be, a community, possessing mutual hopes, mutual fears, and mutual affection. Officers and men have learnt to know one another and to rely on one another, and if they are worth their salt, the spiritual bond uniting them is far stronger and more effectual for good than the power conferred by rank and authority.

In the 10th Division the bonds uniting all ranks were unusually

---

1. *Eugene of Savoy* is also published by Leonaur.

strong. In the first place came love of Ireland shared in equal degree by officers and men. Second to this, and only second, was pride of regiment, happiness at forming part of a unit which had had so many glorious deeds recorded of it and resolution to be worthy of its fame. The names of the battalion, Dublins, Munsters, Inniskillings, Connaught Rangers, spoke not only of home, but also of splendid achievements performed in the past, and nerved us to courage and endurance in the future.

Above and beyond these feelings, common to all Irish soldiers, the 10th Division had a peculiar intimacy gained from the circumstances of its formation. It was the first Irish Division to take the field in war. Irish Brigades there had often been; they had fought under the *fleur-de-lys* and the tricolour of France and under the Stars and Stripes as well as they had done under the Union Jack. But never before in Ireland's history had she sent forth a whole division (but for one battalion) of her sons to the battlefield.

The old battalions of the Regular Army had done magnificently, but they had necessarily been brigaded with English, Scotch and Welsh units. The 10th Division was the first division almost entirely composed of Irish battalions to face the enemy. Officers and men alike knew this and were proud of their destiny. As the battalions marched through the quiet English countryside, the drums and fifes shrilled out "St. Patrick's Day" or "Brian Boru's March," and the dark streets of Basingstoke echoed the voices that chanted "God Save Ireland" as the units marched down to entrain. Nor did we lack "the green." One unit sewed shamrocks on to its sleeves, another wore them as helmet badges . Almost every company cherished somewhere an entirely unofficial green flag, as dear to the men as if they were the regimental colours themselves. These constituted an outward and visible sign that the honour of Ireland was in the division's keeping, and the men did not forget it.

There was singularly little jealousy in the division. Naturally, where there were two battalions of one regiment in the same brigade, each one of them cherished the belief that they and they alone were the true representatives of the old regiment, but this was only wholesome emulation. Where this cause for rivalry did not exist units were on very good terms, and at Basingstoke, where the different messes first really got to know one another, there was any amount of friendship and good fellowship. Every battalion, of course, believed that it was the finest service battalion in the army, but it was also convinced that the remainder of the division, though inferior to itself, reached a very much higher standard than any other unit in K.1.

Having regard to this sentiment it was with great regret that officers and men found that the division was not destined to take the field as a whole. The first shock was the loss of the artillery, and the realisation that we should be compelled to rely on the support of strange gunners when we took the field. Next came the fact that the 29th Brigade was detached and sent to Anzac, where in turn it met with yet further sub-division, its battalions going into action as isolated units.

Finally, the mischance that sent the 5th Inniskillings, the two battalions of Munster Fusiliers, and the Pioneer battalion into action on the Kiretch Tepe, while the remainder of the 30th and 31st Brigades were fighting under General Hill at the other end of the Suvla area, destroyed the last chance that the division as a whole might place some distinct achievement to its credit.

Of the dash and eagerness of the men there was no doubt. All they needed was to be told what they were to do, and they would carry it out whatever the cost. They showed, too, on the 16th August, that in addition to eagerness in the charge, a quality never lacking in Irish soldiers, they possessed the rarer and finer military quality of dogged tenacity. Whoever may be blamed for the small success achieved in Gallipoli, no discredit rests on the rank and file of the 10th Division.

The circumstances attending the formation of absolutely new units had brought officers and men into a somewhat unusual relationship. In the old Regular Army, except for a few N.C.O.'s and old soldiers who have wives and families in married quarters, and an occasional indiscreet youth who marries off the strength, the family life of the soldier never comes under the officers' notice at all. In the New Army things were very different. The rapid expansion of our military forces that took place in August and September, 1914, had placed a tremendous strain on the resources of paymasters and record officers. The confusion and delay inevitably caused by this often meant considerable hardship to the soldier's family, and he had no one to turn to for help but his officer.

First came the question of men whose employers were prepared to increase their pay to the level of their previous wages provided they could prove that they had enlisted. As a rule, the official papers were long in coming, and in consequence company-commanders made out certificates that the men were serving, which, though unofficial, proved effective. Next came the question of allowance; separation allowance and allowance to dependants, which involved an enormous amount of work and entailed a close acquaintanceship with the details of each man's family history. Finally came the work of stamping and keeping up-to-date the National Insurance cards, which formed the last remaining bond that linked the soldier to his civilian life.

Meanwhile, officer and man had been gaining insight into each other's character. The company commander had watched his men change from a mob in civilian clothes to a disciplined body in khaki. He had been busy picking out the intelligent, encouraging the backward, stimulating the lazy, and checking the first steps of a few towards drunkenness and vice. In all this he had had the invaluable assistance of his company sergeant-major, and an intimacy had grown up between them of no ordinary kind. When it was severed, as it too often was, on the field of battle, the survivor felt that he had been maimed and deprived of an invaluable m support.

On a smaller scale a similar relationship arose between the subaltern and his platoon-sergeant, while among the specialists, signallers and machine-gunners, the bond between officer and men was even closer as became those who shared a common mystery. The whole unit had grown up together; the men in the ranks had watched the subaltern who had joined ignorant of the rudiments of drill acquire knowledge and self-confidence, and in the process had learned to trust him themselves. The officers had seen with pleasure a boy selected for a lance-corporal's stripe because he showed signs of intelligence, gradually gaining experience and the power to command men, until sometimes he graduated into an excellent sergeant. There were many common memories; wet days on the Curragh, long treks in the Hampshire dust, scuffles in the hedgerows during a field-day, bivouacs in a twilight meadow, all combined to cement the feeling of friendship between officer and men. Sometimes these memories went back to a period before the war.

Nearly all the officers were Irish, and most of them were serving in their Territorial units, with the result that they often found privates who were their near neighbours and knew the woods, and the bogs, and the wet winding roads of home. All this was good; it gave the division a character that it could not otherwise have obtained, but it had its black side when men began to fall. It was not merely Number So-and-so Private Kelly who was killed, it was little Kelly, who had cooked (very badly) for the mess at Basingstoke, or Kelly who had begged so eagerly not to be left behind with the first reinforcements, or Kelly, the only son of a widowed mother, who lived on the Churchtown Road, three miles from home.

To the staff and the High Command, men must necessarily be no more than ciphers on a casualty list, but to the regimental officer it is very much otherwise, and every man who falls causes a fresh pang to his commander's heart. Few things are more distressing to an officer than to hear the roll of his unit called after an engagement, to look in vain among the thinned ranks for many familiar faces, to hear no answer given to name after name of the men with whom his life has been bound up for months. This and not any extreme of physical suffering is the hardest ordeal that a soldier has to face.

Nor was this loss of friends and comrades the only cause of sorrow. The same feelings have been felt in every unit of the New Army after a strenuous engagement, but the 10th Division had a special reason for regret since the 10th Division was a thing unique in itself. Ireland is a land of long and bitter memories, and those memories make it extremely difficult for Irishmen to unite for any common purpose. Many have believed it impossible, and would have prophesied that the attempt to create an Irish Division composed of men of every class, creed and political opinion would be foredoomed to failure. And yet it succeeded. The old quarrels, the inherited animosities were forgotten, and men who would have scowled at one another without speaking became comrades and friends. Only those who know Ireland can realise how difficult this was.

The division was not composed of professional soldiers; many of the officers and men had played, or, at least, had relatives who had played, an active part in the agrarian and political struggles that have raged in Ireland for the last forty years. Yet all this went for nothing; the bond of common service and common sacrifice proved so strong and enduring that Catholic and Protestant, Unionist and Nationalist, lived and fought and died side by side like brothers. Little was spoken concerning the points on which we differed, and once we had tacitly agreed to let the past be buried we found thousands of points on which we agreed. To an Englishman this no doubt appears natural, for beneath all superficial disagreements the English do possess a nature in common and look on things from the same point of view, but in Ireland up to the present things have been very different. It is only to be hoped that the willingness to forget old wrongs and injustices, and to combine for a common purpose, that existed in the 10th Division, may be a good augury for the future.

No doubt the experience of the two other Irish Divisions of the New Army has been the same. Both of them have since won abundant glory in France. When the war is over, all these combats shared together, and dangers faced side-by-side, should count for something in the making of the new Ireland.

No doubt it may seem to the outsider that all this is founded on an unstable foundation, and that the 10th Division did not do so much after all. Measured by the scale of material results he may seem correct. At Suvla, indeed, they claim to have taken Chocolate Hill and to have gained ground along the Kiretch Tepe Sirt, part of which they were unable to hold. At Anzac two battalions seized part of the Chunuk Bair and held it until they were driven off, a third succeeded in maintaining its position on Rhododendron Ridge, while the fourth captured the wells of Kabak Kuyu and gained a footing for a time on Hill 60. All these were but incidents in what was itself an unsuccessful campaign, yet officers and men did all that was required of them. They died. There was no fear or faltering, there was no retirement without orders.

The 10th Division, young soldiers without knowledge or experience of war, were plunged into one of the hardest and fiercest campaigns ever waged by the British Army, and acquitted themselves with credit. They make no claim to exclusive glory, to have done more than it was their duty to do, but they have no cause to be ashamed. Their shattered ranks, their enormous list of casualties, show clearly enough what they endured, and the words used by Sir Ian Hamilton of one brigade are true of the whole division. He wrote:—

> The old German notion that no unit would stand a loss of more than 25 *per cent,* had been completely falsified. The 13th Division and the 29th Brigade of the 10th (Irish) Division had lost more than twice that proportion, and in spirit were game for as much more fighting as might be required.

This may reasonably be applied to the 30th and 31st Brigades as well as to the 29th, for the best proof of the enduring spirit of the division may be found in the fact that when after having lost nearly 75 *per cent,* of its original strength, it was hastily filled up with drafts and sent under-officered and barely rested to fight a new and arduous campaign single-handed, it did creditably.

In some quarters, particularly in Ireland, which is a sensitive and suspicious country, it has been suggested that the services of the division have not been adequately recognised. Little is to be gained by engaging in a controversy on this point. No doubt if on the grounds that the Gallipoli campaign was unsuccessful, the men who fought there are refused a clasp to their medals, and the regiments who took part in it are not permitted to add its name to the battle honours on their colours, much resentment will be aroused, but it is hardly likely that this will occur. If precedents are needed, Talavera and Busaco, both of which figure as British victories, were followed by retirements and by no definite result other than the exhaustion of the enemy's forces. Corunna, too, which was merely a repulse of a pursuing enemy, followed by embarkation and evacuation, is considered a victory, and while these names are emblazoned among the battle-honours of regiments there is little reason for excluding Gallipoli, where men suffered as much and fought as bravely.

But, after all, these considerations, though sentiment endears them to the soldier, are minor matters. The soldier's true reward is the gratitude of his fellow-countrymen, and that we have in full measure obtained. Ireland will not easily forget the deeds of the 10th Division.

Appendix

APPENDIX A
On Authorities

In writing this book I have in the main been guided by my own memory and by information obtained from other officers, but I have also read almost every book dealing with Gallipoli that has been published up to the present (February, 1917). Three of these have been of great value to me, since their authors served with the division. The first (*At Suvla Bay* by John Hargrave.) was written by a sergeant in the 32nd Field Ambulance and describes in graphic language the experiences of a stretcher-bearer. It is illustrated by a number of sketches from the author's hand. The second book (*Suvla Bay and After*, by Juvenis.) is also a record of individual experiences. Though the author is anonymous and is very reticent in giving detailed information of any kind, yet he appears from internal evidence to have been an officer in the 5th Royal Inniskilling Fusiliers. His narrative describes life on the Peninsula from the 8th to the 15th, on which date he was wounded. It also gives a vivid account of hospital life at Mudros.

Both these works are first-hand evidence of the doings of individuals, but the third is of greater value to the historian. It is a record of the services of the 5th (Service) Battalion of the Connaught Rangers between the 19th of August, 1914, and the 17th of January, 1917, compiled by its commanding officer. This work not only provides a clear and vivid narrative of the movements of the battalion, but also gives invaluable information as to orders, strength and casualties. If a similar work were compiled for each unit, the task of the historian would be easy.

I regret that the book dealing with the history of "D" Company of the 7th Royal Dublin Fusiliers, which has been written by Mr. H. Hanna, K.C., was not published in time to allow me to read it before writing this work. Mr. Hanna has, however, been kind enough to allow me to read part of his proof-sheets, and the information which I obtained from him has been of great assistance to me.

I have also studied the letters from officers and men which appeared in the Irish Press in the Autumn of 1915, but I have not as a rule considered their statements as unimpeachable unless they were confirmed by some independent authority.

Appendix B

CASUALTIES TO OFFICERS
(STAFF AND INFANTRY ONLY)

STAFF:

Killed:
Capt. G. W. Nugent, Staff Capt., 29th Brigade.

Wounded:
Brig.-Gen. R. J. Cooper, G.V.O., 29th Brigade.
Major D. J. C. K. Bernard, G.S.O. III.
Capt. A. H. McCleverty, Brigade-Major, 29th Brigade.
Capt. T. J. D. Atkinson, Staff Capt., 31st Brigade.

5TH ROYAL IRISH REGIMENT (PIONEERS).

Killed:
Lieut. R. MacAndrew.
2nd Lieut. J. P. Costello.

Wounded:
Major J. L. Fulda.
Capt. E. C. Morel.
Capt. J. R. Penrose Welsted.
Lieut. E. C. Beard.
Lieut. J. N. More.
2nd Lieut. C. Bewicke.
2nd Lieut. L. M. Lefroy.

Missing:
Lieut. J. R. Duggan.

5TH ROYAL INNISKILLING FUSILIERS.

Killed:
Lieut.-Col. A. S. Vanrenen.
Capt. R. W. Robinson.
Capt. C. E. G. Vernon.
Lieut. H. H. McCormack.
Lieut. J. E. T. Nelis.
2nd Lieut. D. J. Grubb.

Died of Wounds:
Lieut. J. R. Whitsitt.

Wounded:
Major T. A. D. Best.
Major C. S. Owen.
Capt. W. C. G. Bolitho.
Capt. V. H. Scott.
Lieut. F. C. Stigant.
Lieut. T. T. H. Verschoyle.
Lieut. T. E. Hastings.
Lieut. F. M. McCormac.
Lieut. O. G. E. MacWilliam.
2nd Lieut. G. C. Ballentine.
2nd Lieut. R. R. A. Darling.
2nd Lieut. L. F. Falls.
2nd Lieut. M. W. F. Hall.
2nd Lieut. I. A. Kirkpatrick.

6TH ROYAL INNISKILLING FUSILIERS.

Killed:
2nd Lieut. W. S. Collen.
2nd Lieut. I. J. Smyth.

Wounded:
Lieut.-Col. H. M. Cliffe.
Major G. C. B. Musgrave.
Lieut. and Qrmr. J. J. Dooley.
Lieut. S. T. Martin.
Lieut. A. B. Douglas.
2nd Lieut. J. F. Hunter.
2nd Lieut. W. Porter.

10TH HAMPSHIRE REGIMENT.

Killed:
Capt. C. C. R. Black Hawkins.
Capt. W. H. Savage.
Lieut. G. L. Cheeseman.
Lieut. P. C. Williams.
2nd Lieut. S. A. Smith.
2nd Lieut. O. S. Whaley.

Died of Wounds:
Capt. G. E. Hellyer.
Wounded:
Lieut.-Col. W. D. Bewsher.
Major L. C. Morley.
Capt. T. A. Shone.
Capt. C. C. Waddington.
Capt. F. M. Hicks.
Lieut. L. Whittome.
Lieut. J. H. Tanner.
Lieut. C. C. Griffith.
Lieut. J. Clement.
2nd Lieut. I. H. German.
2nd Lieut. J. Morse.
2nd Lieut. C. Grellier.
2nd Lieut. G. S. H. De Gaury.

Wounded and Missing:
Major A. L. Pilleau.
Capt. C. B. Hayes.
Lieut. P. L. Bell.

6TH ROYAL IRISH RIFLES.

Killed:
Major and Adjt. W. Eastwood.
2nd Lieut. J. H. B. Lewis.
2nd Lieut. A. W. Richardson.

Died of Wounds:
Capt. J. F. Martyr.

Wounded:
Lieut.-Col. E. C. Bradford.
Major A. L. Wilford.
Major H. J. Morphy.
Capt. P. D. Green Armytage.
Capt. F. E. Eastwood.
Capt. R. H. Lorie.
Capt. R. O. Mansergh.
Lieut. N. McGavin.
Lieut. T. W. E. Brogden.
Lieut. D. Campbell.
Lieut. J. H. Pollock.
2nd Lieut. A. F. Harvey.
2nd Lieut. G. B. J. Smyth.
2nd Lieut. J. Murphy.
2nd Lieut. J. G. Martry.
2nd Lieut. W. G. Ryan.

5TH ROYAL IRISH FUSILIERS.

Killed:
Major W. F. C. Garstin.
Capt. W. J. Hartley.
2nd Lieut. C. Crossly.

Died of Wounds:
Capt. G. G. Duggan.
Capt. A. W. Scott-Skirving.

Wounded:
Major F. W. E. Johnson.
Capt. E. M. McIlwain.
Capt. and Adjt. P. E. Kelly.
Capt. J. A. D. Dempsey.
Capt. H. G. Whyte.
Lieut. J. B. Atkinson.
Lieut. W. A. Beattie.
Lieut. C. F. N. Harris.
Lieut. C. A. Murray.
Lieut. R. V. Murray.
Lieut. J. A. Blood.
2nd Lieut. J. L. Chalmers.
2nd Lieut. P. H. D. Dempsey.
2nd Lieut. E. A. Evanson.
2nd Lieut. F. A. Nowell.
2nd Lieut. L. C. Fitzgerald.
2nd Lieut. J. L. Bennett.

6TH ROYAL IRISH FUSILIERS.

Killed:
Major H. M. Taylor.
Capt. and Adjt. J. C. Johnston.
Capt. B. V. Falle.
Lieut. L. Tolerton.
Lieut. J. S. Schute.
2nd Lieut. H. M. MacDermot.
2nd Lieut. G. F. Dobbin.
2nd Lieut. P. S. Snell.
2nd Lieut. W. A. Birmingham.

Wounded:
Lieut.-Colonel F. A. Greer.
Capt. W. A. Woods.
Capt. F. G. M. Wigley.
Capt. H. F. Belli Biver.
Capt. F. R. M. Crozier.
Capt. P. Jackson.
Lieut. G. H. Gallogly.
Lieut. F. H. Ledgerwood.
Lieut. A. L. Gregg.
Lieut. P. C. Tudor Craig.
2nd Lieut. J. C. McCutcheon.
2nd Lieut. C. F. Kennedy.
2nd Lieut. R. S. Trimble.
2nd Lieut. W. R. Egar.
2nd Lieut. C. E. T. Lewis.

Missing (believed killed):
2nd Lieut. C. M. A. Barker.
2nd Lieut. J. J. Beasley.
2nd Lieut. F. G. Heuston.

5TH CONNAUGHT RANGERS.
Killed :
Lieut. A. J. W. Blake.
2nd Lieut. J. E. Burke.
2nd Lieut. G. R. Bennett.

Died of Wounds :
Major N. C. K. Money.
Capt. A. S. Hog.

Wounded :
Major H. J. Nolan Ferrall.
Capt. and Adjt. H. W. B. Maling.
Capt. A. Webber.
Capt. F. C. Burke.
Capt. G. J. B. E. Massy.
Capt. B. W. Bond.
Lieut. J. W. Cartmell Robinson.
Lieut. T. S. P. Martin.
Lieut. F. J. Charlton.
Lieut. O. M. Tweedy.
2nd Lieut. A. D. Mulligan.
2nd Lieut. J. Wallace.
2nd Lieut. T. W. G. Johnson.
2nd Lieut. E. J. G. Kelly.
2nd Lieut. A. St. J. Mahony.

Wounded and Missing :
Lieut. S. T. H. Lewis.

6TH LEINSTER REGIMENT.
Killed :
Lieut. N. J. Figgis.
Lieut. G. W. B. Gough.
2nd Lieut. A. R. Toomey.
2nd Lieut. W. S. C. Griffith.
2nd Lieut. H. G. Hickson.
2nd Lieut. J. V. Y. Willington.

Wounded :
Lieut.-Col. J. C. Craske, D.S.O.
Major T. R. Stannus.
Lieut. A. J. Jennings.
2nd Lieut. H. D. Little.

Missing (believed killed) :
Capt. C. C. D'Arcy Irvine.

6TH ROYAL MUNSTER FUSILIERS.
Killed :
Major E. P. Conway.
Lieut. J. B. Lee.
Lieut. G. W. Burrowes.

Died of Wounds :
Major J. N. Jephson.
2nd Lieut. L. A. Gaffney.

Wounded :
Lieut.-Col. V. T. Worship, D.S.O.
Capt. H. G. Oldnall.
Capt. H. G. Livingston.
Capt. C. Y. Baldwin.
Lieut. G. W. N. N. Haynes.
Lieut. A. T. Lee.
Lieut. E. A. Thornton.
2nd Lieut. H. M. Chambers.
2nd Lieut. T. E. Hearn.
2nd Lieut. J. I. Comerford.
2nd Lieut. J. W. L. Rathbone.
2nd Lieut. S. C. Webb.

Missing :
Capt. J. B. T. Grant.

7TH ROYAL MUNSTER FUSILIERS.
Killed :
Capt. R. H. Cullinan.
Capt. J. V. Dunn.
Lieut. K. E. O'Duffy.
Lieut. S. R. V. Travers.
2nd Lieut. E. M. Harper.
2nd Lieut. F. E. Bennett.
2nd Lieut. W. H. Good.

Wounded :
Major C. L. Hendricks.
Capt. A. L. Cooper Key.
Capt. W. F. Henr.
Capt. M. Wace.
Capt. H. Aplin.
Lieut. W. E. McClelland.
Lieut. H. G. Montagu.
Lieut. T. D. Hallinan.
Lieut. C. E. Longfield.
Lieut. R. E. Lawler.
2nd Lieut. V. J. Magnier.
2nd Lieut. F. S. L. Stokes.
2nd Lieut. J. L. Fitzmaurice.

6TH ROYAL DUBLIN FUSILIERS.
Killed :
Capt. A. J. D. Preston.
Capt. and Adjt. W. R. Richards.
Lieut. J. J. Doyle.
2nd Lieut. W. C. Nesbitt.
2nd Lieut. F. B. O'Carroll.
2nd Lieut. W. F. C. McGarry.

Died of Wounds:
2nd Lieut. W. L. G. Mortimer.

Wounded:
Capt. W. H. Whyte
Capt. P. T. L. Thompson.
Capt. R. B. C. Kennedy.
Capt. J. Luke.
Capt. J. J. T. Carroll.
Capt. W. S. Lennon.
Lieut. C. A. Martin.
2nd Lieut. R. W. Carter.
2nd Lieut. C. F. Healy.
2nd Lieut. M. Moloney.

Wounded and Missing:
Major J. G. Jennings.
Lieut. D. R. Clery.
2nd Lieut. R. Stanton.

[All these are believed to have been killed.]

7TH ROYAL DUBLIN FUSILIERS.

Killed:
Major C. H. Tippet.
Major R. S. M. Harrison.
Capt. P. H. Hickman.
Capt. G. Pige Leschallas.
Capt. R. P. Tobin.
Lieut. M. J. Fitzgibbon.
Lieut. A. J. Russell.
2nd Lieut. E. T. Weatherill.

Died of Wounds:
Lieut. E. L. Julian.

Wounded:
Lieut.-Col. G. Downing.
Capt. L. S. N. Palmer.
Lieut. C. B. Girvin.
Lieut. A. W. MacDermott.
2nd Lieut. C. D. Harvey.
2nd Lieut. H. L. Clover.
2nd Lieut. G. Hicks.
Lieut. A. M. Eynaud (Royal Malta Regiment of Militia attached.)

Missing:
2nd Lieut. A. G. Crichton.

I regret that I have been unable to compile a full list of casualties in the Royal Artillery, Royal Engineers, Army Service Corps and Royal Army Medical Corps. Among those who were killed and wounded were :—

Killed:
Capt. H. J. Sudell, Army Service Corps.

Wounded and Missing (probably killed):
2nd Lieut. M. W. Prettyman Royal Engineers.

Wounded:
Capt. C. R. Satterthwaite, Royal Engineers.
Lieut. C. Patteson, Royal Engineers.
Lieut. L. Cassidy, Royal Army Medical Corps.

APPENDIX C

NAMES OF OFFICERS, NON-COMMISSIONED OFFICERS, AND MEN MENTIONED IN GENERAL SIR IAN HAMILTON'S DESPATCHES

JANUARY AND MARCH, 1916

STAFF:

Lieut.-General Sir B. T. Mahon, K.C.V.O., C.B., D.S.O.
Colonel (temporary Brigadier-General) F. F. Hill, C.B., D.S.O.
Lieut.-Col. (temporary Brigadier-General) J. G. King King, D.S.O., Res. of Officers.

ROYAL INNISKILLING FUSILIERS

No. 12,519, Corporal J. Matchett.
No. 12,515, Private A. Mason.
No. 13,272, Private R. Bannon.
No. 13,981, Private J. Cox.
Temporary Lieut.-Colonel H. M. Cliff.
Temporary Lieut.-Col. M. P. B. Frazer.

Major M. J. N. Cooke Collis, Royal Irish Rifles.
Capt. A. H. McCleverty, 2nd Rajput Light Infantry.

ROYAL ENGINEERS.

Lieut.-Col. F. K. Fair.
Temporary Lieut. C. Patteson.
Temporary Lieut. J. H. de W. Waller.

ROYAL IRISH REGIMENT.

Temporary Lieut.-Col. Rt. Hon. B. A. W. P., Earl of Granard, K.P., G.C.V.O.
Temporary Major V. M. B. Scully.
No. 5,615, C.S.M. R. Gallagher.
No. 223, C.S.M. M. McGrath.
No. 2,797, Lance-Corporal A. Laughlin.
No. 2,821, Lance-Corporal W. Grant.
No. 1,251, Private J. C. Keefe.
No. 4,545, Sergeant T. Sturges.
No. 10,205, Private F. Biddicombe.
No. 9,871, Private J. C. R. Moxham.
No. 14,938, Private F. Dyer.
No. 14,295, Private E. P. Shawe.

ROYAL IRISH RIFLES.

Lieut.-Colonel E. C. Bradford.
Temporary Major W. Eastwood.
Temporary Major H. L. Wilford.
Regimental Sergeant-Major P. Mulholland.

ROYAL IRISH FUSILIERS.

Temporary Lieut.-Col. M. J. W. Pike.
Major F. W. E. Johnson.
Capt. P. E. Kelly.
Temporary Capt. H. S. C. Panton
2nd Lieut. C. Crossley.
Temporary Capt. G. M. Kidd.
Temporary Lieut.-Col. F. A. Greer.
Temporary Major M. J. Thompson.
Temporary Capt. P. C. Tudor Craig.
Temporary Lieut. A. L. Gregg.

Temporary Major G. C. B. Musgrave.
Temporary Capt. R. H. Scott.
Temporary Lieut. C. G. Barton.
Temporary Second-Lieut. G. B. Lyndon.
No. 7,817, Sgt. M. Garrett.
No. 17,986, Lance-Corporal W. Wynne.
No. 11,792, Lance-Corporal J. Maple.
No. 19,955, Private P. O'Kane.
No. 11,832, Private J. Lamont.
No. 12,720, Private T. Millar.

HAMPSHIRE REGIMENT.

Temporary Lieut.-Col. W. D. Bewsher.
Temporary Capt. F. M. Hicks.
Temporary Capt. P. H. Hudson.
Quartermaster and Hon. Lieut. W. J. Saunders.
No. 4,410, Temporary Sergeant-Major J. Smith.
No. 42,196, Company Sergt.-Major W. T. Groves.
No. 3,010, Temporary Sergeant-Major J. Hudson.
No. 319, Acting C.Q.M. Sergeant M. Nealon.
No. 652, Sergeant J. O'Connell.
No. 6,757, Sergeant J. McIlwaine.
No. 824, Acting Corporal J. Doyle.
No. 83, Private J. Geehan.
No. 3,831, Private J. Sweeney.
No. 529, Private M. Kilroy.

LEINSTER REGIMENT.

Lieut.-Col. J. Craske, D.S.O.
Temporary Capt. C. Lyster.
Temporary Capt. C. W. D'Arcy Irvine.
Capt. H. W. Andrews (Adjt.)
Temporary 2nd Lieut. H. G. Hickson.
No. 8,120, Company Sergeant-Major H. H. Anderson.
No. 833, Sergeant J. Henry.
No. 1,201, Sergeant E. W. Bruce.
No. 3,134, Private J. Carolan.

ROYAL MUNSTER FUSILIERS.

Temporary Lieut.-Col. M. A. Tynte.
Major J. N. Jephson.

Quartermaster and Hon. Lieut. S. L. Cleall.
Temporary 2nd Lieut. F. G. Heuston.
No. 12,169, Sergeant J. Donohoe.
No. 12,166, Sergeant G. O'Neill.
No. 11,892, Sergeant G. Thirkettle.
No. 1,991, Lance-Corporal G. Cassells.
No. 15,641, Private C. Kipps.
No. 13,703, Private C. Lees.

CONNAUGHT RANGERS.

Temporary Lieut.-Col. H. F. N. Jourdain.
Temporary Major N. C. K. Money.
Temporary Major B. R. Cooper.
Capt. H. B. W. Maling (Adjt.)
Capt. G. J. B. E. Massy.
Temporary Lieut. A. J. W. Blake.
Lieut. S. H. Lewis.

ROYAL DUBLIN FUSILIERS.

Temporary Lieut.-Col. P. G. A. Cox.
Temporary Major W. H. Whyte.
Capt. A. J. D. Preston.
Capt. P. T. L. Thompson.
Capt. W. R. Richards.
Qr. Master and Hon. Lieut. R. Byrne.
No. 13,507, Temporary Sergeant-Major J. Campbell.
No. 17,141, Sergeant J. West.
No. 13,197, Corporal E. Bryan.
Lieut.-Col. G. Downing.
Major R. S. M. Harrison.
Major M. P. L. Lonsdale.
Temporary Major C. B. R. Hoey.
Temporary Capt. R. P. Tobin.
Temporary Capt. L. S. N. Palmer.

Temporary Capt. B. R. French.
No. 250, Company Sergeant-Major J. Murphy.
No. 26, Sergeant J. Ring.
No. 176, Sergeant W. Connors.
No. 545, Corporal R. Saunders.
Temporary Major G. Drage.
Temporary Major H. Aplin.
Temporary Lieut. H. Fitzmaurice.
Temporary Lieut. E. M. Harper.
Temporary Capt. G. H. Davis.
Temporary Lieut. S. R. V. Travers.
Temporary 2nd Lieut. F. T. S. Powell.
Qr. Master and Hon. Lieut. C. Lindsay.
No. 10,397, Sergeant-Major M. Stacey.
No. 2,364, Company Sergeant-Major R. Mason.
No. 2,501, Private W. Bellamy.
No. 2,521, Private H. Carbult.
Temporary Capt. G. N. Williamson.
No. 14,153, Regimental Sergeant-Major A. Guest.
No. 14,133, Company Sergeant-Major W. Kee.
No. 14,972, Company Sergeant-Major T. Haig.
No. 14,275, Company Sergeant-Major H. Robinson.
No. 14,150, Sergeant A. E. Burrowes.
No. 14,645, Sergeant E. C. Millar.
No. 13,852, Private A. E. Wilkin.
No. 25,563, Company Sergeant-Major C. Lynch.

CHAPLAIN'S DEPARTMENT.

Rev. R. A. McClean.

APPENDIX D

HONOURS AWARDED TO OFFICERS NON-COMMISSIONED OFFICERS AND MEN OF THE TENTH DIVISION

C.B.

Col. (temp. Brig.-Gen.) R. J. Cooper, C.V.O., Res. of Off.

C.M.G.

Temp. Capt. H. S. Panton, Royal Irish Fusiliers.
Temp. Lt. J. F. Hunter, Royal Inniskilling Fusiliers.
Temp. Lt. C. Patteson, Royal Engineers.

Col. (temp. Brig.-Gen.) F. F. Hill, C.B., D.S.O.
Lt. Col. J. Craske, D.S.O., Leinster Regt.
Major (temp. Lt.-Col.) H. F. N. Jourdain, The Connaught Rangers.

D.S.O.

Major (temp. Lt.-Col.) W. D. Bewsher, Res. of Off.
Capt. (temp. Major) N. C. K. Money, Indian Army (att. Connaught Rangers).
Capt. (temp. Major) A. L. Wilford, Indian Army (att. Royal Irish Rifles).

To be Brevet Colonel in the Reserve of Officers.

Lt.-Col. (temp. Brig.-Gen.) J. G. King-King, Res. of Off.

MILITARY CROSS.

Temp. Capt. G. M. Kidd, Royal Irish Fusiliers.
Temp. Capt. C. C. J. Lyster, Leinster Regt.
Capt. G. J. B. E. Massy, The Connaught Rangers.
No. 14153, Acting Sergt.-Major A. Guest, 7th Royal Dublin Fusiliers.
No. 32611, Sergt. G. Hughes, 30th Field Ambulance.
No. 15641, Pte. C. Kipps, 6th Royal Irish Fusiliers.
No. 11832, Pte. J. Lamont, 6th Royal Inniskilling Fusiliers.
No. 11782, C.-Sergt.-Major C. Lynch, 5th Royal Inniskilling Fusiliers.
No. 12515, Pte. A. Mason, 5th Royal Inniskilling Fusiliers.
No. 2464, Acting C.-Sergt.-Major R. Mason, 7th Royal Munster Fusiliers.
No. 17792, Lance-Corpl. J. Meckle, 6th Royal Inniskilling Fusiliers.

Qr.-Master and Hon. Lt. W. J. Saunders, Hampshire Regt.
Qr.-Master and Hon. Lt. R. Byrne, Royal Dublin Fusiliers.
Temp. Sec. Lt. F. G. Henston, Royal Irish Fusiliers.
Temp. Sec. Lt. G. B. Lyndon, Royal Inniskilling Fusiliers.

D.C.M.

No. 8120 Sergt. H. Anderson, 6th Leinster Regt.
No. 2501, Pte. W. Bellamy, 6th Royal Munster Fusiliers.
No. 1470, Pte. F. Biddlecombe, 10th Hampshire Regiment.
No. 10205, L.-Sgt. S. Bowers, 10th Hampshire Regt.
No. 41627, Pioneer T. L. Campbell, Royal Engineers.
No. 3134, Pte. J. Carolan, 6th Leinster Regt.
No. 177, Sergt. W. Connors, 6th Royal Munster Fusiliers.
No. 12169, Sergt. J. Donohoe, 6th Royal Irish Fusiliers.
No. 33452, Corpl. S. A. Fitch, 30th Field Ambulance.
No. 83, Pte. J. Geehan, 5th Connaught Rangers.
No. 250, C.-Sergt.-Major J. Murphy, 6th Royal Munster Fusiliers.
No. 642, Sergt J. O'Connell, 5th Connaught Rangers
No 1251, Pte J. O'Keefe, 5th Royal Irish Regiment.
No. 4545, Acting C.-Sergt.-Major T. Sturges, 10th Hampshire Regiment.
No 17986, L.-Corpl. St. C. P. Wynne, 6th Royal Inniskilling Fusiliers.

Clasp to D.C.M.

No. 3010, Sergt.-Major J. Hudson, 5th Connaught Rangers, was awarded a clasp to the D.C.M. won by him in South Africa when serving with the Irish Guards.

With the Ulster Division in France

Contents

Preface 191
Part 1 193
Part 2 237
Part 3 246
Part 4 251
Appendix 258

This Book
is
Dedicated to the people of Ulster

In remembrance of those who have given
their lives for their King and Country.

The sequel of today unsolders all
The goodliest fellowship of famous knights
Whereof this world holds record:
Such a sleep they sleep—the men I loved,
I think that we shall never more, at any future time,
Delight our souls with talk of knightly deeds
Walking about the gardens and the halls
Of Camelot, as in the days that were.
　　　　　　　　From *The Passing of Arthur,*
　　　　　　　　　—Lord Tennyson.

THE KING REVIEWING THE ULSTER DIVISION.

Preface

The appearance of this little book needs a word of explanation. While at the front with the Ulster Division, the late Captain A. P. I. Samuels, had kept a very complete record of events, and collected all the material available, with the object of being in a position, some day, to publish an account of the doings of the division, and particularly of his own battalion, the 11th Royal Irish Rifles (South Antrim Volunteers.) It has been willed, however, that he should not be spared to carry out his intention. Like so many of his gallant comrades he gave his life for his country, being killed in action on September 24th, 1916. His name is now on Ulster's Roll of Honour, among those whose death has brought unspeakable grief to thousands of our homes, and yet has filled the hearts of Ulstermen and women with pride, and bequeathed such renown to our Province as will last while it endures. His papers, and the materials he had gathered have naturally come into my hands, and I have endeavoured, though in a very small and inadequate manner, to carry out the purpose for which they were collected.

This little book does not profess to be in any way a history of the Ulster Division, nor even of the 11th Batt. Royal Irish Rifles. Being compiled from the diary of Captain Samuels, supplemented by the records he was able to obtain, its scope is necessarily limited, and the story closes with the historic advance of the Ulster Division on the Somme at Thiepval on 1st July, 1916. In some respects this necessary limitation is a fitting one. To many in Ulster this great event marks in reality the passing of the glorious division recruited during the first six months of the war, trained by battalions in various camps in Ireland, and finally, as a complete division, at Seaford and Borden, before being sent to France. True, those permitted to survive that awful shock of July 1st, and those drafts in reserve at home remained to carry the fame of Ulster to Messines Ridge and Cambrai, but the division was never again quite the same as before that memorable day.

At that time it was unique. All its members were identified with the Northern Province. Each battalion was recruited from some particular part, and even small districts and villages were represented separately in the companies and platoons. It was inevitable that after the Somme battle distinctive units should become merged, and that as the war progressed officers and men should find their way to the 36th Division who were not strictly representative of Ulster.

It is hoped that these memoirs may be of interest to Ulster people as describing the everyday life of a unit of their division during its first eight months in France before the novelty of the life in billets and in trenches had worn off, and become merely monotonous, and while the point of view was still that of the native Ulsterman rather than the British soldier.

Part 1

We fell in at 4 o'clock on the afternoon of October 4, 1915, on the parade ground of St. Lucia Barracks, Borden. So mechanical a proceeding is a regimental parade, and so extremely heavy were the packs that we carried, that there was little opportunity for pondering over the changed conditions that we were soon to undergo. As far as the men were concerned—and the same applied to a large number of the officers—they had left their homes and all that home implied when they left Ireland three months before.

As we marched to the station we were struck by the apathy displayed by the few civilians we saw. There was no cheering, waving of handkerchiefs, or kissing of hands; even the children, making mud pies on the side of the road did not trouble to look up. We were only one of the many units that had passed down that same road during the previous fourteen months. It was almost an everyday sight now for the people who lived there to see regiments entraining for France. So it was, that as we marched down the short road to Borden station, we felt that we were only going on our business, and that those plain-clothed civilians—many of them young and physically fit men—were going on theirs. At Borden station the somewhat questionable spirits of the men were revived by large cups of excellent tea, brought round by ladies, a parting kindness which was greatly appreciated, and which none of us will forget

. The first train, with Brigade Headquarters, Battalion Headquarters, and "A" and "B" Companies, steamed out of the station at 5-10 p.m., followed at 5-35 by the second train with "C" and "D" Companies. Blinds were drawn in the carriages soon after starting, and with only one stop the train ran through to Folkestone Pier, where we went on board the transport *Onward*. At 9-35 p.m. we left the shores of England, bound for France and the unknown. A war-time cross-

The Review of the Ulster Division

channel steamer, converted into a troopship for short runs, is as uncomfortable a form of craft as one can wish to sail in, and the *Onward* was no exception to the rule. In addition to our battalion there were several drafts, principally from Scotch regiments, on board. Luckily it was a fine, warm night, and the sea was as smooth as glass. The dining-room and lounge were boarded up and stripped as bare as a barrack floor, while the corridors, and every available inch of accommodation below were packed with men, in all those extraordinary attitudes, recumbent and sprawling, which the sleeping Tommy can only adopt.

On deck it was just the same, and quite impossible to walk from one end of the boat to the other. There were strict orders against smoking on deck, and the task of the unfortunate officer, whose sense of duty was sufficiently strong to prevent him from winking at any breach of discipline, was unenviable. A cigarette, like Nerissa's candle, throws a long beam, and every effort to reach the culprit was fraught with such curses and mutterings from the bodies over which one stumbled, that it would have disheartened even the adamant spirit of the Secretary for War himself.

We reached Boulogne at 11-30 p.m., and, after the usual disembarkation formalities, in which the Disembarkation Officers and R.T.O.'s always seem to exercise their unlimited powers to the full, the battalion fell in by companies about 300 yards down the pier. In the darkness and heavy rain which now began to fall this proceeding took a considerable amount of time, but after half an hour we moved off, all thoroughly soaked through. At the best of times the way from the pier at Boulogne to the Rest Camp, some distance out of the town, is not pleasant, but that October night it was particularly bad. The streets were wet and slippery, the men heavily laden with blankets and equipment, and the road up to the Rest Camp led up a steep incline. The leading company, however, stepped out at their normal pace. A few, mindful of the landing of the original Expeditionary Force, and the ever famous "Tipperary" scenes, burst into song, but the Frenchman retires early to bed, and, with the exception of one long, thin arm fluttering a pocket handkerchief from a top window, we saw no sign of life in the deserted streets.

After a very steep climb of about two miles, we came to the Rest Camp, and a series of gasoline flares lit up the muddy flats on which the tents were pitched. The mud, ankle deep, sucked up round our boots, and torrents of rain danced in the puddles. It was a matter of ten minutes before each company was allotted its area, and after that, in less time than it takes to tell, the sleep, which only those who have spent a night in a Rest Camp at Boulogne know, had fallen on all.

The day after we landed was an easy one. No orders came as to moving, and the time was spent by our men in parading about the camp, sleeping, and talking to the numerous women and small boys who wandered round the railings, clamouring for "biscuit," "penny," or "bully beef." So urgent was the appeal for these commodities, that the men took it for granted that the entire population of France was starving, and handed over that somewhat elusive "unconsumed portion" of the previous day's ration, or any that remained of it. As the day wore on and word was received that there would be no move until the following morning, some of the officers were allowed into town in the afternoon. Boulogne in war-time is not an interesting place, and an hour was sufficient for exploration purposes.

With the exception of a few French territorials, guarding the bridges and railway station, the town seemed to be entirely handed over to the British, whose motor ambulances glided in every direction. The *Cambria*, with her green and white topsides and large Red Cross flag at her masthead, lay alongside at the quay, a sight to make one home-sick, which brought one's mind back to Dublin Bay and Kingstown Harbour in the days of peace. It rained off and on all day, and was bitterly cold, an early foretaste of the bitter winds we were to experience in France. We fell in next morning, Wednesday, 6th October, at 10-15, and marched to the Central station, where we entrained. Speculation was rife as to where we were going, whether Belgium, which savoured of Ypres and all that that name implied, or the new line between Arras and the Somme. The latter was a sector taken over by the British from the French in the July preceding, and had the name of being quiet and pleasant compared to the more northerly parts of the line.

As the day wore on and we steamed South through Abbeville, and finally came to Amiens, there was no doubt as to our destination. From Amiens we moved on to a side line, and at 6-15 came to Flesselles, a small town about 15 miles south of Amiens, where we detrained. It was a lovely autumn evening, and with a slight breeze blowing from the East, and as we stood fallen in ready to move off from the station, we heard the low rumble and occasional growl of a big gun. From Flesselles we had to march some twelve kilometres to Rubenpre, which was to be our billeting town. Very heavily laden as we all were, officers and men, again the mistake was made of setting too fast a pace. It was an exceptionally warm evening, the men were tired, hungry and thirsty, after the long train journey, and as an hour, and then two, passed by, and we still appeared to be some distance from our town, the softer hearts in the battalion collapsed. There is no necessity to dwell on the unpleasant memories of our first route march in France; it was the most trying experience for both officers and men that we had for many a long day. As we marched East, and as the night grew darker, the flares, and the lurid flashes of gunfire became more vivid, and helped to keep up the interest of the men and distract their attention from the general weariness; at any rate we were, after eleven months' training, getting to the "Front" at last.

When we reached Rubenpré, at 11 o'clock at night, many of the men done up and all very tired, we halted at the head of the village. The second in command had gone on the previous day with the advance party to arrange the billeting, but in the darkness, of a more than usually dark night, the result of his effort was practically impossible to find. The village consisted, as far as one could judge by the light of electric torches or matches, of a series of long barns with doors most of which were barred and bolted, and presented a remarkably inhospitable appearance. A few days before we had left Borden we had been paraded, and in the course of a ten minutes' harangue, the commanding officer had dwelt upon the good name of the battalion, and its excellent conduct while in England. He told the men that he relied on them to maintain that high record in the country to which they were going. Especially he told them to respect the religious susceptibilities of the people.

> Hanging over your beds in your billets you will find crucifixes, pictures of the Virgin Mary, and the Saints, and other emblems of the Roman Catholic Church and religion. You will respect these emblems, and remember that you and your Allies have come to free these people from the Germans.

So throughout that march from Flesselles to Rubenpré, the men had before them the vision and anticipation of feather beds which all the saints in the catalogue might adorn, so long as it was a bed. No such luck, however, as feather beds could be hoped for in the land which the men had already christened "No man's land." So dark was the night, and so impossible to find were the billets allotted to each company, that after nearly half-an-hour's halt at the entrance to the village, company commanders and officers took the matter into their

Rubenpré.

own hands, threw off their packs and equipment on the side of the street, and led their worn-out men down the village. They burst open the doors of barns, and put in, here 20, there 30, men, despite the irate remonstrances of the owners, often punctuated by some shrill scream from some female proprietor, who thought that at any rate her last hour had come.

At length, on straw and hay, on floors hard and soft, everyone found a bed, and, tired, as they were, one or two were heard to mutter, Orangemen though they might be, that they wouldn't mind a bed even if the picture of the Pope himself hung at the head. In this part of France there are no farms. The country is dotted at intervals of a kilometre or two with villages, some small, some large, mostly the same in appearance, with their orchards, and grey church spires sticking up above the knots of trees. All round these villages the country stretches away in gently rolling plains, like a great checkerboard, no ditches or hedges, reminding one of what England must have looked like in the days of the "common field" system. This part of the country is intensely cultivated, not an inch of land is allowed to go to waste, and in war time the work is done entirely by young girls and old women. A young man was never seen, either in the fields or villages; there seemed to be few old men, and the small boys spend most of their day at school.

These Picard villages are intensely dirty, and Rubenpré was even dirtier than most of them. The barns were in a bad state of repair, and the yards were swimming with filthy water from the great heaps of manure which were piled up in front of each house, often right up against the windows, yet, curiously enough, the houses themselves were in most cases neat and clean. The houses are built of laths, plastered with mud and straw, poor in construction, and, owing to lack of men, in many cases whole villages presented a dilapidated and tumbled-down appearance. Rubenpré was, therefore, an inhospitable place, and the reception we received from the people themselves was not what we expected. We felt that we had come to the country to fight for the people, and to free them from the enemy; in other words we looked upon ourselves in a mild way as deliverers, and felt to a small extent that we were entitled to be received as such.

But our eyes were soon opened,—those bolted barns and inhospitable entrances were an index of the regard in which the people held us; we were received with suspicion, and often with dislike, in every village to which we came during our long peregrinations in Picardy. It speaks volumes for our men to be able to say, as we can say with truth, that we always went away with the good wishes and blessings of the people, and there were many in the battalion who, when a day off came, would walk eight or ten miles to revisit some of their French friends. It was only after we had been some time in the country that we discovered the reason for this coldness. Robbed first of all by the Germans, they had endured successive invasions of Zouave, English, Scotch, and Indian troops, and now an Irish division, a form of terror formerly unknown was thrust upon them in its entirety. We saw that there was a certain amount to be said for their apparent inhospitality, and put up with it.

The first couple of days at Rubenpré were devoted to "shaking down." As far as my company was concerned, we were, on the whole, fortunate with regard to our billets. There was at first a lack of straw, but this was soon remedied, and the men very soon accustomed themselves to the novelty of their surroundings. Large fatigue parties were put on from each company, and within a week the town was cleaner than it had been for many a long day. The people looked on with quiet amusement, but they too soon became resigned to what they considered the British mania for cleaning.

Battalion headquarters were in a cottage, and at first a battalion officers' mess was tried in an estaminet which had a room in which a stove was riveted in the centre. In a short time, however, the difficulty of running a four company and headquarters mess in the same house became apparent, and two companies, "A" and "B", seceded and formed a mess of their own in another *café*. "C" Company and headquarters remained in the same house, but before we had been many weeks in France the advantages of company messes became evident. Our company headquarters was in a disused and rather tumbled down house, but it had a good orchard and field behind, which we used for musketry and range finding. In return for the use of the house, we lent the owner a few men every day as a help to thresh his corn and milk his cows. There was no lack of fresh milk, eggs, potatoes, and apples. Eggs cost three *sous* each, milk four *sous* per litre.

We remained at Rubenpré for about two weeks, and during that time had the usual routine of parades and training as at home. We were inspected by the G.O.C. Third Army, Sir Charles Munro, who expressed himself very pleased with our bearing on parade. We had two or three brigade field days and one divisional day, the latter the first divisional exercise under the eyes of our new G.O.C. Division, General Nugent. The remarks of our general on the day's performance

MAILLY-MAILLET.

MAILLY-MAILLET SUCRIER.

were, to say the least of them, hardly as complimentary as we should have wished. They left an impression on the minds of those who heard them that will never fade, and they had their effect on all ranks.

On 18th October we left Rubenpré to go up to the line for that instruction period which everyone in the New Army in France knows so well. As we got nearer to the line the sound of the guns became more distinct, and the tiny puffs of white smoke in the sky from the German aircraft guns was the first sign of the nearness of the trenches. The country was just the same as at Rubenpré every inch cultivated. At Varennes we were met by a band of the South Lancs., and played through the town and along the road as far as Forceville. Here we halted in a field for dinners. After dinners we fell in, and marched off by companies at ten minutes' interval, for we were now within the zone of artillery fire, being about 3½ miles from the trenches. It was only when we left Forceville that we saw any change in the aspect of the country. We now passed several lines of heavily wired trenches, which made long, white streaks across the otherwise brown and regular landscape.

In other respects there were the same signs of intensive agriculture as far behind the line. We reached, at length, Mailly-Maillet, which was to be our billeting town during the instructional period. In peace time Mailly-Maillet had evidently been a very pretty little town of about 1,000 to 1,500 inhabitants, considerably better built and evidently much more prosperous than any of the villages we had seen since we came to France. There was a *château* with a fine avenue of elms which had its entrance on one side of the main street. The *château* was a brigade headquarters, while the avenue of elms was used as a park for transport, and was crowded with limbers and G.S. waggons up to the axles in mud. There was not a pane of glass to be seen in any of the houses; many were without doors, and some were pierced by great shell holes. Generally Mailly-Maillet had a dejected and war-worn appearance.

A battery of howitzers close by caused all the window-frames in the place to shake, and every now and then a few slates would come tumbling down. As the town was full of troops, and we were an additional battalion, our billets were very poor. The men were in a very bad outhouse with little straw, while "C" Company Headquarters was an empty room with a tile floor in an extremely rickety condition. The first few days in Mailly were devoted to working parties. "A" Company was attached to the 1st Batt. Essex Regt., "B" Company

IN TRAINING BEHIND THE LINES.

to the 8th South Lancs., and "C" to the 1st Batt. Kings Own Royal Lancaster Regiment, and "D" Company to the 2nd Royal Lancaster Fusiliers; all belonging to the 12th Brigade of the 4th Division.

The more or less eventful period of instruction which "C" Company experienced with the King's Own began on the night of 19th October, when No. 11 and 12 platoons working at the second line trenches on the Mailly-Serre Road, were fired on by a machine gun. It was the christening. On the 21st we paraded at 5-30 a.m. and with guides from the King's Own supplied to each platoon, marched to the trenches by platoons at five minutes' interval. The front held by the King's Own ran from the Serre Road on the right to slightly below and to the left of La Ligny farm. On our left was the Essex Regiment, while on our right were the Lancs. Fusiliers. No. 12 platoon was attached to "A" Company of the King's Own on the right of the Batt. line; No. 10 was attached to "C" Company in the centre; No. 11 to "B" Company on the left, and No. 9 to "D" Company in reserve. I was with "B" Company on the left with Vance. The line held by the 12th Brigade formed part of the trenches taken from the Germans by the French in the preceding June.

These trenches, known as the "Toutvent" trenches, had been subjected to a prolonged bombardment by the French. The latter would cease firing at intervals, during which the Germans would man the front line, and on the bombardment recommencing would retire to their dugouts. This sort of thing went on for over a fortnight, and finally, one morning, the Germans got tired of coming out of their dugouts when the bombardment stopped, and the French swept down from their trenches behind La Ligny farm, and caught them. The victorious French advanced as far as the village of Serre, but had to fall back in the face of a terrific German counter attack, and eventually took up their position in what had been the old German second line. This trench they consolidated and held. The regiment which took the trenches was a local one, consisting of men from the region around Hebuterne, Mailly, and Bapaume. There had been reports of terrible outrages committed by the Germans on the villages behind the lines, and evidence was found in the trenches themselves to prove the truth of these reports. The story goes that little quarter was given, and the French took few prisoners, the Germans, caught like rats in a trap, being bombed in their dugouts.

"B" Company of the King's Own, to which I was attached, had its headquarters in a dugout known as "The Catacombs." Built by the

Germans, no labour had been spared to make it shellproof and comfortable. Twenty feet deep, cut out of solid chalk, it was about twenty yards long by seven feet broad. It was divided into sections for signallers, mess, and servants' quarters, but into the wall from the mess were nooks containing beds for six officers. The whole inside of this dugout was riveted with massive planks four to six inches in thickness. There were five entrances approached by flights of steep, narrow steps. This was typical of the living dugouts in this hive of trenches. The English never built dugouts like this one in front line trenches, owing to the difficulty of getting men out of them in a hurry in case of emergency, and time after time they have proved death traps to the Germans themselves. The method of training for a battalion up for instruction is as follows:—Officers, N.C.O.'s and men are attached to their opposite numbers. Company commander to company commander, platoon commander to platoon commander, sergeant to sergeant, corporal to corporal, and sentry to sentry.

For three nights this proceeding is carried out, then, on the fourth night, the instructing companies withdraw to reserve, and each company takes over a sector of line on its own. Thus, bit by bit the officers and men are broken in. The first night we were in the trenches was an ideal one. A full moon made things easy, and it was quite possible to get the lie of the trenches and those of the enemy. Opposite "B" Company the Germans were about 100 to 120 yards away; in the centre their trenches ran to within 40 yards, and on the right about 100. There were a number of "saps" formed out of what had originally been old German communication trenches. Sandbag barricades built by each side in these formed the "sap heads." In one "sap" these barricades were about 15 feet from each other.

One may forget the incidents of one's first night in the trenches, but one never forgets the first dawn. Gradually, out of the darkness, things begin to take upon themselves their proper shapes. The first impression is that of desolation, for there is nothing so utterly forsaken or forlorn as "No man's land" at first grey dawn. A maze of misty barbed wire, some in loose coils lying on the ground, some draped from stumps and stakes driven in at all angles, some in shell holes, all in a shapeless and indescribable jumble, stretches for about three yards in depth in front of the parapet. Then there is that desolate and shell-pocketed strip of land which terminates with the German wire, and beyond that again great heaps of chalk and brown earth begin to appear as the daylight comes. These are the German trenches, and

One of the sergeants of "C" Company in the trenches.

In the trenches.

behind them is the rolling country out of which the sun now begins to rise; country that is in the hands of the Germans, away beyond the pale. Those coils of rusty wire, hung on the rickety posts, form the boundary of civilization.

The 22nd of October promised to be the most lovely day. Except for the usual amount of desultory rifle and machine-gun fire at "stand to," there was nothing to show that the Germans were about to depart from the normal state of inactivity that characterised the warfare on this sector of the front. About 8 a.m. a corporal of the King's Own who had been doing observation work reported that the Germans had removed all their own wire, with the exception of a few strands, on their front opposite the sector held by "C" and "B" Companies. This Captain Woodgate, commanding "B" Company, confirmed himself. In the *Comic Cuts*, or Corps' Summary, of the previous day it was noted that the enemy had also removed his wire opposite the line held by the French, north of Hebuterne. The natural conclusion was, therefore, that he was going to attack. The state of the wire in front of our own trenches was wretched. A month before, during the period of fighting in Champagne and the battle of Loos, the wire all along the front had been removed in readiness for a possible advance, and little trouble had been taken to replace it afterwards.

At 9-35 a.m., Woodgate, Vance, Brown (one of Woodgate's subalterns), and myself were having breakfast in the "Catacomb." Suddenly—"*whiz-bang, whiz-bang*" right at the door of the dugout. The blast from the shells knocked the cups and plates off the table. There was a pause for a second, then a terrific explosion which shook the whole earth. In half a minute we had on our equipment, and Woodgate, followed by myself, Brown, and Vance, ran up the stairs of the dugout. The air was full of dust, and the ground in front of us seemed to be in a blaze of bursting shells. "This way," called Woodgate, and following him we ran down a communication trench leading to the front line. We had only gone a few yards when we ran into a man rushing back, blood pouring from his shoulder and arm. Woodgate stopped and caught hold of him, calling to us to run on. We ran down the trench, bending low, for a hail of shells was passing us and bursting on all sides. In a few seconds Woodgate caught us up again. I led, then Brown, Woodgate, and Vance.

Suddenly, just round a curve in the trench, and about ten yards in front of me, there was a terrific explosion. I was lifted clean off my feet into the air, and thrown flat on my stomach on the ground. Almost simultaneously another shell hit the top of the trench, and before I could think where I was, or recover my breath, the whole side of the trench leant over, and fell on top of me. It was a wonderful sensation, and I remember saying to myself aloud: "I wonder when this is going to stop." Still the earth kept falling, and the weight on my shoulders and the small of my back became oppressive.

One thing was pleasing, there was dead silence under ground. I began to heave with my shoulders, and took a deep breath. There was no difficulty in breathing as the earth seemed full of air. On the second heave I felt I was able to move, and after what seemed ages I got my head and shoulders clear. I was firmly fixed from my waist down, but in less than a minute had dragged myself out. I looked round, and saw that the entire trench had been filled in. There was no sign of any of the others, but a small bit of British warm coat was sticking out of the hole where I had been which represented Brown. I got hold of it and pulled hard. Gradually Brown emerged, cursing like a trooper, and spitting clay out of his mouth. With little difficulty we got Woodgate out, and Vance appeared behind him.

We then ran on, and when we came to the fire trench Woodgate called out: "Get the men out of the living trench into the front line." The living trench was one running just behind and parallel to the fire trench. In it were a large number of what were called "funk holes," scooped out of the front of the trench, in which the men slept when off duty. Leading from each company in the fire trench there was a passage to the living trench. It should be explained that by day the minimum number of men possible are on duty in the fire trench. Sentry duty is most exhausting work, and it is possible for one man by day to suffice where it would take ten or even twenty men by night. In a company frontage of perhaps 500 to 600 yards three sentries, one to each platoon would be ample in the firing line provided there was a clear field of view to the front; but of course it is entirely a matter of situation and the nature of the ground.

Woodgate called to me: "You take the two centre platoons and get everyone into the trench as quickly as possible." I ran along the living trench rousing the men, who despite the terrific din of bursting shells were mostly sound asleep, and telling them to get out. Shells were falling mostly in the living trench and just behind it, and I had to go round by way of the fire trench as the passage behind was blocked up. Meanwhile the air was thick with flying debris of every kind—posts, iron sheets, great baulks of timber were flying everywhere as the enemy blew our wire to bits. In particular I watched with fascination, a sheet of corrugated iron, blown from the roof of a dug-out, which flew about in the air like a card, and dashed hither and thither, finally coming down with a great slant on the parados of the bay next to where I was. It is no easy matter to wake the sleeping soldier, and as I worked my way down the living trench I thought I would never get the men out of the dug-outs. Here and there, however, where a bit of trench had been blown in, men were creeping out, pulling their rifles from under the fallen clay. At last, after what seemed an age, they began to file into the bays. The front trench was very narrow, deep, and well sand-bagged, and once they had thoroughly realised what was going on they knew it was the safest place.

Owing to the double number in the trenches nearly every bay was manned by at least two men. Bayonets were fixed, and ten rounds fixed into the magazine, and we felt quite ready for what I expected would come any minute. The shell fire now became terrific, and practically the whole living line was filled in, the shells just missing the front line and lighting on the step of ground some ten yards inside separating it from the living trench. Curiously enough no shells were lighting in the fire trench. Two bays on the right of the two platoons under my charge had been knocked in during the first few minutes of the bombardment. They formed a small salient, and presented a very easy target to the enemy, whose artillery was mostly operating from Serre wood. Once the fire trench was manned there was little to do except go up and down the trench and see that all was well.

The stuff the Germans were sending over was composed of every imaginable form of ordnance. The biggest shells were probably eight inch, and the air was thick with aerial torpedoes, *minenwerfer*, and oil drums. The latter came hurling through the air turning over and over and exploding with a terrific crack, making a very large crater. Aerial torpedoes, designed more for moral effect than to cause actual damage, burst with a nerve shattering explosion. I noticed that the closer one was to a bursting shell or aerial torpedo the less the noise, it was more of a sharp click, the greatest effect would be at almost 30 yards, under that the sound did not seem so great, though the concussion of course was terrific. Meanwhile the Germans, though they had blown most of our wire away showed no signs of attacking.

It was just one of those small intensive bombardments known at the front as "a morning hate" or "*straffe*." When this had lasted about an hour and a half, our artillery began to retaliate. Those were the days when ammunition was precious, and each battery strictly limited. It was a pleasant sound, however, to hear the whiz of our own shells overhead and see a great mass of earth rise from the German lines, and this had a marvellous effect on the men. They at once became cheerful, the Lancashire men especially. "Thar goes a Lloyd George for you," as the whiz of a heavy shell like an express train overhead was heard. "Bah, he's a dud." "Say, Jock, the lassie 'as made 'im forgot to put in the vital spark." "There goes Fritz's iron rations" as a salvo of shrapnel burst over the first line. On the whole, however, our artillery retaliation was poor.

About 11-30 the bombardment began to die down, and by 12-30 it was over. The damage done, considering the number of shells fired into such a small sector was very small. Two bays on the right of "B" Company were completely flattened, otherwise there was no damage done to the fire trench. The living trench and communication trenches suffered more. Two of the latter had been knocked in, while the living trench along the company line had been badly battered. One very gruesome effect was noticed. There were a large number of Frenchman's graves in the parapet of the fire trench, for the French have a habit of burying a man where he falls, whether at his post or not. A hole was opened in the side of the trench, the body was shoved in, and the grave filled up. A little cross surmounted by the dead man's cap, and often his bayonet and rifle, marking the spot. In places where the fire trench had been hit or shaken many of the remains stuck out, and in many cases buttons and badges were "souveneered" by the men.

When the bombardment was over Woodgate told me it was the most severe they had experienced since May 8th, at Ypres, and quite an unusual occurrence on that front. Two men were killed and sixteen wounded, very small casualties taking into consideration the intensity of the fire. That night we dug a new trench behind the small sector blown in. There was a full moon, and walking about on top was very interesting. The ground was honeycombed with shell holes, while in all directions unexploded shells were lying about. A trench which had been used by the French for the purpose of burying dead had been unearthed in many places and the ground was littered with old equipment, clothes, and bones. I remember thinking it was the most appalling refuse heap I had ever seen. Next day was very quiet, we began work on the new trench at about 7-30, and I took charge of the three working parties in it.

A considerable amount of work had been done the night before, and only a short piece remained to be dug in the centre. At 8-55 I told the men to take a ten minutes "easy" and went up to the left platoon to see one of the sergeants about rations. I had gone about five minutes when a salvo of "whiz bangs" (77 mm shells) burst right in the trench where the men had been working, and immediately afterwards very heavy rifle fire broke out on our right. The "stand to" was passed down and the rifle fire went on for about half-an-hour, especially in the direction of "C" Company. All had quieted down about 10 o'clock. I then ascertained that a party of Germans had endeavoured to bomb "C" Company's trenches. A very large number of bombs were thrown, and in all sixteen men were wounded. For their coolness in this attack our men were greatly commended, and one man, Andrew Marshall, of No. 11 platoon, was specially recommended for devotion to duty. Badly wounded in the hand, and unable to use his rifle, he refused to leave the trench, and kept loading rifles for the men on the fire step.

The remainder of our time in the trenches was very quiet. On Sunday, 24th October, we took over the line held by "A" Company King's Own as a company the King's Own going back into support, and the following evening we marched back to our billets in Mailly-Maillet. Our period of instruction had been most useful, for "C" Company in particular. We had experienced a bombardment and a bomb attack in both of which the men had proved their metal, and shown what was in them. As far as the officers of "C" Company were concerned, those who came in contact with Capt. Woodgate will never forget the lesson they learned from him. "A" and "B" Companies attached to the Essex and South Lancs. Regiments had a quiet time, but "D" Company attached to the Lancs. Fusiliers in the Redan salient had their initiation into mine warfare, a platoon being in the salient when the Germans blew up a mine without, however, causing any loss of life. A good story is here told of Lieutenant W. He was out one night with a small patrol, the password being "Shakespeare." A large German patrol was sighted and W and his patrol had to retire in some haste. W himself fell headlong into a sap on the top of the astonished sentries with the ejaculation "For God's sake let's in, Shakespeare."

We left Mailly early in the morning of October 26th, and marched down through Forceville and Varennes to Puchvillers where we stayed the night. Next day we marched to Fienvillers and went into billets. Fienvillers was a better town than Rubenpré. There were better barns

Fienvillers.

Fienvillers.

for the men, and for a company headquarters mess we were lucky to get a lovely house standing in its own grounds with bedrooms for each officer. We now had heard our fate, it was that the 107th Brigade was to go up to the trenches to take the place of the 12th Brigade of the 4th Division, which was coming out and going to be attached to our division. Our two remaining brigades were to be in army reserve for about three months. Our battalion, with the 14th R.I.R. from the 109th Brigade, was attached to the 12th Brigade under General Auley, taking the places of the Essex Regiment attached to the 109th Brigade, and Lancashire Fusiliers attached to the 108th. We joined the 12th Brigade at St. Leger-les-Domarts on the 5th November, the King's Own being billeted in the same town. We now began a new and extensive system of training, both in march discipline and attack. General Auley, during the first week that we were in his brigade gave the officers a series of lectures on the retreat from Mons and the subsequent advance to the Marne.

We heard the story from his own personal point of view, which made it a fascinating narrative rather than a tactical lecture. During the five weeks in which we were attached to his brigade we obtained much practical and useful knowledge. In march discipline, especially, we improved greatly. We were taught that the most men can do with comfort is 112 paces to the minute. The pace was set from the rear and not from the head of the column. Company commanders riding at the rear of their companies were made to check the pace. The utmost importance was paid to keeping in step, and keeping the sectors of fours well dressed and well covered down. The rifle was carried at the sling, never over the shoulder, the reason for this being that men, when they get tired, will let their butts drop, and keeping hitting the man in the sector of fours behind, thus causing loss of space in the section, in the company, and so on down to the brigade and division on the march. We did many long route marches, and the general used to hide in all sorts of weird places to watch us go past, and take us unawares.

During the time we were in St. Leger, Major Clarke (Officer Commanding "C" Company) left the Battalion and joined the 108th Brigade as Staff Captain. I took over command of "C" Company on November 12th. Our company headquarters were in the Cure's house, the Cure, like most of his confreres in France, having gone to the front. On 27th we moved from St. Leger to Buigny l'Abbe, a small village about three kilometres from St. Requier where we were bil-

ST LEGER
LIEUT. VANCE, CAPTAIN SAMUELS, LIEUT. YOUNG, LIEUT. ELLIS.

"C" COMPANY, ST. LEGER.

leted until December 10th. Buigny was an unhealthy low lying village, and we experienced a considerable amount of sickness, principally influenza. Our stay of a fortnight was unpleasant, it rained most of the time, and the people were inhospitable. This, we found, was due to bad conduct on the part of a regiment which had preceded us there. The triangular pond, which is a feature of all Picard villages, had in former days formed the fish pond of the ancient monastery of Buigny l'Abbe; and for this reason was held in more respect by the villagers than most ponds of its kind.

Unfortunately, whether by accident or design, some bombs were thrown into this pond one night, and in the morning the villagers woke up to find their pond gone, and in its place a chasm of liquid mud. On investigation it was found that the bombs had burst in what proved to be the roof of a subterranean passage leading from the monastery, and through this the water had disappeared. During our stay in the town we had working parties engaged in making good the damage.

On December 10th we rejoined the 108th Brigade, moving from Buigny l'Abbe to St. Mauguille, a faubourg of St. Requier. This proved to be the most pleasant town in which we had as yet been billeted. Two companies "B" and "C" were in St. Mauguille at Neuville, about one mile from St. Riquier. We had excellent billets both for officers and men, and as we had now thoroughly acquired the knack of making ourselves at home, settled down very comfortably. The people were most hospitable. There were excellent hot and cold shower baths for the men, and a battalion laundry was set up. For our Company Mess, Monsieur Vivien, the manager of a big phosphate works gave us the greater part of his house, and he and Madame Vivien with their daughter, did all they could to make us feel at home. St. Requier was a most interesting old town. It had successfully stood siege by Henry V. and the English on two occasions, but had been sacked and burnt by the Burgundians in the end of the 15th century. Large portions of the walls still remain, and some of the old towers. In a moated farmhouse just outside the town Jeanne D'Arc spent a night on her way to her trial at Rouen. Another fact of great interest was that the ancient Abbey of St. Requier had been founded by our own countrymen in the 6th century.[1]

We spent a happy Xmas at St. Requier, and as we were in billets decided to make the best of it. The men were in excellent health and

---
1. See note, Appendix 1.

Tomb of the First Irish Saints.

Monsieur Vivien and Family.

spirits, football, shooting, and route marches keeping them in training. The 18th of December being "Lundy Day," was celebrated by some Derry men and other Ulster boys, the following being a description of the celebration by an officer. Two Lundy's had been prepared, one large and the other small. Some of the inhabitants suggested that they were father and son. The father was about eleven feet long, stuffed with straw, and with rockets put in unexpected places. He had large wooden feet and wire knees, and his head filled with gunpowder and surrounded by a large yellow trimmed hat in the shape of an admiral's. On his chest was a placard bearing the words "Lundy the traitor."

The procession, headed by torchlights and band, marched through the village playing such airs as "No Surrender," "Derry Walls" and "The Boyne Water." Lundy was then let down on a wire rope from a tree where he had been strung up, and set on fire, amidst great cheering and boohing. He was well soaked with petrol and burnt excellently. Every now and then someone gave him a shake and his knees wobbled in most realistic fashion. Bombs made of jam tins were thrown into a pond just beside him, and of course broke the windows of houses in the vicinity. The procession then reformed, and marching to the top of the village, where Lundy junior was burnt with like ceremony.

Christmas, of course, produced a series of dinners given by the Officers Commanding Companies and Battalion Headquarters. To read the menu cards it was hard to believe we were in France, and that this was the second year of the war. One particularly elaborate dinner was given on Christmas day, to which we invited Madame Vivien, our kind hostess, and her family. The following is a copy of the menu in which most of the guests are represented.

Potage Vivien.
Poulets Roti au Capitaine.
Petits pois Lieutenant.
Rosbif au Docteur.
Pommes de terre Louis (the little son).
Fruits, plumb pudding, Xmas desserts.
Cafe.
Vins—Muscatel—Bordeau—Whiskey.
    Toasts.
Le Presedent de la Republique.
Le Roi D'Angleterre.

Three Sergeants of "C" Company.

At St. Riquier

Mesdames, Messures Vivien.
Les Allies au paix glorieuse.

A service was held in the ancient Abbey of St. Requier on Christmas Day, and a sacred concert, which gave our men an opportunity of listening to Christmas music.

An incident happened about this time at St. Requier which caused no little excitement. A French billet belonging to the Downs (13th Battalion Royal Irish Rifles) went on fire. At the sound of the fire alarm everyone turned out to assist the French people who stripped to the waist were hard at work trying to save their farm. The fire was raging fiercely round the stables and outhouses, and it was quite impossible to save all the horses, some of whom were burned to death in their stalls. It was a horrible sight.

On January 8th, our battalion moved to Bernavillers. We were now beginning to think of the trenches again, and many were the rumours. Everyone seemed to know for certain our exact peregrinations during the next few months, but in truth no one could tell from day to day what our next move would be. There were also rumours of a more pleasant character, but so far only spoken of with bated breath, the one and only hope of our existence—"Leave" had begun. Our first "leave" and all that the word means. There is no doubt of it that the first leave is the best, but your first leave you are then indeed a hero, whether from billets or trenches, and your dear people who have not yet become accustomed to those short ten days have waited and watched for it with an intense longing and pride in their hearts; is it any wonder one's blood thrills with the thought of that never-to-be-forgotten home coming.

At Bernavillers an excellent concert party was formed by Lord Farnham, called "The Divisional Follies" or "The Merry Mauve Melody Makers." Their first concert was honoured by a visit from The Most Rev. Dr. Crozier, Lord Primate of Ireland, who had come to France on a tour among the Irish Divisions. He had already paid a visit to the 107th Brigade, who had been having a strenuous training in the trenches ever since October. They had escaped with very few casualties.

My company now got orders to move to Beauval, where we took over billets from the Y.C.V.'s (14th Battalion Royal Irish Rifles). They were the cleanest billets I can remember in France, and the Y.C.V.'s deserve great praise for the way in which they were left for us. After

Officers of "C" Company.

St. Leger.

a week of preparation we moved on to Canaples, and from there to Martinsart where we again manned the trenches, and went in alongside the 9th Inniskilling Fusiliers by companies, "C" and "D" Companies in front with "A" and "B" in reserve. The next week we went into support with "D" Company, and "A" and "B" took our place in front. This time we were not attached to a regular battalion for training, but took over part of the line ourselves. Our period in the trenches was uneventful, it was a quiet part of the line, and the trenches were deep and well made. This time we gave the Bosche 500 to every 50 of theirs, so all taken into consideration we were lucky. The weather, however, was by no means favourable, the trenches being full of slush and water. A heavy fall of snow also made the ground in a bad condition, and the men suffered greatly from the cold, which was intense. Several new officers joined our battalion about this time, for which we were very thankful, as leave was able to proceed without difficulty, two officers being sent each week.

On February 29 our first death occurred, poor young Watt of No. 12 platoon. He was killed by a shell while standing outside the door of his billet in Mesnil, and buried in Mesnil Ridge Cemetery. From this time on we went into the trenches by battalions, alternately with the Downs (13th Royal Irish Rifles). Our casualties were not great, but always a few, the expected result of trench warfare. Indeed, if it had not been for a tot of rum at "stand to" on those very cold mornings, I feel sure there would have been more work for the hospitals. About March 6th the weather began to improve and we occasionally felt dry. We now began to think about giving Jerry something to stir him up as he seemed to have gone underground completely during the cold weather. Evidently battalion headquarters also felt that the time had come to stir for we received a message to supply a specimen of German wire as it was wanted by the corps. The job was given in "C" Company to Young, our scout officer, and four other scouts.

On a dark and snowy night they crept out on patrol, and procured a good specimen about a yard long. The other companies also procured specimens and the corps appeared satisfied with results. Our batteries also began to wake up, and we kept them well informed as to the position of the German transports, which from this time on never got a moment of peace. The 10th Inniskillings on our right, under command of Colonel Ross-Smyth, got a terrific shelling from the Bosche on the night of the 10th-11th of March. Shells came over at the rate of 60 to the minute, but the 10th showed splendid coolness and gallantry, keeping up a steady fire from the front trenches throughout the bombardment, which was evidently intended by the Germans to cover a raid on our lines, similar to one which took place elsewhere the same night. An officer, describing the bombardment in a letter, writes—

> The Bosche has been very prodigal of shells for a day or two, all along the front, but particularly on the somewhat unpleasant sector occupied by the "Derry's." On this particular afternoon he had subjected it to a smart bombardment with "heavies," field guns, and trench mortars. Then he fell short and waited. At eleven o'clock precisely he opened fire with guns of all calibres. Over the Derrys he burst shrapnel, reserving his high explosive for the Donegals and Fermanaghs, and for the brigade on their right. Not content with peppering the line, the supports, and the reserves, he shelled half a dozen villages to the rear, with which he did not as a rule concern himself. It was a very dark night, and the flashes of the guns seemed to cut through the darkness like spear points.
>
> Before the Bosche had been firing five minutes our guns had begun to reply to him, and the eighteen pounders commenced to whiz over our heads on to their front line, and soon the men in the trenches heard the welcome whistle of a high travelling howitzer over their heads in the right direction. Then indeed the din was indescribable, so fast and furious did the game become that at one time it seemed as if the boom of the big guns, the harsher bark of the small, the explosion of the shells, and the tearing crash of bursting mortars were all blended into one continuous roar. The trenches of the "Derrys" had an ugly time of it. Dugouts were caved in, and traverses smashed down, one whole sector of the front line being practically ploughed up.
>
> At one time the enemy proceeded to pound the flank out of one company with high explosives for several minutes, then lifted to the opposite flank and gave it the same measure. This evidently appeared to him a satisfactory idea as he repeated the manoeuvre. But the company officer had by now appreciated his tactics, and by his work undoubtedly prevented a great number of casualties. Gradually the German fire on the front line slackened and ceased, though it still continued overhead, and our "heavies" now warmed up to their work showed no

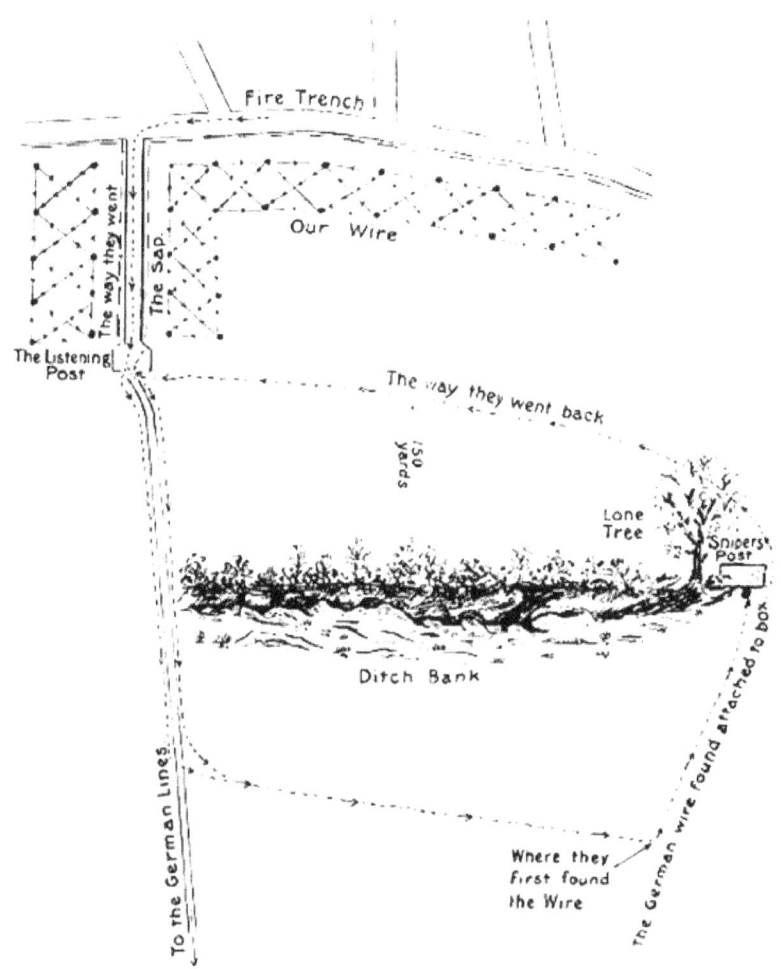

Bombs found on night patrol just in front of Beaumont Hamel, March, 1916.

inclination to give up. It was at this juncture that a sentry came running back from the sap head to report that he had seen Germans moving in front of the wire. The order was given to the men to stand up on the fire step, and send bursts of rapid fire in the direction of the German line.

If the raiders had intended coming over this caused them to change their minds. The "Derrys" stood to till morning, but nothing fresh occurred. Through the night the men prayed their officers to lead them over to vengeance, but for that they will have to wait. The loss was slight considering the intensity of the bombardment. When morning came the "Derrys" learned that the famous raiders had entered the trenches of the battalion on their right, which, by the way, did not belong to the Ulster Division, and carried off an officer and nine men as prisoners. It was a workmanlike job without a doubt, for the raiding party had come and gone within ten minutes.

Several of the men of the Inniskillings earned commendation from Colonel Ricardo for conspicuous gallantry on this occasion; their names were Private D. Little, Private J. J. Young, Lance Corporal Black, and Private W. Dinsmore. They were serving as company officers, orderlies, signallers, and messengers. Captain Cruickshank, of Omagh, also showed great coolness and valour on that occasion.

The weather still continued fine, and our time was spent in building new traverses, and riveting and sandbagging the parados and firesteps. Bosche aeroplanes, taking advantage of the fine nights, crossed our lines, and green flares were sent up from the enemy to show our positions. The Germans would then send over a number of shells, and we had several casualties, Lieutenant Waring of "A" Company being hit by shrapnel, and Privates Moffat and McBride of "C" Company badly wounded. Poor Moffat subsequently died from his wounds.

We were now stirred to think of raids and night patrols. The following is an example of a patrol done by one of my officers and some men of "C" Company. Lieutenant Young, Sergeant Renshaw, Riflemen Storey, Pollock, M'Dowell and M'Kelvey. March 16th. "C" Company Patrol Report.

Patrol went out from Sap in Sector 41 at 7-30 p.m., consisting of one officer, one sergeant, and four Riflemen. On leaving our wire we turned north, striking sunken road which runs north-east in direction of German trenches. After going about

Thiepval Château.

Mesnil Château.

100 yards down this road we turned off under a ditch running north-west from the road. There were a number of small thorn trees on this ditch, and we could distinctly see footprints and elbow marks round them, also pits had been dug which could be used by snipers. Further along the ditch we came to a lone tree, which can be seen from Sector 49 in our lines, here we halted. About 20 yards from the tree we discovered a wire which came from the direction of the German lines. Following this we found it entered the parapet of a sniper's pit, just beneath the lone tree. We then dug out the wire, and discovered it was attached to a square box covered with felt. This box we opened, thinking it contained a telephone, but instead found four German grenades with the detonators attached to the wire. We quickly disconnected the wire, and dug out the box. Not far from the spot we found another German grenade which we also took with us. At 10 p.m. we returned to our own trenches. A working party of the enemy could be heard, but it was difficult to say from which direction the sound came. Otherwise, everything was normal.

G. O. Young, Lieutenant.

On March 18th we went into reserve, and were billeted in Englebelmer, being relieved on 24th by the 13th Royal Irish Rifles (The Downs). This time the 11th Battalion East Yorks. were attached to us for instruction. They saw a fair amount of shelling for their first period in the trenches, the Germans putting a lot of trench mortars over on Thiepval hill. All that remained of the *château* at Thiepval being the walls, about as high as the hall door, and a few holes where windows once had been, in all about 7ft. high by 20ft. long. The German trenches lay in front of it, on the carriage drive, and ours right up to the other side of the avenue, almost into them. Not a pleasant place, with an active sniper in the *château*. Our trenches also ran through Thiepval wood, in which the trees were now thick with foliage. The birds built their nests and sang merrily enough on those Spring mornings. They did not appear to mind the shelling, even a cuckoo could sometimes be heard, reminding us that winter was over "this winter of our discontent."

Spring had indeed come, a time when the birds call, the trees call, all nature calls for life, while we were there to kill and to be killed. There were moments when a lull came in the busy day's work, when the monotony of trench warfare left time to think, that thoughts such as these arose.

We spent Easter in billets, in Martinsart village. The 23rd of April being Easter Sunday, a general holiday was given to the battalion. Amiens, once the capital of Picardy, was about twenty-five miles distant, a long ride, but an interesting old town, and well worth visiting. Its fortifications have been turned into Boulevards, but it still retains its old citadel, and the Cathedral of Notre Dame is indeed a masterpiece of Gothic architecture. The great straight road that leads from Amiens to the front, or Albert, is the great *route nationale*, running from Rouen through Amiens, Albert, Pozieres, Le Sars and Bapaume on to Mons and Valenciennes. It was on this road that the famous Gordon Bennet races took place, and a better road for riding on or motoring on, it would be hard to find. The road is lined on either side with poplar trees, and a screen used to be hung from tree to tree to hide the traffic to and from Albert. There are few trees left now, and only the barest stumps, owing to bombardment.

Amiens, as a rule, was out of bounds to both officers and men, unless they were the possessors of a pass, but on Easter Monday official permission was granted to all, and many availed themselves of the opportunity to explore the ancient town. It was a chance to see civilization again, and to dine in a restaurant. At that time Amiens had not been badly shelled, even the Bosche aeroplanes seemed to be busy elsewhere, and life went on much the same as in towns at the base. People went about their business and pleasure with very little thought of the enemy who were comparatively few miles away.

The ride back at night from Amiens was rather an interesting experience. After the first six miles the sky was lit up like sheet lightning. Then the villages all became dark, no lights to be seen, then came the halts at the different outposts, the constant flashes and rockets in the sky, awful, yet fascinating. Nearer Albert the sound of the guns became clearer, and in the distance could be seen the great church tower of Notre Dame de Brebieres with the leaning figure of the Virgin holding the infant Christ above her head. For over a year she had hung at an angle of 15 degrees below horizontal, face downwards to the street below. The French people believed that the day the holy figures fell, would see the end of the war, and that the German shell which threw down the blessed Virgin of Brebieres would shatter the throne of the Hohenzollerns.

Our battalion being now out of the trenches the companies were

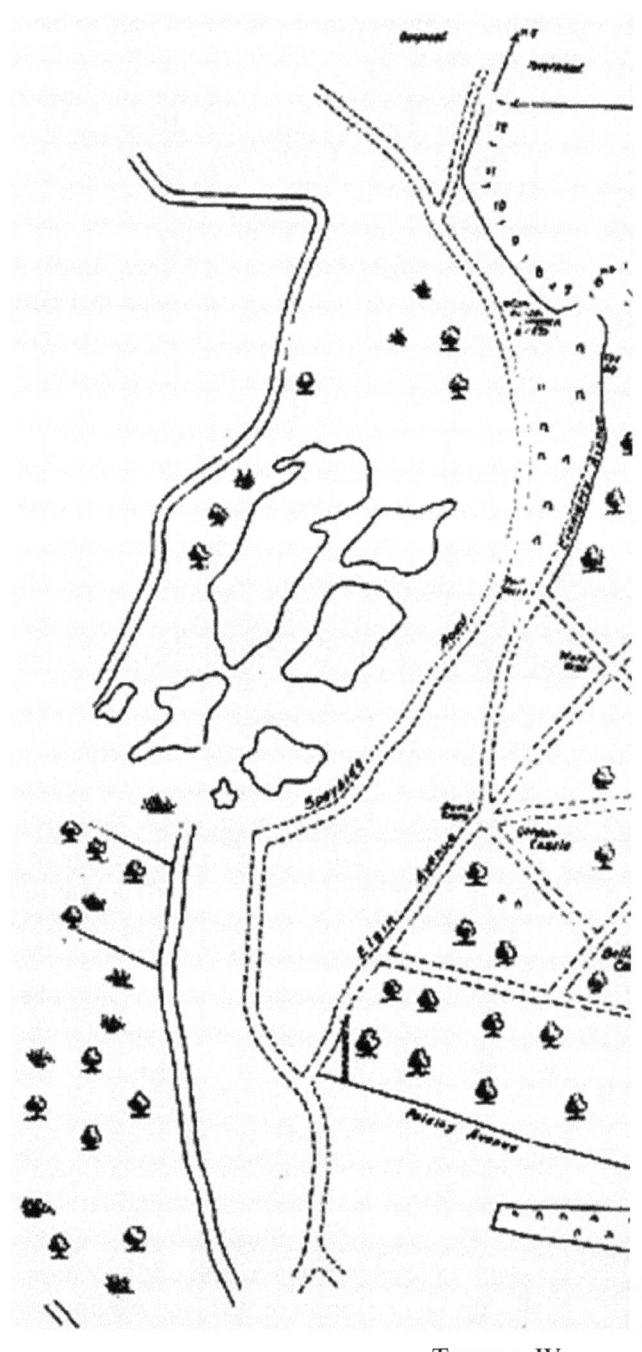

THIEPVAL WOOD.

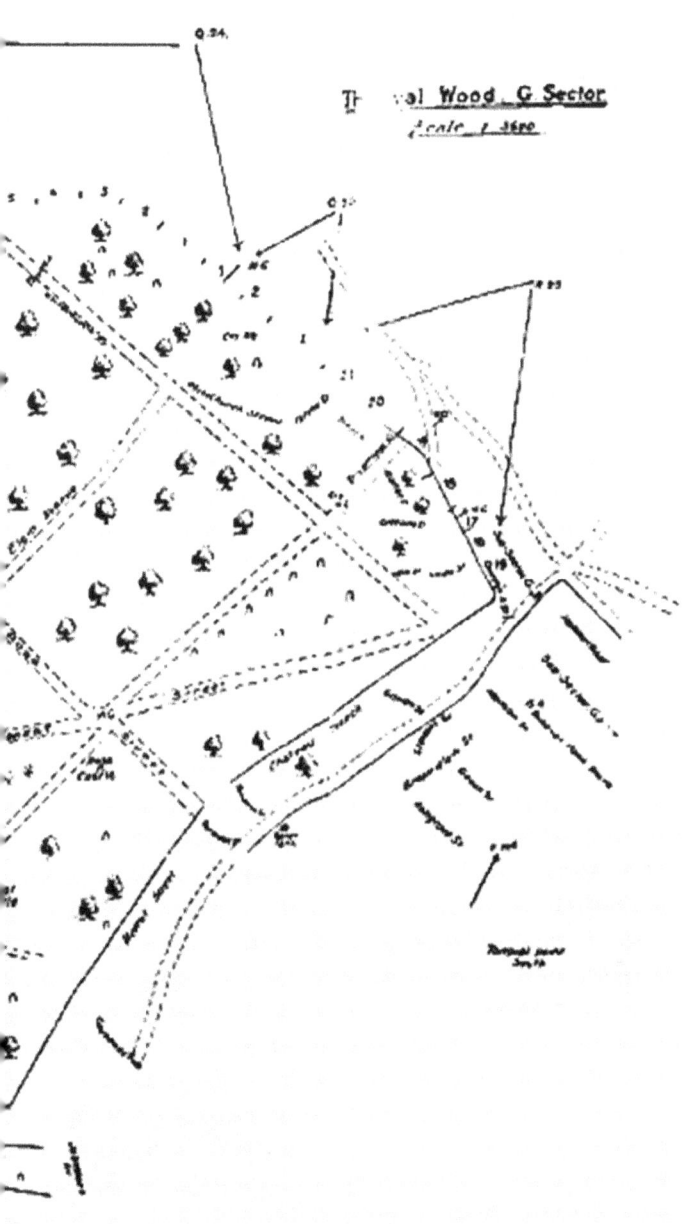

G. SECTOR.

Albert.

Ruins of Albert.

divided among the small villages around. My company had the luck to be billeted in Autuille, a small village on the Ancre. We were able to get plenty of amusement there between rat hunting, fishing and bathing. Captain E. and I spent several afternoons trying for trout, and sent our finest specimen to "B" Company with compliments. The Ancre at Autuil was an excellent place for fishing, and this would have been a pleasant occupation were it not for the fact that snipers found us out in a short time. The bathing place was hardly 600 yards from the German lines. On May 7th the "Tyrones" had the honour of carrying out the first raid made by the division. The following is contained in a special order of the day issued by Major General O. S Nugent, D.S.O., Officer Commanding Division.

> A raid on the German trenches was carried out at midnight on the 7th inst., by the 9th Battalion Royal Inniskilling Fusiliers, the raiding party consisting of Major W. J. Peacock, Captain J. Weir, Lieut. W. S. Furness, Sec.-Lieut. L. W. H. Stevenson, Sec.-Lieut. R. W. M'Kinley, Sec.-Lieut. J. Taylor, and 84 other ranks. The raid was completely successful and was carried out exactly as planned. Six German dugouts, in which it is certain there were a considerable number of men, were thoroughly bombed, and a machine gun was blown up, while a lively bombing fight took place between the blocking detachments of the raiding party and the Germans. Having accomplished the purpose of the raid the party was withdrawn with the loss of one man killed and two wounded. The raid was ably organised by Major Peacock, and was carried out by the officers and men in accordance with plan, the discipline and determination of the party being all that could be desired. The Divisional Commander desires that his congratulations should be extended to all who took part in it.

Brigadier-General Hickman in a special Brigade Order says—

> The arrangements and plans reflect the greatest credit on Colonel Ricardo, Major Peacock, and the officers concerned. The whole scheme was executed with great dash and determination, with cool judgment and nerve.

The following awards were issued—Major Peacock received the D.S.O., Sec.-Lieutenant Stevenson the Military Cross, Sergeant Barker, D.C.M., and Lance-Corporal D. Armour, M.M.

THE RUINS OF ALBERT CATHEDRAL.

At this time an important change took place in the command of the 11th Battalion Royal Inniskilling Fusiliers. Lieutenant-Colonel W. F. Hessey was promoted to Brigadier-General, and given Command of the 110th Infantry Brigade. His place was taken by Major G. H. Brush, Second in Command of the 10th Battalion (Derry Volunteers). The following farewell order was issued by Lieutenant-Colonel Hessey to his battalion.

Lieutenant-Colonel Hessey wishes God Speed to all members of the 11th Inniskillings, and thanks them for the loyal support they have given him from the raising of the battalion to this day. He leaves the battalion with very sincere regret, but with feelings of great pride that he has had the privilege of commanding such a fine lot of officers, N.C.O.'s and men, and that their *esprit de corps* has made the battalion a worthy part of the 27th Inniskilling Regiment of Foot.

During the following days we spent alternate periods in and out of the trenches, with little excitement to keep our spirits up. On May 16th we again took over from the 13th Battalion Royal Irish Rifles (Downs), and this time a spell of beautiful weather favoured us and the trenches were quite dry and habitable. We had the usual machine gun fire at night, especially from the direction of Thiepval Château, also a large number of shrapnel shells and whizbangs fell in our Sector. The enemy was apparently very busy during the night on his front line opposite our company. We could hear the sound of picking and shovelling going on, and stakes being driven into the ground. During 18th-19th the enemy gave us little peace, between trench mortars, heavies, and whizbangs.

Several salvoes of shrapnel managed to do considerable damage to our inspection trench and Whit Church Street. During a heavy bombardment, while the shells went over and round us at a tremendous rate I was lying flat on my stomach to avoid some shrapnel that burst near. I looked round to see if there were any casualties among the men following, and noticed a head emerging from the earth which had fallen in all round; suddenly there was a splutter, the head moved, and a very solemn voice said "Boys o' boys it's aboot time the referee blew his whistle," his thoughts must have been far away on the Balmoral football ground, perhaps he was thinking of a tough fight Malone v. Queen's, in the old days.

We were glad to notice that the German trenches opposite suffered severely on the retaliation of our artillery. The following nights were busy putting up wire and sending out patrols. On one occasion a sentry reported having seen an aeroplane fall in flames some distance to the east of Thiepval, just before it fell three planes had been observed very high in the air, and the sound of machine-gun fire heard coming from them.

On the 20th there was considerable enemy machine gun activity, and a very large number of flares were sent up during the night from the German lines. At 9-30 p.m. two red flares were sent up apparently from the German salient opposite "Mary Redan." Immediately afterwards two salvoes of shrapnel were fired, and appeared to burst in the neighbourhood of "Mary Redan," while enemy search lights could be seen near Serre.

During the 21st the enemy continued his constant machine gun fire, and at night our wiring parties were much hampered on this account, one being forced to come in. At 10-30 p.m. on the 22nd, red rockets were sent up from the German lines north of the Rriver Ancre. Immediately afterwards a heavy bombardment by enemy artillery began, apparently on our lines in front of Thiepval, which lasted about half-an-hour. We had a more or less quiet day on the 23rd, and on the 24th were relieved by the 13th Royal Irish Rifles. "C" Company was sent to Autile, "B" to South Antrim Villas, and the other two Companies to Mesnil. We spent a pleasant few days in billets, the usual rat hunts and bathing in the Ancre gave plenty of amusement to the men.

On May 31st we got our orders to join "D" Company in Martinsart, and the following day moved to Harponville *via* Bouzincourt and Varrennes, where we rejoined our brigade, and started Divisional exercises on a large training ground known as the Clairfaye trenches. These trenches had been dug from aeroplane photographs, and were an exact reproduction of the German trenches opposite Thiepval. It was here that we heard the terrible news of the death of Lord Kitchener, to whose genius we owed so much. During our period of training the 107th Brigade held the trenches at Thiepval.

On June 15th, at 3 p.m., the battalion marched off, and with the 9th Royal Irish Fusiliers bivouacked in Martinsart Wood. Martinsart village was already occupied by numerous troops sent up in readiness for the great battle of the Somme. We sent working parties down to Thiepval wood to help in the digging of assembly trenches. Our working party was very unfortunate, and out of No. 11 platoon we

Thiepval Village

had six men wounded, Miller, Lyle, Brown, Galloway, Quinn, and "B" Company also lost eleven men.

On 17th several new officers joined the battalion in Martinsart Wood, among them Lieut. J. Marshall, posted to "B" Company, afterwards proved to be the only officer of the 11th Battalion who went over the top on the 1st July without getting wounded. All was bustle and excitement, we heard we were to hold the line from Thiepval Wood to La Boiselle and Fricourt.

On 22nd the Tyrones went into the trenches. We had a fine concert in "D" Company Mess, and I had a last talk to the N.C.O.'s. On 23rd we paraded at 7-45 p.m. and marched to our trenches in Thiepval Wood. Our company officers consisted of the following—myself, in command, Captain Ewart, Lieutenants Vance, Ellis, Young, Carson and Murphy. It was a very hot march but a glorious day, and all of us were in good heart. "C" and "D" Companies manned the front line, with "A" and "B" behind, "C" holding from Elgin Avenue to Garden Gate at the head of Cromarty Avenue. "C" Company Headquarters were in Thurso Street, and Battalion Headquarters in Cromarty Avenue. On the 26th, at 2-30, we had planned a gas attack, but there was not much wind, and the gas did not go well. Young and myself happened to be the next casualties, luckily both of us slight. Young was gassed while on duty at a gas cylinder, and I got a touch of shrapnel from a whiz bang. It meant No. 29 C.C.S. for both of us, and very reluctantly we had to leave our men just on the eve of the first and greatest battle ever fought by the division.

Part 2

THE CHARGE OF THE ULSTER DIVISION.
         Ulster's Sacrifice.
Ah! fair July of tear and sigh
Sad was the news you brought
To many an ancient noble Hall,
And humble peasants' cot,
Within our old courageous land
Of honour, truth and worth
Grave Ulster of the Iron Will,
Proud Province of the North.
                  H. G. Gallagher.

The following account of the great battle is taken from different stories and official accounts given by officers and men who came through that memorable day. It has been censored by several commanding officers in the division, who ascertain to the correctness of it in detail. In a letter received by General Sir George Richardson, K.C.B., commanding the Ulster Volunteer Force, from General Nugent, commanding the Ulster Division, the following passages occur:—

> Before you get this we shall have put the value of the Ulster Division to the supreme test. I have no fear of the result. I am certain no general in the army out here has a finer division, fitter or keener. I am certain they will be magnificent in attack, and we could hardly have a date better calculated to inspire national traditions amongst our men of the North.[1] It makes me very sad to think what the price may be, but I am quite sure the officers and men reck nothing of that.

---

1. General Nugent's reference is of course to the First of July, a date sacred to Orangemen.

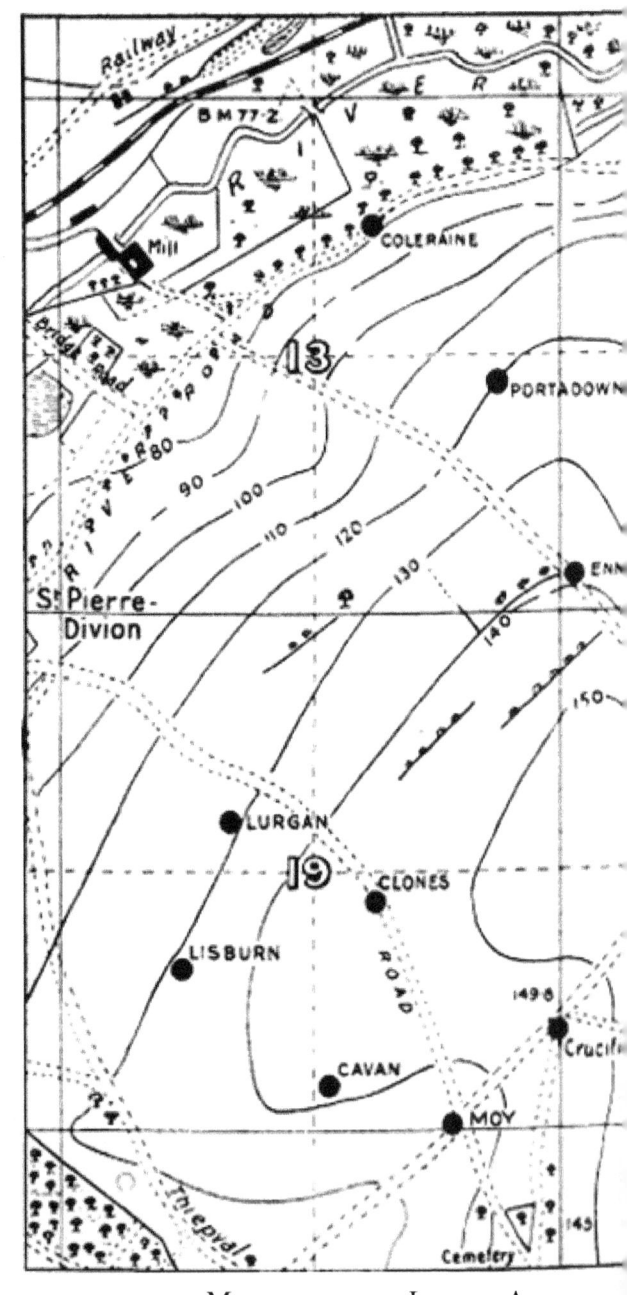

Map showing the Lines of Advance

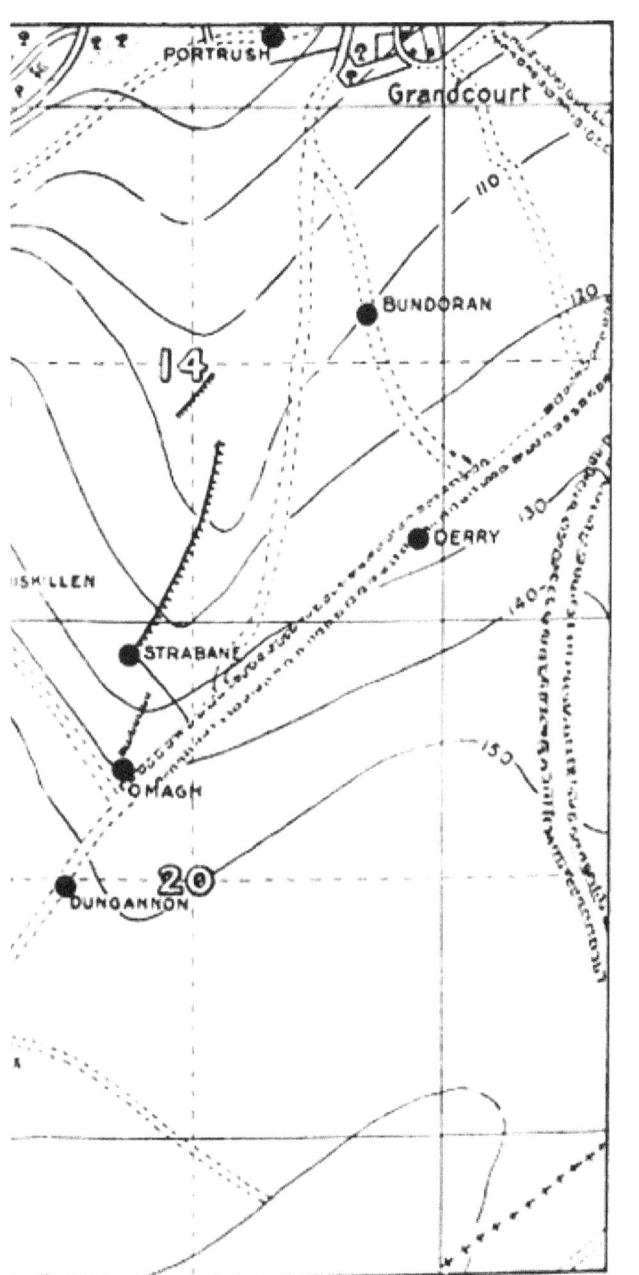

taken by Ulster Division, July, 1st, 1916.

Our divisional line on the right ran through Moy and Crucifix (see map), and on the left from "Mary Redan" on the other side of the river. The 109th Brigade held the line on the extreme right, 9th Inniskilling Fusiliers, and 10th Inniskilling Fusiliers in front, with 11th Inniskilling Fusiliers and 14th Royal Irish Rifles behind. Of the 108th Brigade, our battalion was on the right nearest the 10th Inniskilling Fusiliers, then came 13th Royal Irish Rifles with 9th Royal Irish Fusiliers and the 12th Royal Irish Rifles on the extreme left. Our battalion formed "B" and "A" Companies in front, with "D" and "C" Companies in support, "C" supporting "A" on the right, "D" supporting "B" on the left. Our object was the line marked "Omagh" "Strabane." "C" Company was to consolidate "Omagh" and "A" Company "Strabane." "D" and "B" Companies commanded by Captain Webb and Captain Craig, "Strabane" and "Enniskillen". That was as far as we had to go, which meant consolidating the 3rd German line running through "Coleraine," "Portadown," "Enniskillen," "Strabane," "Omagh."

The 107th Brigade were in support behind the 108th, and we were supported by the 15th Battalion Royal Irish Rifles. The object of the 107th Brigade was then to pass through to the 4th German line, "Portrush," "Bundoran," "Derry," and consolidate it. This was as far as the division was to go. We were to be relieved by the 49th Division when we had "done our bit." After an intense bombardment the great day of battle broke in "sunshine and mist" the mist almost obscuring the brilliant sunshine as the morning advanced.

The previous night had been passed quietly in the trenches, the enemy submitting in silence to the terrific gun fire. The German lines were pulverised, shells being discharged at the rate of 140 rounds of shell per minute. In spite of this their dug-outs mostly remained uninjured. For half-an-hour it seemed as if the guns had gathered themselves together for one grand final effort before the British lines should be let loose on their prey. Presently the mist cleared away and heavy black smoke clouds could be seen drifting across the German lines on a slight south-westerly breeze, the result of the bursting of our heavy shells. This proved small assistance to us later on, when, with the sun in their faces, our men advanced from the trenches.

At seven o'clock, eight of our 'planes flying over the German lines were fired at, but not much damage done. The Germans still lying low, not a single German aviator could be seen at any time that morning. Soon after 7 a.m. there was a perceptible slackening of our fire, and at 7-30 a.m. the attack began, our gallant soldiers leapt from their trenches and advanced against the enemy. The very moment that our men slipped over the parapet they were met with a hail of machine-gun bullets and shrapnel played on them. It was then that Captain Webb, of "D" Company fell, and many others. They advanced in waves 50 yards apart, and were mown down like hay. "A" Company was soon wiped out, and "C" Company, supporting it, suffered very severely; but they pressed on, gaining all their objectives. By this time there had been a severe thinning out of officers and others in command, and the men, too eager, shoved on towards the 4th line very quickly, and got into the fire of our own artillery. Some of "B" and "D" Company actually got into Grandcourt. A war correspondent said:

> The gallantry displayed by the carrying parties at this part of the fight was most conspicuous, and tiny escorts showed complete contempt of danger in bringing prisoners across an area which was being ploughed up by shell fire. One man, unaided, shepherded across the valley of death a party of fifteen Germans who showed extreme reluctance to risk the fire of their own guns; they wanted to lie down and wait. 'Not at all,' said the Ulsterman, covering them with his rifle, 'just you go across, and they'll look after you when you get there.' In the course of a brief conversation several of the prisoners said that the effect of our bombardment prior to the launching of the attack had been terrific. They had been in the front lines, and while they had a reserve supply of food, our barrage fire had prevented them getting any water. Their machine-guns, they said, had been protected by being placed in deep dugouts, and were brought up and used against our troops when they advanced.

Within an hour and a half after the opening of the battle our men had taken five lines of German trenches and captured several hundred prisoners, advancing wave after wave like an irresistible tide. We were in advance of the division on our left, who were to take Beaumont Hamel, and consequently the whole left flank was exposed to batteries of machine-guns: it was through this that the 12th Battalion Royal Irish Rifles suffered so severely, also the 9th Royal Irish Rifles, who supported them. "The men advanced as if on parade; one or two remembering the ancient watchwords, sang out "Dolly's Brae" and "No Surrender," but for the most part they kept the stiff upper lip and clenched teeth that meant death or victory."

There was no thought of giving way, merely duty to be done and a task to be completed. Into the very furnace heat of the German fire our gallant lads went, and as shot and shell raked their ranks, others pressed forward to take their places. From both flanks they were enfiladed by machine-gun fire. On the right, Germans lying low in dugouts came up from the cellars in Thiepval village with machine-guns and poured a hail of bullets into the 109th Brigade and 108th Brigade from behind. "As they emerged from Thiepval Wood they fell in hundreds, the German fire at this point being protracted and perfect." The trees were slashed and cut till nothing but bare stumps remained. No one could cross that No Man's Land and escape the fire; even the wounded were shot through and through on the ground as they lay.

The 107th Brigade, passing through in support to the 108th, did magnificent work. All day long the remnants of the battalions held on to the lines of the German trenches which had been captured, though nearly all the officers were gone, but no supplies of bombs or ammunition could be got across. In the evening, about six o'clock, a big German counter-attack was made, and we had to fall back, leaving our wounded, who were too bad to be moved, in dugouts. These advanced points could not be held for long; the enemy might be killed and captured, but the place had developed into a dangerous salient, while the flanking fire from right and left made the position a terrible one, the division on either side being held up by insurmountable obstacles. The order to retire was given, and on Saturday night, July 1st, we were once more on our old front line.

Apparently all the sacrifice had been in vain. At 1 o'clock on Sunday afternoon the remnants of the 107th Brigade and all that was left of our battalion and the 13th Royal Irish Rifles counter-attacked and easily retook the three German lines. The crucial point was the ridge that ran through "Omagh," and unless that could be held we could not hope to hold Serre and the line to La Boiselle. On the left, Beaumont Hamel commanded all, and on the right Thiepval village was the strong point. Unless these were captured our divisional line became a salient raked by machine-gun fire. The 32nd Division actually passed through Thiepval village, but the Germans, who were hidden in the cellars and concrete dugouts, allowed them to pass, and then came up from behind, and the casualties were appalling. The 12th Royal Irish Rifles and the 9th Royal Irish Fusiliers, on our left, were practically wiped out.

The Germans staked all on holding the ridge. 70 of the 15th Royal Irish Rifles and 113 of our 11th Battalion answered their names on

Saturday night, and that was before the fierce fighting of Sunday. One of the most remarkable facts was the enormous number of slightly wounded men among our casualties; and as for the medical organisation, nothing could surpass it; no tribute could be great enough for the divisional medical staff. It was a magnificently heroic fight, and one of which Ulster has every reason to be proud.

THE RED HAND OF ULSTER.
Somme—July 1st, 1916.

When one great wave has shatter'd
A coast that gleamed in light,
We look, and share the wonder,
Amazement and affright;
But what can hide its grandeur,
And what can veil its might?

On grey and heathy hillsides,
In valleys bowered in leaves;
In wide and flowery meadows,
Where peaceful sheep and beeves
Strayed thro' the days of waiting,
No change the eye perceives.

The mist-clouds veil the mountains,
The mist-rains drift and wing
Across the ancient castle,
The homely cot, where cling
The climbing sprays of woodbine,
Where wild birds hop and sing.

Now comes the news of battle—
The long-awaited roll
Of our great Western rampant—
A wall of thews, and soul—
And Ulster's sons are writing
Their names upon a scroll.

That rain-swept mist-land gathers
Before their eyes, as forth
They sweep—the watched-for Ulsters,
For honour of the North;
For Freedom's best and dearest,
For Britain's word and worth.

That wave of Northern valour
Is like the advancing tide,
And nought can cool or curb it,
And nought can change its stride;
In "Derry," "Enniskillen,"
And Omagh they reside!

'Tis Lurgan and Dungannon,
Armagh and proud Belfast,
St. Johnston, Londonderry,
And Donegal's grey vast
That flit before their vision
As trench by trench is passed.

The roar of bursting cannon
Breaks voices faintly heard—
The voices of their youth-time,
Familiar jest and word;
But, hark! the call is "Onward!"
And visions grow more blurred.

Hurrah! the drive so eager,
So long-continued, deep,
The firmly-driven bayonet,
The stumble and the leap
Grow less intense; the foeman
Has wavered in the sweep!

And in the lone, grey cottage
A trembling hand essays
To hold the fateful message
Which speaks a proud son's praise:
"He nobly did his duty,
And fell—there is a haze. . . . ."

Read in another homestead—
A loftier home, now chill;—
The page tells of a soldier
Who led his men, until
There came the hue of sunset—
He lives in honour still.

"Dead," do you call these heroes?
Dead?—who have given birth
To all that makes life living—

To all that is of worth;
No, never, never write it—
This "death" is Freedom's girth!

This wounding is for homeland—
For Britain's winsome weal—
Through all the years advancing,
A theme for song, a peal
That swings in jubilation—
How Ulster met the steel!

How Ulster claimed the expected,
Already-given cheer;
How Ulster's hand directed
The torch which yet shall sear
The remnant of the Prussian,
And make the future clear!
     William J. Gallagher.
Galdonagh, Manorcunningham,
Co. Donegal.
10th July, 1916.

Part 3

In a specially written account of the part taken in the big advance of July 1st by the Tyrone Battalion of the Royal Inniskilling Fusiliers, Lieut.-Col. Ricardo, D.S.O., commander of the battalion, says:—

Just now it is a hard struggle between pride and sorrow, and every moment the latter surges up, and it takes a mighty effort to keep our chins up; but we shall see it through and begin again, however hard. Out of 19 officers who went over, 12 have gone, the very best, and all dear pals; four came back untouched, and three wounded got back—one of these lay out for 24 hours, and one for 48—whilst the casualties in the rank and file were numerous. Early on the 1st July (the boys were convinced the date had been chosen for their especial benefit) the battle began. Every gun on both sides fired as fast as it could, and during that din our dear boys just walked out of the wood and up gaps we had cut through our parapet, and out through lanes in our wire. I shall never forget for one minute the extraordinary sight. The Derrys, on our left, were so eager they started a few minutes before the ordered time, and the Tyrones were not going to be left behind, and they got going without delay—no fuss, no shouting, no running; everything orderly, solid, and thorough, just like the men themselves.

Here and there a boy would wave his hand to me as I shouted "good-luck" to them through my megaphone, and all had a happy face. Many were carrying loads. Fancy advancing against heavy fire carrying a heavy roll of barbed wire on your shoulders! The leading battalions suffered comparatively little getting out, but when they came close to the German front line they came under appalling machine-gun fire, which obliterated whole platoons. And alas! for us, the division on our right could not get on, and the same happened to the division on our left, so we came in for the concentrated fire of what would have been spread over three divisions.

But every man who remained standing pressed on, and without officers or N.C.O.'s they "carried on," faithful to their job. Not a man turned back, not one. Eventually, small knots belonging to all the battalions of the division (except two) gathered into the part of the German line allotted to the division and began to consolidate it. Major John Peacocke, a cousin of Lady Carson, a most gallant and dashing officer, was sent forward after the advance to see how matters stood. He took charge, and gave to the representatives of each unit a certain task in the defence. The situation after the first few hours was indeed a cruel one for the Ulster Division. There they were, a wedge driven into the German line, only a few hundred yards wide, and for 14 hours they bore the brunt of the German machine-gun fire and shell fire from the sides; and even from behind they were not safe.

The parties told off to deal with the German first and second lines had in many cases been wiped out, and the Germans sent parties from the flanks in behind our boys. The division took 800 prisoners, and could have taken hundreds more, but could not handle them. Major Peacocke sent back many messages by runners. They asked for reinforcements, for water, and for bombs, but no one had any men in reserve, and no men were left to send across. We were told reinforcements were at hand and to hold on, but it was difficult, I suppose, to get fresh troops up in time. At any rate, the help did not come. I sent off every man I had—my own servant, my shorthand clerk, and so on—to get water out of the river; the pipes had long before been smashed. On their way, many, including both above-named, were killed by shell fire.

At 10-30 p.m. the glorious band had to come back; they had reached the third line. At 8-30 a.m. they fought to the last, and threw their last bomb, and were so exhausted that most of them could not speak; and shortly after they came back, help came, and the line they had taken and held was re-occupied without opposition, the Germans, I suppose, being as exhausted as we were. Our side eventually lost the wedge-like bit, after some days. It was valueless, and could only be held at very heavy cost.

We were withdrawn late on Sunday evening, very tired and weary. There are many instances of outstanding gallantry, but it is almost impossible to collect evidence. We may hear more of it when some of our wounded come back.

A correspondent to the *Times* wrote:—

I am not an Ulsterman, but yesterday as I followed their amazing attack I felt I would rather be an Ulsterman than anything else in the world. My position enabled me to watch the commencement of their attack from the wood in which they formed up, but which long prior to the hour of assault was being overwhelmed with shell fire, so that the trees were stripped and the top half of the wood ceased to be anything but a slope of bare stumps, with innumerable shell holes peppered in the chalk. It looked as if nothing could live in the wood, and indeed the losses were heavy before they started, two companies of one battalion being sadly reduced in the assembly trenches. When I saw the men emerge through the smoke and form up as if on parade, I could hardly believe my eyes. Then I saw them attack, beginning at a slow walk over No Man's Land, and then suddenly let loose as they charged over the two front lines of the enemy's trenches, shouting "No surrender, boys!"

The enemy's fire raked them from the left, and machine-guns in a village enfiladed them on the right, but battalion after battalion came out of that awful wood as steadily as I have seen them at Ballykinlar, Clandeboye, or Shane's Castle. The enemy's third line was soon taken, and still the waves went on, getting thinner and thinner, but without hesitation. The enemy's fourth line fell before these men, who could not be stopped. There remained the fifth line. Representatives of the neighbouring corps and division, who could not withhold their praise at what they had seen, said no human man could get to it until the flanks of the Ulster Division was cleared. This was recognised, and the attack on the last German line was countermanded.

The order arrived too late, or perhaps the Ulstermen, who were commemorating the anniversary of the Boyne, would not be denied, but pressed on. I could see only a small portion of this advance, but could watch our men work forward, seeming to escape the shell fire by a miracle, and I saw parties of them, now much reduced indeed, enter the fifth line of the

German trenches, our final objective. It could not be held, as the Division had advanced into a narrow salient. The corps on our right and left had been unable to advance, so that the Ulstermen were the target of the concentrated hostile guns and machine-guns behind and on both flanks, though the enemy in front were vanquished and retreating. The order to retire was given, but some preferred to die on the ground they had won so hardly.

As I write, they still hold the German two first lines, and occasionally batches of German prisoners are passed back over the deadly zone; over 500 have arrived, but the Ulstermen took many more, who did not survive the fire of their own German guns. My pen cannot describe adequately the hundreds of heroic acts that I witnessed, nor how yesterday a relieving force was organised of men who had already been fighting for 36 hours to carry ammunition and water to the gallant garrison still holding on.

The following letter sent to the *Times*, July 3rd, is a description of the great day by a senior officer:—

The 1st of July should for all time have a double meaning for Ulstermen. The attack carried out by the Ulster Division was the finest thing the new armies have done in this war. Observers from outside the division who saw it say it was a superb example of discipline and courage. We had to come through a wood which was being literally blown to pieces, form up in successive lines outside of it under a devastating fire, and then advance across the open for 400 yards to the German first line trenches. It was done as if it was a parade movement on the barrack square. The losses were formidable before we ever reached the first line, but the men never faltered, and finally rushed the first line, cheering and shouting, "Boyne" and "No Surrender!"

From then onwards they never checked or wavered until they reached the fifth line of German trenches, which was the limit of the objective laid down for us. They captured and brought in many hundred prisoners, and actually captured many more who were either killed by the German fire before they reached our lines, or were able to get away in the maze of trenches owing to the escort being knocked over. I can hardly bring myself to think or write of it. It was magnificent—beyond description. Officers led their men with a gallantry to which I cannot do justice, and the men followed them with equal gallantry; and when the officers went down, the men went on alone. The division was raked by machine-gun and shell fire from in front and from both flanks, and our losses have been very severe.

Ulster should be very proud of her sons.

Part 4

Messages of tribute to the Ulster Division from:—

The Corps Commander.
The Divisional Commander.
The Commanding Officer of the Ulster Volunteer Force.
Sir E. Carson.
The Lord Primate.
The Bishop of Down.
The Bishop of Clogher.
Belfast.

Lieut.-General Sir T. L. N. Morland, K.C.B., D.S.O., commanding the Army Corps in which the Ulster Division was serving, has issued the following order:—

The General Officer Commanding the Corps wishes to express to the General Officer of the Division and all ranks his admiration of the dash and gallantry with which the attack was carried out, and which attained a large measure of success under very unfavourable conditions. He regrets the heavy and unavoidable losses sustained, and feels sure that after a period of rest the division will be ready to respond to any call made upon it.

G. Webb,
Brigadier-General, D.A. and Q.M.G.

The General Officer Commanding the Ulster Division has issued the following special order:—

The General Officer Commanding the Ulster Division desires that the division should know that in his opinion nothing finer has been done in the war than the attack by the Ulster Division on July 1st. The leading of the company officers, the discipline and courage shown by all ranks of the division will stand out in the future history of the war as an example of what good troops, well led, are capable of accomplishing. None but troops of the best quality could have faced the fire which was brought to bear on them, and the losses suffered during the advance. Nothing could have been finer than the steadiness and discipline shown by every battalion, not only in forming up outside its own trenches, but in advancing under severe enfilading fire. The advance across the open to the German line was carried out with the steadiness of a parade movement under a fire from front and flanks which could only have been faced by troops of the highest quality.

The fact that the objects of the attack on one side were not obtained is no reflection on the battalions which were entrusted with the task. They did all that men could do, and in common with every battalion in the division, showed the most conspicuous courage and devotion. On the other side the division carried out every portion of its allotted task in spite of the heaviest losses. It captured nearly 600 prisoners, and carried its advance triumphantly to the limits of the objective laid down. There is nothing in the operations carried out by the Ulster Division on July 1st that will not be a source of pride to all Ulstermen. The division has been highly tried, and has emerged from the ordeal with unstained honour, having fulfilled in every particular the great expectations formed of it. Tales of individual and collective heroism on the part of officers and men come in from every side, too numerous to mention, but all showing that the standard of gallantry and devotion attained is one that may be equalled but is never likely to be surpassed.

The General Officer Commanding the Division deeply regrets the heavy losses of officers and men. He is proud beyond description, as every officer and man in the division may well be, of the magnificent example of sublime courage and discipline which the Ulster Division has given to the army. Ulster has every reason to be proud of the men she has given to the service of our country. Though many of our best men have gone, the spirit which animated them remains in the division, and will never die.

The following orders of the day have been issued by General Sir

George Richardson, K.C.B., G.O.C., Ulster Volunteer Force:—

1. The General Officer Commanding wishes to take this opportunity of recording an appreciation of the gallantry of the officers and men of the Ulster Division. Perhaps it may serve as a solace to those on whom will fall the heaviest burden of sorrow, and that it will help to sustain them in the knowledge that duty was nobly done, and that the great warm heart of Ulster goes out to them in affectionate sympathy and takes an unfathomable and unforgettable pride in every man of them.

2. Perhaps more especially the officers and men U.V.F. offer their heartfelt sympathy to the relatives of those who fell on the 1st July, 1916. They were put to the supreme test, and history will claim its own record.

3. For those who fell in the service of their King, the Empire, and the glory of Ulster, we mourn, but we have no regrets. We are proud of our comrades. Our path of duty is clear. Every effort must be made to fill up the casualties in the division, and maintain the glorious lead given by the brave men of Ulster.

4. The attack of this division is already talked of outside the division as a superb example of what discipline, good leading and magnificent spirit can make men capable of performing. Much was expected of the Ulster Division, and nobly they have fulfilled expectation.

5. I will quote from a letter received:—"There was never a sign of falter. On the right two battalions of the 108th, the 109th and the 107th swept over four successive lines of German trenches, capturing nearly 600 prisoners and reaching the objective laid down for them absolutely on the stroke of the hour fixed as the time they might be expected to get there. On the left the 12th Royal Irish Rifles made a magnificent effort, but were swept away by machine-gun fire. They did all that men could do. The 9th Royal Irish Rifles went to them, and succeeded in getting into the German trenches, and were held up there by weight of munition and machine-guns."

6. It fills me with pride to think how splendidly our men were capable of performing.

7. On the 30th September, 1915, His Majesty the King was graciously pleased to say to the Ulster Division:—"I am confident

that in the field you will nobly uphold the traditions of the fine regiments whose name you bear." This mandate has been faithfully obeyed with a heroism and devotion that will establish a rich record in the annals of the British Army, and conveyed to us by the war cry of Ulster—"No Surrender."

Geo. Richardson,
Lt.-General, G.O.C., U.V.F.

Sir E. Carson has issued the following message to the Ulster people:—

I desire to express, on my own behalf and that of my colleagues from Ulster, the pride and admiration with which we have learnt of the unparalleled acts of heroism and bravery which were carried out by the Ulster Division in the great offensive movement on July 1st.

From all accounts that we have received they have made the supreme sacrifice for the Empire of which they were so proud, with a courage, coolness, and determination, in the face of the most trying difficulties, which has upheld the great tradition of the British Army. Our feelings are, of course, mingled with sorrow and sadness at the loss of so many men who were to us personal friends and comrades; but we believe that the spirit of their race will at a time of such grief and anxiety sustain those who mourn their loss and set an example to others to follow in their footsteps.

His Grace the Lord Primate of All Ireland, who was in Dungannon holding a visitation of the clergy of the rural deaneries of Dungannon, Aghalo, and Tullyhogue, has given us the following message to the people of Ulster:—

All Ireland is proud of the noble gallantry of the Ulster Division. I have lived amongst these officers and men for the greater part of my life, and I expected nothing else. They are of the stock from which our heroes come and to whom our Empire owes so much—unconquered and unconquerable.

Today our hearts are bowed with woe for their relatives at home who have been so grievously bereaved. For many years to come the gallantry of these sons of Ulster will be an inspiration to fresh generations of Irishmen.

I spent a considerable time with them last January in France, and I can testify to their patience and pluck, as well as to their chivalry and courtesy. Oh! the wild charge they made! Their services for honour and truth, after they have passed on into the near presence of God, will never be forgotten.

The Right Rev. Dr. D'Arcy, the Bishop of Down, in a message, says:—

> The 1st of July will for all the future be remembered as the most glorious in the annals of Ulster. Terrible indeed are the losses sustained. Many of our noblest and best young men, to whom we looked for help and leadership in the time to come, have given their lives in the service of their country and for the welfare of humanity. But our deep sorrow is permeated by the sense of the joyful exultation at their splendid heroism. They have proved themselves worthy of the grandest traditions of their race. They have, indeed, surpassed all records of ancient chivalry. Wherever Ulstermen go they will carry with them something of the glory of the great achievement of the 1st July. The spirit of willing sacrifice for the sake of those great ideals of liberty and progressive humanity which belonged to all that is best in the British race, and which has inspired Ulster throughout all her recent struggles, was never more magnificently exhibited.

The Right Rev. Dr. Day, the Bishop of Clogher, writes:—

> I most heartily join with the Lord Primate, the Bishop of Down and others in offering my congratulations to the Ulster Division on the record of their noble deeds at the front in taking a prominent part in the great offensive which was begun on July 1st by the united forces of France and England. While we regret the heavy roll of casualties with which their great achievements were carried out, and sincerely sympathise with the sorrowing relatives of those who have fallen in the cause of their king and country, the "order of the day" issued by General Nugent is a testimony to valour and determination which may well rouse the admiration of everyone who is associated with Ulster.
>
> Maurice Clogher.

The following paragraph, taken from the *News-Letter,* July 12th, 1916, shows how Belfast and the people of Ulster paid a tribute to their glorious dead:—

This year, for the first time in the history of the Orange Institution, the celebration of the anniversary of the Battle of the Boyne was abandoned, while the customary holidays were to a great extent postponed until next month, to enable the shipyards and munition works to complete immediate orders. At the suggestion of the Lord Mayor, all work, business and household, was temporarily suspended for five minutes following the hour of noon today, as a tribute to the men who have fallen in the great British offensive. Viewed from the City Hall, on the steps of which the Lord Mayor and Lady Mayoress were standing, the scene was most impressive.

On the stroke of 12 all traffic came to a standstill, men raised their hats, ladies bowed their heads, the blinds in business and private houses were drawn, and flags were flown at half-mast. The bells at the Assembly Hall tolled, and after the interval of five minutes chimed the hymn 'Abide with Me.' Intercessory services were held in the cathedral and other churches. Shortly before noon the following telegram was received by the Lord Mayor from Sir Edward and Lady Carson:—'Our prayers and solemn thoughts will be with you all at 12 o'clock, in memory of our illustrious dead, who have won glory for the Empire and undying fame for Ulster. May God bless and help their sorrowing families.'

THE EXTERIOR OF ST. RIQUIER CATHEDRAL.

Appendix 1

NOTE ON ST. RIQUIER.

A beautiful description of St. Riquier and the foundation of the Abbey is given in a book by Margaret Stokes, *Three Months in the Forests of France*.

About the year 589, two Irishmen, named Caidox and Fricor, disembarked on the coast at the little town of Quentovic, on the mouth of the Somme, with twelve companions, and they followed the great Roman road, now called the Chaussée Brunehaut, preaching the Gospel on their way. They reached Centule (now St. Riquier), and remained there some days to rest.

Some say they came to France with Columban, and that when Columban resumed his journey towards the Vosges, he left behind him these two monks that they might give instructions to the half-barbarous inhabitants, and initiate them into the mysteries of the Christian religion. "They fought on," said the old chronicler, "perceiving that the inhabitants of Centule (St. Riquier) were blinded by error and iniquity, and were subjected to the most cruel slavery; they laboured with all their strength to redeem their souls, and wash them in the Saviour's Blood."

But the people could not understand the language of these heavenly messengers, and they rebelled against a teaching so holy and sublime. They demanded what these adventurers, who had just escaped out of a barbarous island, could be in search of, and by what right they sought to impose their laws on them. The voice of charity was met by cries, menaces, and outrage, and the natives strove to drive them from their shores by violence, when suddenly a young noble, named Riquier, appeared upon the scene. He commanded silence, and arrested the most furious amongst the mob, and taking the two strangers under his protection, he brought them into his house. He gave them food

THE INTERIOR OF ST. RIQUIER CATHEDRAL.

and drink, and in return they gave him such nourishment of the soul as he before had never tasted. He learned to know God and love Him beyond all things.

When he had taken orders he became the founder of the celebrated Abbey of Centule (now St. Riquier), and the bodies of the two Irishmen from whom he had learned Christianity were interred with splendour in this church.

When St. Angelbert, in the year 799, restored this church, he also restored the half-ruined tombs, decorated their shrines with such magnificence, and inscribed verses upon them in letters of gold. The relics of the two saints lay beneath the monument till the year 1070, when St. Geroinus transferred them to a silver shrine adorned with precious stones, and in this shrine also were laid the relics of another Irish saint, Mauguille.

Their festival is celebrated on June 3rd. On the road from Abbeville to Doullens, on the edge of the wood of St. Riquier, and below the slope of a smiling hill, an ancient church, majestically seated in the valley below, comes into view. It is the Abbey Church of St. Riquier. The town rises from the foot of the church like an amphitheatre round the enclosure of its ancient walls. The great tower rises above the fertile fields around and above the summits of the distant hills and woodland glades. The little stream of Seardon, which almost threatens to disappear at its very source, passes through the lower town and on towards the south-west.

The old chroniclers called it Reviere au Cardons, from the little flower cardoon. This little thread of water, rising at Bonnefontaine, under Isinbard's tomb, is swelled by the junction with the river Mirandeuil, or Misendeuil, a name derived from the fact that it was at this spot the ladies of St. Riquier first heard the fatal news that their husbands had fallen in the Battle of Crecy.

The labours of the Irish Church in Picardy, commenced by these two missionaries, Caidox and Fricor, and carried on by the disciples of Columban from Luxeuil, were destined to receive a fresh impetus from the parent country. Another mission, this time from the shores of Lough Corrib, in Galway, was undertaken. Fursa and his twelve companions, who landed at Mayoc, at the mouth of the River Somme, A.D. 638, went up the river to St. Riquier, a monastery in which he must have found traditions of his native Church.

OFFICERS 11TH BATTALION ROYAL IRISH RIFLES. JULY. 1915

Top Row—Lieut. Waring, 2nd Lieut. Ellis, 2nd Lieut. P. B. Thornely, Lieut. F. G. Hull, 2nd Lieut. D. J. Brown, Lieut. E. Vance, Lieut. R. H. Neill (Assistant Adjutant), 2nd Lieut. C. C. Canning.

Second Row (standing)—Lt. and Q.M. W. L. Devoto, Lieut. R. Thompson (Transport Officer), Lieut. C. F. K. Ewart, 2nd Lieut. C. G. F. Waring, 2nd. Lieut. S. A. M'Neill, 2nd Lieut. D. S. Priestly, 2nd Lieut. W. C. Boomer, 2nd Lieut. T. H. Wilson, 2nd Lieut. G. O. Young (Scout Officer), Lieut. K. M. Moore, Lieut. M. C. Graham (Medical Officer), Captain S. D. B. Masters.

Third Row (sitting)—Captain Smyth, Capt. C. C. Craig, M.P, Capt. A. P. Jenkins, Capt. R. Rivers Smyth (Brigade Major, 108th Inf. Brigade), Major P. L. K. Blair Oliphant (2nd in Command), Lt.-Col. H. A. Pakenham (Commanding), Major W. D. Deverell (Adjutant), Capt. O. B. Webb, Capt. A. F. Charley, Capt. A. P. I. Samuels.

Two Officers sitting in front—2nd Lieut. C. H. H. Orr, 2nd Lieut. J. C. Carson.

BIOGRAPHIES OF OFFICERS OF 11TH ROYAL IRISH RIFLES (SOUTH ANTRIM VOLUNTEERS,) WHO WERE KILLED OR WOUNDED DURING THE BATTLE OF THE SOMME.

In some cases Photographs could not be obtained.

CAPTAIN C. C. CRAIG.

Commanding B Company; wounded and prisoner; M.P. for South Antrim.

MAJOR A. P. JENKINS, LISBURN

Commanding A Company; wounded and prisoner; first reported missing; received Commission as Captain in 11th Royal Irish Rifles, September, 1914, served in France till July 1st, 1916, when wounded and made prisoner, released from Germany owing to wounds in December, 1916, spent from December, 1916, till November, 1917, as a repatriated prisoner of war in Switzerland, returned to England November, 1917.

Captain O. B. Webb.

Commanding D Company, killed in action; son of the late Mr. Charles J. Webb, J.P., the Old Bleach Linen Company, Randalstown.

Captain A. P. I. Samuels.

Commanding C Company; wounded during bombardment previous to advance, afterwards killed at Messines, September, 1916; son of the Right Hon. Mr. Justice Samuels.

Captain E. F. Smith.

Wounded; son of Mr. Smith of Banbridge; before the war was an officer in the Lisburn contingent of the U.V.F.

Lieut. E. B. Vance.

Died of wounds a prisoner in Germany; C Company; son of the late Mr. William Vance, Antrim.

CAPTAIN CECIL EWART.

Killed in action; second in command of C Company; he took Command of the Company after Captain Samuels was wounded. Captain Ewart is the second son of Mr. F. W. Ewart, Derryvolgie, Lisburn.

LIEUT. R. H. NEILL.

Killed; only son of Mr. Reginald Neill, Colingrove, Dunmurry; educated at Mourne Grange, Kilkeel, Co. Down, and Malvern College, Worcestershire. He was formerly an officer in the 2nd Batt. South Antrim Regiment, U.V.F.

LIEUT. W. ELLIS.

C Company; wounded; son of Mr. Ellis, Toomebridge.

LIEUT. G. O. YOUNG.

C Company, Scout Officer; gassed in bombardment previous to advance; son of Mr. George L. Young, J.P., Culdaff House, Co. Donegal, and Millmount, Randalstown.

Sec.-Lieut. B. W. Gamble.

A Company; wounded; son of Mr. Baptist Gamble, 2 Elmwood Avenue, G.W.R., Belfast.

Sec.-Lieut. G. N. Hunter.

Wounded; second son of Mr. Samuel Hunter, Gracepark Gardens, Dublin, Public Valuer to His Majesty's Treasury in Ireland.

SEC.-LIEUT. E. DANIEL.

Shell-shock; son of Mr Daniel, Dungannon.

SEC.-LIEUT. J. W. SALTER.

B Company; prisoner; first reported killed.

SEC.-LIEUT. C. J. H. SAMUELS.

D Company; wounded; nephew of the Right Hon. Mr. Justice Samuels.

SEC.-LIEUT. F. B. THORNELY.

Wounded; B Company; nephew of Major Blair Oliphant, second in command of the battalion; received his commission from Uppingham School.

Sec.-Lieut. J. C. Carson.

C Company; wounded; only son of Mr. J. Carson, of Parkmount, Lisburn, and the Stock Exchange, Belfast.

Sec.-Lieut. J. C. Orr.

Wounded; son of Mr. J. C. Orr, Londonderry. Was in the Hong Kong and Shanghai Bank, London, before the war. He was with the 108th Brigade Trench Mortar Battery during the advance.

Sec.-Lieut. C. R. B. Murphy

Wounded; son of the Rev. Dr. Murphy, Rector of St. George's Parish Church, Belfast.

Sec.-Lieut. D. S. Priestly.

Killed, attached 108th Brigade Machine Gun Corps. This officer had been with D Company until January, 1916.

Sec.-Lieut. W. C. Boomer.

D Company, Lisburn; wounded previous to July 1st.

Sec.-Lieut. Bramhal.

Wounded during bombardment previous to advance.

Sec.-Lieut. S. Waring.

A Company, Glenavy; wounded previous to July 1st.

Sec.-Lieut. W. P. Vint.

Wounded; was with the Machine Gun Company, 108th Brigade.

★★★★★★

Orders No. 237.
Royal Irish Rifles (South Antrim Regiment).
16th July, 1916.

313 Casualties.
Killed—1/7/16.

"A" Company.

Cpl. Dunlop, Q.
L/Cpl. Lennox, F. J.
R'man. Allen, W. J.
    "   Clelland, G.
    "   Harvey, J.
    "   Marks, R.
    "   Morrow, R.
    "   Leckey, W.

"B" Company.

R'man. Bell, H.
   "   Brown, E.
   "   Gaussen, C. L.
   "   Haddock, T.
Cpl. Lunn, J.
R'man. Lewis, E.
L/Cpl. M'Kechnie, R.
R'man. M'Keown, W.
   "   Neill, J.
Cpl. Stewart, P. M.
L/Cpl. Walker, G. F.
R'man. Welch, Alex.

"C" Company.

Sgt. Buick, J.
R'man. Andrews, J.
   "   Knox, F.
   "   Magill, R. D.
   "   Pollock, A.
   "   Wallace, J.

"D" COMPANY.

C.S.M. Bell, J.
L/Sgt. Bell, J.
L/Cpl. Foster, J. B.
   "   Cathcart, T.
R'man. Ansell, J.
   "   Dunleavy, J.
   "   Gorman, D.
   "   Hoy, S.
   "   Harper, J.
   "   Morrow, J.
   "   M'Clean, J.
   "   M'Mullen, J.
   "   M'Clughan, R.
   "   M'Gimpsey, J.
   "   Nixon, R. W.
   "   Robinson, E.
   "   Smith, R.

" Sloan, W.
" Steadman, J.
" Stephenson, J.
" Toman, H.
" White, J.
" Weir, W.

Died from wounds.

R'man. Boyd, D.

614 Casualties.
Wounded—1/7/16.
"A" Company.

Sgt. Abbott, J.
" Patton, J.
L/Sgt. Gillespie, G.
" Beattie, V.
L/Cpl. Atkinson, M.
" Kerr, A.
" Lynch, E. W.
Upd.
L/Cpl. M'Neice, E.
L/Cpl. Corkin, W.
R'man. Allen, S.
" Beck, J.
" Bell, R.
" Buchanan, J.
" Barrons, A.
" Conway, W. C.
" Corkin, J.
" Connaughty, R.
" Dodds, S.
" Frazer, R.
" Fulton, J.
" Hawthorne, J.
" Hunter, R.
" Keery, S.
" Lavery, Jas.
" Lavery, John
" Lewis, G.

" Logan, W. J.
" Lyness, C.
" Maginess, W.
" Morgan, J.
" Murdock, J.
" Morrison, T. G.
" Mulligan, D.
" Mulholland, C.
" M'Cann, E.
" M'Cann, J.
" Matier, R. (2)
" M'Neice, J. (1)
" Orr, W.
" Patterson, T.
" Reid, J. E.
" Salley, R.
" Sewell, F.
" Smyth, W.
" Spratt, S.
" Steele, J.
" Semple, W.
" Savage, E.
" Ward, T.
" Watson, A.
" Weir, A.
" M'Gorkin, R.
" Hillis, J.
" Hanna, B.
" Coburn, J.
" Abbott, T.
" Agnew, J.
" Atkinson, T.
" Beattie, E.
" Cassidy, J.
" Chapman, Jas.
" Fox, W. J.
" Herron, J.
" Hanna, R.
" Murdock, T.
" Rainey, S.

" Williamson, R.
" Watson, C.
" Beattie, R.
" Freeland, S.

"B" Company.

R'man. Benson, A.
" Blakes, T.
" Bleaks, W.
" Briggs, R.
" Bryson, S.
Sgt. Burke, F. G.
L/Cpl. Crawford, W. J.
R'man. Curry, W.
" Crowe, J.
" Crozier, W.
" Dickson, C.
" Dodds, J.
" Duff, J.
" Foreman, J.
L/Cpl. Gill, D.
R'man. Green, T.
" Hawthorne, A.
" Hill, S.
L/Cpl. Hull, W. J.
R'man. Hyndman, R. J.
" Lewis, W.
" Moore, R.
" Mulholland, T. J.
Sgt. Munn, H.
R'man. Maybin, J.
" Moody, T.
" Marshall, G.
Sgt. M'Clenahan, W. J.
R'man. M'Cormick, J.
" M'Donald, J.
" M'Gurk, J.
" M'Henry, J.
" M'Knight, R.
" M'Williams, F.

  " M'Williams, J.
  " M'Gall, J.
  " M'Cluskey, W.
  " O'Neill, J.
  " Patterson, T.
  " Ramsey, J.
L/Cpl. Rennix, E.
R'man. Scott, H.
  " Spears, D.
  " Smith, A.
  " Thompson, J.
  " Trousdale, G.
  " Verner, T.
Sgt. Waring, G. D.
R'man. Webb, H.
  " Webb, Jos.
  " Woods, J.
  " Woods, A. C.
  " Rea, S.
  " Dowling, A.
  " Matchett, J. H.

"C" COMPANY.

Sgt. Steele, M.
 " Kelly, A.
 " Whiteside, A.
 " Kernaghan, J.
L/Sgt. Swann, J.
Cpl. Flemming, H.
 " M'Burney, J.
A/Cpl. M'Burney, T.
L/Cpl. Reid, B.
  " Crookes, C. E.
  " Wallace, J.
  " O'Neill, J.
R'man. Andrews, R. J.
  " Alderdice, R.
  " Bates, R.
  " Campbell, S.
  " Cullen, W.

"   Doole, I.
"   Dawson, J.
"   Ewart, H.
"   Ewart, H.
"   Esler, R.
"   Foster, W.
"   Greer, A.
"   Gillespie, J.
"   Hamilton, J.
"   Hughes, J.
"   Hamilton, T.
"   Hanlon, A. T.
"   Harvey, J. S.
"   Hume, J.
"   Kirkpatrick, S.
"   Harbinson, A.
"   M'Cammond, J.
"   Linton, W.
"   Millar, J.
"   Moore, J.
"   Magill, T.
"   Milligan, J.
"   Manning, R. J.
"   M'Kee, J.
"   M'Lean, W.
"   M'Connell, J.
Upd.
L/Cpl. M'Grugan, H.
R'man. M'Clay, S.
"   M'Calmont, W. J.
"   Nicholl, S.
"   Patterson, J.
"   Sterling, D.
"   Storey, D.
"   Sergeant, T.
"   Shannan, A.
"   Stewart, J.
"   Thompson, S.
"   Thompson, J.
 "   Wallace, A.

" Woods, R.
" Young, W.
" Young, S.
" Scullion, J.
L/Cpl. Eakin, T.
R'man. Bailey, W.
" Millar, J.
" Mulree, J.

"D" COMPANY.

Sgt. Higginson, W.
" Mercer, J.
Cpl. Matier, T.
" Adamson, R. M.
L/Cpl. O'Neill, E.
" Wallace, W.
" Shaw, J.
" Allen, W.
R'man. Ayre, S.
" Adair, G.
" Adair, B.
" Adams, K. G.
" Allen, D.
" Ashe, E.
" Boomer, R.
" Boggs, J.
" Calvert, W.
" Christie, J.
" Corkin, T.
" Cochrane, G.
" Cunningham, D.
" Duffy, R. J.
" Dalton, A.
" Doole, G.
" Dickson, S.
" Dawson, A.
" Fleming, W.
" Harbinson, R.
" Horner, J.
" Hill, S.

- " Johnston, W.
- " Johnston, H.
- " Kennedy, G.
- " Leathem, W.
- " Stratton, W. J.
- " Jenkins, T.
- " Lowery, J.
- " Kerr, J.
- " Lyttle, J.
- " Millar, B.
- " M'Pherson, R.
- " M'Kee, J.
- " M'Kibben, R. M.
- " M'Cloy, W.
- " M'Kibben, L.
- " M'Dowell, W.
- " Martin, T.
- " Mawhinney, S.
- " M'Connell, W.
- " M'Garth, J.
- " M'Ilroy, H.
- " M'Dowell, D.
- " Neeson, J.
- " Peel, A.
- " Russell, J.
- " Ringland, G.
- " Rodgers, J.
- " Steele, J.
- " Stewart, W.
- " Smyth, W. J.
- " Smith, W.
- " Shields, S.
- " Todd, J.
- " M'Clelland, S.
- " Ingram, H.

615 Missing
"A" Company.

R'man. Chambers, J.
- " Cowan, Jos.

" Doherty, A.
" Davidson, J. H.
" Emerson, D.
" Freeland, S.
" Kerr, D.
" Kain, W.
" Kidd, Jas.
" Lightbody, J.
" Logan, T.
" Lyttle, S.
" Russell, W.
" Singleton, T.
" Topping, S.
" Totten, W.
" Wright, W.
" Kidd, R.

"B" Company.

R'man. Beattie, G.
" Blakely, S.
" Bruce, W. J.
Cpl. Cairns, E.
Sgt. Cairns, T. G.
R'man. Crowe, J.
" Gordon, R.
" Green, J.
" Hawthorne, T.
" Herron, W.
" Henninger, W.
" Hanna, D.
" Irvine, W.
" Kidd, G.
" Kennedy, R. J.
" Kennedy, R.
" Logan, T.
" Lowry, H.
" Lyness, J.
" Marks, T.
" Murdock, H.

Upd.
L/Cpl. Murphy, T.
R'man. Morrow, J.
  " Morrow, R. J.
  " M'Ilhatton, R.
  " M'Larnon, G.
  " Patterson, W.
  " Reid, D.
  " Stevenson, J.
  " Semple, S.
  " Sample, S. J.
  " Tollerton, R.
  " Wills, S.

"C" COMPANY.

Sgt. Stewart, W.
 " Miller, W.
L/Cpl. Scott, J.
  " Ellis, S.
R'man. Anderson, W. H.
  " Bell, A.
  " Clarke, A.
  " Coulter, J.
  " Drennan, R.
  " Dyers, J.
  " Derby, G.
  " Graham, D.
  " Greer, A.
  " Houston, W.
  " Linton, H.
  " Lyttle, F.
  " Marshall, A.
  " Mairs, E.
  " M'Dowell, J.
  " M'Fall, J.
  " Newell, T.
  " Nelson, W.
  " Orr, J.
  " Smith, W. J.
  " Wilkinson, W.

"D" Company.

Sgt. Lavery, G.
A/Cpl. Moore, W.
Cpl. Glendinning, D.
" Williamson, W. J.
Upd.
L/Cpl. Purdy, R.
" M'Aleece, J.
" Smyth, J.
" Robinson, W.
R'man. Bushe, S.
" Bell, A.
" Easton, S.
" Goudy, J.
" Heaney, T.
" Logan, W.
" Moore, H.
" M'Curdy, W.
" Moore, J.
" M'Allister, J.
" Patterson, R.
" Skillen, W.
" Thompson, J.
" Williamson, A.
" Wilson, T.
" Hamill, J.
" Graham, J.
" Boyd, W.
" Boyd, D.
" Henderson, J.
Upd.
L/Cpl. Millar, S.

Prisoner of War.

R'man. Fisher, J.
" Walker, H.
" Frouten, A.

Adjutant,
11th (S.) Bn. R.Ir.Rif.

Embarkation List of Officers

Embarkation List of Officers 11th Royal Irish Rifles who left Bordon Camp for France, October, 1915.

Lieut.-Col. H. A. Pakenham, Commanding Officer.
Major P. Blair Oliphant.
Major Devonish Deverell, Adjutant.
Lieut. R. Thompson, Transport Officer.
Capt. Graham, Medical Officer.
Lieut. F. Hull.
Lieut. Devoto, Quartermaster.

"A" Company.

Major A. P. Jenkins.
Capt. E. F. Smith.
Capt. C. Ewart.
Lieut. C. G. F. Waring.
Lieut. T. G. Thornely.
Lieut. S. Waring.

"B" Company.

Captain C. C. Craig.
Captain A. T. Charley.
Lieut. R. N. Neill.
Lieut. Wilson.
Lieut. Webb.

"C" Company.

Major Cavendish Clark.
Lieut. Vance.
Captain A. P. I. Samuels.
Lieut. Ellis.
Lieut. Young.
Lieut. Vint.

"D" Company.

Captain O. B. Webb.
Captain Masters.
Lieut. Canning.
Lieut. Waring.
Lieut. W. C. Boomer.
Lieut. Priestly.

Embarkation List of N.C. Officers & Men.

Sgt. Abbott, James
R'man. Abbott, Thomas
" Abbott, Wm. Robert
" Allen, Samuel
" Allen, Wm. John
" Andrews, James
" Andrews, James
" Andrews, Thomas
" Atkinson, Moses
" Atkinson, Thomas
" Atkinson, Moses
" Atkinson, Thomas
" Adams, R.
" Adams, John
" Addis, David
" Addis, Henry
" Agnow, Edward
" Andrews, William
" Adams, Henry
" Adams, James Alex.
" Adams, Oliver
" Allen, John
" Anderson, Samuel A.
" Anderson, Wm. Hy.
L/Cpl. Andrews, Robt. John
R'man. Ardery, Francis
" Armstrong, William
" Adair, Ben
" Adair, George
" Adams, Kenneth K.
" Adams, Robert
" Adamson, Robt. M'K.
" Addis, James
Cpl. Addis, Wm. Hy.
R'man. Allen, William
" Anderson, John Jos.
" Ansell, John
" Archer, Bertie
" Ashe, Edward

" Ayre, Samuel
" Baxter, Isaac
" Beattie, Ernest
" Beattie, Robert
Cpl. Beattie, Victor
R'man. Beck, James
" Bell, Robert
" Bingham, William
L/Cpl. Black, James
R'man. Blakley, Edward Chas.
" Boyd, David
Sgt. Breathwaite, Samuel
R'man. Brown, George
" Brown, Isaac
" Brown, Samuel
" Buchanan, John
C.Q.M.S. Bullick, Edwin
L/Sgt. Bullick, Wm. Parker
R'man. Barr, David Geo.
" Barr, John Nathaniel
" Beattie, George
" Beck, Hg. Hy
" Bell, Hy.
" Bell, John
L/Cpl. Brown, Samuel
R'man. Benson, Albert
L/Cpl. Benson, John
R'man. Birney, Thomas
" Black, William
" Blakes, Thomas
" Blakely, Alexander
" Blakely, Samuel
" Blakely, Thomas
" Bleaks, William
" Bloomfield, Sl.
" Briggs, Robert
" Brown, Edmund
" Brown, George
Cpl. Brown, James
R'man. Brown, John

" Brown, Samuel
" Bruce, Albert E. G.
" Bruce, William
" Bruce, William
" Bryans, David
" Bryson, Samuel
L/Sgt. Burke, Fk. Geo.
R'man. Bankhead, Robt.
" Barbour, Robt.
" Barkley, Arthur
" Bates, Robert
" Beattie, Robert
" Beattie, Robt. Jas.
" Beattie, William
" Beck, James
" Bell, Andrew
" Boyd, David
" Brown, Fred Chas.
" Brown, John
" Brown, John
" Brown, Robert
Sgt. Buick, Jackson
R'man. Buick, James
" Burrowes, Hy.
" Barkely, James
" Beggs, James
" Bell, Andrew
" Bell, Alexander
" Bell, Joseph
C.S.M. Bell, John
R'man. Bell, William
" Brides, Michael
" Brown, James
Cpl. Bushe, James Hy.
R'man. Campbell, Wm. Saml.
C.M.S. Caton, Jack
R'man. Ceaser, Hugh
" Clarke, Arthur
" Cairns, Robert
" Calvert, William

" Campbell, James
" Campbell, John Hy.
" Caskery, Francis
" Cathcart, Thomas
" Chapman, Jos.
" Chapman, William
" Christie, Jos.
" Clarke, Hugh
" Clarke, William
" Clarke, Wm. Robt.
" Cooper, William
" Coulter, James
Sgt. Chambers, Jas. Orr
R'man. Chambers, Robert
" Chapman, David
" Chapman, James
L/Cpl. Chapman, Joseph
R'man. Chapman, William
" Clarke, Chas.
" Clarke, George
Sgt. Clarke, Joseph
R'man. Cleland, George
" Coburn, James
" Coburn, John
" Collington, Edward
" Connolly, John
" Connor, James
" Conway, William Chas.
" Cordiner, Samuel
" Cordner, George
" Cordiner, Thomas
Cpl. Corkin, Hy.
R'man. Corkin, John J.
Cpl. Corken, Robert J.
R'man. Corkin, William
" Corry, John
" Cowan, Albert Wm.
" Cowan, Joseph
" Cowan, Samuel
" Cowan, Thomas

"   Creighton, Robert
"   Crone, William
"   Crowe, Francis
"   Coulter, Thomas
"   Craig, Alexander
"   Craig, David
L/Cpl. Crooks, Chas. Edward
R'man. Crooks, Cecil
"   Cullen, William
"   Campbell, Edward
"   Cassidy, Joseph
Cpl. Cathcart, David
R'man. Chambers, James
Cpl. Cairns, Edward
R'man. Cairns, Samuel
Sgt. Cairns, Thos. John
R'man. Campbell, John
C.Q.M.S. Campbell, William
R'man. Carson, Robert
"   Carson, William
"   Caughey, Joseph
"   Chapman, Arthur
"   Clarke, Alfred James
"   Clarke, John
"   Clay, John
"   Colvin, Robert John
"   Crawford, William Jas.
Sgt. Cree, John
L/Cpl. Crockard, James
Cpl. Croft, John
R'man. Crone, Richard
"   Crothers, James
"   Crothers, Robt. James
"   Crowe, Fred
"   Crowe, John
"   Crowe, Thomas
"   Crozier, William
Sgt. Crump, William
R'man. Curry, William
R'man. Christie, William John

Sgt. Clarke, William
Sgt. Clendinning, John
R'man. Cochrane, George
" Colvin, Samuel
" Corken, Thomas
" Cowan, Archie
" Craig, James
" Cunningham, Dl.
" Currie, Robert
" Dalton, David
" Davidson, James Hall
" Dodds, Samuel
" Doherty, Alexander
Sgt. Donnelly, James
R'man. Douglas, Saml. James
" Dowds, Joseph Hy.
" Dowling, Albert
" Drennan, David
L/Cpl. Dunlop, Quinton
R'man. Dunlop, William
" Davison, Clem.
" Dawson, John
" Dempster, George
" Dobbin, William H.
" Doole, Isaac
" Doole, William John
" Drennan, Robert
" Dalton, Arthur
" Dalton, Thomas
" Dennison, David
" Dick, Samuel
" Dickson, Samuel
" Dole, George
" Doyle, James Hy.
" Duffy, Robert John
" Dunleavy, James
" Dickson, Chas.
Sgt. Dickson, William G.
R'man. Dodds, John
" Doherty, Samuel

" Dowling, Abraham
" Duff, Joseph
" Dunbar, Francis
" Ederton, Henry
" Elkin, Hugh Kelly
" English, Alexander
" English, William Jas.
L/Cpl. Ewart, William Henry
" Eakin, Thomas
" Edgar, John
R'man. Elliott, Samuel
" Ellis, Samuel
" English, Thomas
" Erwin, Frank
" Esler, Robert
" Ewart, Henry
" Ewart, Henry
" Ellis, William
" English, Thomas
" English, Joseph
Cpl. Fleming, Henry
L/Cpl. Fleming, Robert
R'man. Fleming, Thomas
" Foster, William
" Francey, Robt. James
" French, George
" French, John
" Finlay, Hy.
L/Cpl. Fleming, John
" Fleming, Samuel
R'man. Foster, Allen
" Foster, John B.
" Francey, William Jn.
" Fullerton, Francis
" Fleming, James
" Fenton, John
" Ferrin, Joseph
" Flannagan, William
" Fleming, William
" Fox, William John

"   Foye, Silias
"   Fraser, Robert
"   Freeland, Samuel
L/Cpl. Fulton, John
R'man. Ferguson, Andrew
L/Cpl. Fisher, David
R'man. Fisher, Joseph
"   Foreman, Joseph
"   Forsythe, Fred
"   Forsythe, James
"   Frayer, George
"   Frazer, Robert
"   Gorman, James
"   Gausson, Chas. F.
"   Geddis, David
"   Gill, David
"   Gill, William
"   Gillian, William
"   Gillian, William
"   Gordon, Robert
"   Graham, Thomas
Sgt. Graham, William Jn.
R'man. Green, Thomas
L/Sgt. Gillespie, George
R'man. Gill, Robert
"   Gorman, John
Sgt. Goulding, Fred E.
R'man. Gaston, Alex.
"   Gilmore, Thomas
"   Gowdy, Alex.
"   Graham, James
"   Graham, William
"   Graham, William Jn.
"   Grattan, Hugh
"   Gray, Robt. Jn.
"   Gregory, Joseph
"   Griffin, Martin
"   Galbraith, William
"   Galway, Alex.
L/Cpl. Gleghorn, David

R'man. Goudy, Jos.
L/Cpl. Gourlay, David
C.Q.M.S. Gourlay, David H. J.
R'man. Graham, David
" Graham, William
" Greene, David
" Greene, William John
" Greer, Archibald
L/Cpl. Glendinning, Dd.
R'man. Gordon, James
" Gorman, Daniel
L/Cpl. Gorman, Phillip
R'man. Goudy, James
" Goudy, Jos. Hy.
" Graham, John
" Graham, Robert
" Gray, Samuel
Cpl. Gray, William
Sgt. Gregg, Samuel
R'man. Hanna, Boyd
" Hanna, Fk. James
" Hanna, Robert
" Harvey, John
" Haslett, George
" Hawthorn, James
" Hayes, William James
" Heasley, William
" Herron, John
" Higginson, William Jas.
" Hill, Thomas Robert
" Hillis, John
" Hodgin, John
" Holmes, George
" Hull, George Hy.
" Hunter, Robert
" Hamill, John
Sgt. Harbinson, James
R'man. Harbinson, Rd.
" Harbinson, William
R.S.M. Hall, Isaac

R'man. Heaney, Thomas
" Heaney, William E.
" Hyndman, James
" Hyndman, Robt. Jn.
" Hailhwaite, C. J. G. M.
" Hamill, John Edward
Cpl. Hamill, Samuel
R'man. Hamilton, Francis
" Hamilton, James
" Hamilton, Thomas J.
" Hanlon, Alex. T.
" Hanna, Robert
" Hanna, James
L/Cpl. Hannon, James
R'man. Hannon, Samuel
" Harvey, Jos. S.
" Henderson, John
Cpl. Herdman, James
R'man. Hewitt, William John
" Hogg, James
" Houston, John
" Houston, Robert
" Houston, Robert
" Hughes, James
L/Cpl. Hume, James
R'man. Ingram, Henry
" Irvine, David
" Irvine, John
" Irvine, James
" Irvine, John
" Irvine, Robert
" Irvine, William
" Johnston, George
" Jenkins, Thomas
" Johnston, David
L/Cpl. Johnston, George
Sgt. Jamison, John
R'man. Jefferson, Walter
" Johnston, John
" Johnston, William

" Jackson, Samuel
" Johnston, John
" Johnston, Robert
" Johnston, William
" Linton, William
" Linton, John
" Lyle, Samuel
" Lyttle, Francis
" Lyttle, Thomas
" Lamont, William
" Lamour, Alex.
Cpl. Lavery, Alex.
R'man. Lavery, James
" Lavery, John
Sgt. Lavery, William
R'man. Lavery, William John
L/Cpl. Leathem, John
R'man. Leathem, William
" Leckey, William
" Lennox, Fk. John
" Lewis, George
" Logan, Thomas
" Lynass, Matt
" Lynch, Edward Watson
" Lyness, Chas.
" Lyness, Thomas
" Lyttle, Samuel
" Lightbody, James
" Lavery, Joseph
" Lennon, James
" Lewis, Edward
" Lockhart, Robert
" Logan, Thomas
" Long, Richardson
" Lowery, Henry
Sgt. Lavery, George
L/Cpl. Leach, Arnold
R'man. Leathem, William
" Lennon, Osmond
" Lewis, James

Cpl. Lindop, Charles
R'man. Lindsay, Hugh
" Lindsay, Hugh
" Lindsay, William
" Logan, John
" Logan William
" Lowery, John
" Luke, Archibald
L/Cpl. Lyle, John
R'man. Lyness, Charles
" Lyttle, John
L/Cpl. Lunn, James
R'man. Lyness, James
" Lyons, Thomas
" Magill, Thomas
" Mairs, William J.
" Manning, Reg. Jos.
" Marcus, Alexander
" Mawhinney, Robt. J.
" Miller, Hugh
" Miller, James
" Miller, John
" Miller, John
" Marshall, A.
" Magill, William
" Maginnis, John
" Maginnis, Robert
" Maginnis, William
" Marshall, Andrew
" Marks, Alexander
" Marks, Thomas
" Marwood, James
" Matchett, James Hy.
" May, Nathaniel
" Mcgarry, Jos. Edward
" Megrath, William
" Minford, Alfred
R.Q.M.S. Moore, Richard
R'man. Moore, Robert
" Moore, William Geo.

" Morrow, John
" Mount, James
" Mulholland, Albert
" Mulholland, Thos. Jn.
L/Sgt. Munn, Henry
R'man. Murdock, Henry
" Murdock, Samuel
" Murphy, Thomas
" Morrow, James
Cpl. Marsden, James
R'man. Martin, David
" Martin, Samuel
" Mather, Joseph
" Matier, John
L/Cpl. Matier, Thomas
Cpl. Mearns, Jas. Wilson
R'man. Megarry, James
L/Cpl. Mercer, James
R'man. Miller, James
" Mooney, Robert
" Moore, Henry
" Moore, James
" Moore, William
" Morrison, William
" Morrow, James
" Mynes, Charles
" Miller, Samuel
L/Sgt. Miller, William
R'man. Miller, William
" Milligan, David
" Milligan, James H.
" Milliken, Thomas C. C.
" Moffat, Samuel
" Montgomery, Jos.
" Moore, Herbert J.
" Moore, John
" Moore, Walter
L/Sgt. Mulholland, Hugh
R'man. Mulree, Joseph
" M'Aloney, William

"   M'Bride, Thomas
L/Cpl. M'Burney, John C.
"   M'Burney, Thomas
Cpl. M'Callen, James
R'man. M'Calmont, Wm. J.
"   Martin, Hy.
"   Martin, Thomas
"   Matier, Robert
"   Maxwell, James
"   Megran, Thomas
"   Mills, Samuel
Sgt. Mitchell, Aty. W.
R'man. Moag, David
L/Cpl. Moles, Hy. Smyth
R'man. Mooney, Alex.
"   Moore, Alex.
Sgt. Moore, John
R'man. Moore, Norman Wilfred
"   Moore, William Alex.
"   Morgan, John
"   Morrison, Geo. Thomas
"   Morrow, Robert
"   Morrow, Wm. Hy.
"   Mulholland, Chas. Wm.
"   Mulholland, James
"   Mulligan, Jn.
"   Murdock, John
"   Murdock, Thomas
"   M'Allister, Pierce
"   M'Allister, William
"   M'Avoy, Lewis Patton
"   M'Cann, Edward
"   M'Carthy, Jn.
"   M'Caw, James
"   M'Cleery, Samuel
"   M'Cleeland, William
"   M'Cloy, Hy.
"   M'Cartney, John
"   M'Clintock, Thomas
"   M'Clure, William

" M'Connell, John
" M'Coy, William
" M'Donald, James
" M'Dowell, Johnston
" M'adden, John
" M'Fadden, William
" M'Crubb, Daniel
" M'Crugan, Hugh
" M'Ilwaine, Thomas
" M'Ivor, Samuel
" M'Kee, James
" M'Andrews, H.
" M'Bride, Alexander
" M'Cabe, Robert
" M'Cauley, Robert
" M'Clelland, John
" M'Clements, William
" M'Clenahan, John
" M'Clenaghan, Rd.
Sgt. M'Clenaghan, Wm. Jas.
R'man. M'Clurg, Adam
" M'Kee, John
" M'Kee, Robert
" M'Kee, William
" M'Kelvey, Matt
" M'Lean, William
" M'Lean, William
" M'Mullen, Samuel
Cpl. M'Murray, James
R'man. M'Veigh, William
" M'Aleece, James
" M'Allister, Charles
" M'Allister, Jos.
" M'Auley, Chas.
" M'Cartney, John
" M'Clean, John
" M'Clelland, Samuel
" M'Cloy, William
L/Cpl. M'Comb, Edward
R'man. M'Corkey, Matt. Geo.

Cpl. M'Cord, Archie
R'man. M'Court, John M.
    "   M'Dowell, William
    "   M'Dowell, William
    "   M'Gimpsey, Jas.
    "   M'Grath, Joseph
    "   M'Ilroy, Henry
    "   M'Intosh, Patrick
L/Cpl. M'Kee, John
R'man. M'Kee, John
    "   M'Kee, William
L/Sgt. M'Keown, William
R'man. M'Kibbin, Langtry
    "   M'Kibben, Rt. Millar
    "   M'Kinney, David
    "   M'Knight, Alex
    "   M'Knight, William John
    "   M'Mullen, James
    "   M'Pherson, Robert
L/Sgt. M'Quillan, William
L/Cpl. M'Clurg, William
R'man. M'Comb, Francis
    "   M'Comb, James
    "   M'Comb, John
    "   M'Cormick, Joseph
    "   M'Cracken, William
Cpl. M'Cready, Robert
R'man. M'Cullough, Andy
    "   M'Cune, James
    "   M'Curry, Thomas
    "   M'Curley, Felix
    "   M'Curley, James
    "   M'Donald, Joseph
    "   M'Donald, Samuel
    "   M'Donald, William
    "   M'Dowell, Thomas
    "   M'Gurk, John
    "   M'Henry, John
    "   M'Ilroy, Edward
    "   M'Ilroy, Roger

L/Cpl. M'Kechnie, Robert
R'man. M'Keown, Wm. Robt.
" M'Kibbin, Eli
" M'Knight, Robert
" M'Larnan, George
" M'Murray, William
" M'Nair, William
" M'Veigh, William
" M'Williams, Fredk.
" M'Williams, John
" Neill, Thomas
" M'Cloy, James
" M'Clure, Thomas Jas.
" M'Comb, William
" M'Comiskey, Hbt.
" M'Donald, Wm. Ed.
" M'Geown, Samuel
" M'Ilroy, James
" M'Kaveney, John
" M'Keaveney, James
" M'Keaveney, David
" M'Keown, William
Cpl. M'Mullen, William
L/Cpl. M'Mullen, Samuel
R'man. M'Nair, John
" M'Neice, Edward
" M'Neice, James
" M'Neill, Robert
" M'Watters, Alex.
" M'Watters, Alex.
" Nash, Thomas
" Neagle, William Jas.
" Nicholson, John
" Nolan, Rd. John
" Neeson, John
" Neill, John
" Nelson, Robert
" Nicholl, Samuel
" Nicholl, Wm. Hy.
" Nixon, Robt. Wm.

"   Norwood, Joseph
"   Nowell, Thomas
"   Nicholl, Samuel
Cpl. Orr, George
R'man. Orr, Robert Jas.
Cpl. Partridge, John
R'man. Patterson, John
"   Patterson, Thomas
"   Patterson, William
"   Peel, Michael Jos.
Cpl. Phillips, John
R'man. Poots, William
"   Purdy, Samuel
"   O'Neill, James
"   O'Neill, Hugh
"   Orr, John
"   O'Neill, Edward
"   Orr, William John
"   Osborne, William
"   Patterson, Robert
"   Patterson, Thomas
"   Patton, Daniel
"   Peel, Albert
"   Pollock, James
"   Pollock, James
"   Pollock, Samuel
"   Pershaw, John
"   Pritchard, Thomas
"   Purdy, Robert
"   Patterson, James
"   Patterson, Charles
"   Patterson, Samuel
"   Patterson, Thomas
Sgt. Patton, James
R'man. Potts, Stewart
"   Parker, Hugh
"   Patterson, James
"   Pollock, Alexander
"   Pollock, Victor
"   Pershaw, John

"   Quinn, Thomas
"   Quigley, David
"   Quigley, Samuel
"   Quigley, Matthew
"   Quinn, Robert
"   Quinn, William
"   Rainey, John
"   Rainey, Robert
"   Rankin, Thomas Hy.
"   Reford, James A. M.
L/Cpl. Reid, Bristow
R'man. Reid, James
Sgt. Renshaw, James Hy.
R'man. Roy, Matthew
"   Raddick, Jonathan
"   Rainey, Henry
"   Rainey, Samuel
"   Rainey, William John
"   Reford, Fras. Johnston
"   Regan, Hugh
"   Reid, Joseph Edward
"   Reid, William
"   Robinson, Henry
"   Rowan, William
"   Roy, Thomas
"   Roy, William James
"   Russell, William
"   Rea, David
"   Ringland, George
"   Roberts, Francis
"   Roberts, William
"   Robinson, Edward
"   Rodgers, James
"   Robinson, William
"   Rowley, James
"   Russell, James
"   Shaw, John
"   Sherritt, Joseph
"   Sinclair, William
"   Skillen, William

"   Sloan, William
"   Smith, Robert
L/Cpl. Smylie, Samuel
R'man. Smyth, James
"   Smyth, Thomas
"   Smyth, William
"   Smyth, William John
"   Steadman, John
Cpl. Steele, Henry
R'man. Stephenson, Joseph
"   Stewart, Brice
"   Stewart, Francis
"   Stewart, William
"   Stewart, William
Sgt. Surgenor, James
R'man. Surgenor, John
"   Scott, James
"   Scroggie, John
"   Sergeant, Thomas
"   Salley, Robert
"   Sewell, Francis
"   Shaw, John
"   Shields, Joseph
"   Simpson, Joseph
"   Singleton, Thomas
"   Skelly, James
"   Smith, William
"   Ramsey, John
"   Reid, David
"   Reid, John
L/Cpl. Rennix, Edward G.
R'man. Roberts, Samuel
"   Rodgers, Charles
"   Rush, Edward
"   Scott, Henry
"   Scott, Robert
"   Smyth, Thomas
"   Smyth, William Ed.
"   Stevenson, James
"   Stewart, James

L/Cpl. Stewart, Patk. Mich.
R'man. Stift, Arthur, Geo.
" Taggart, Norman
" Tannahill, Harry
" Thompson, Hy. Jas.
L/Cpl. Thompson, Joseph
R'man. Smyth, Hugh
" Smyth, Joseph
" Smyth, Thomas Hy.
" Smyth, William
" Spratt, Samuel
" Steadman, George
" Stevenson, John
" Stewart, Hugh
" Swann, Samuel
" Swindle, William
" Shannon, Alexander
" Skelton, Arthur
" Sloan, John
" Smith, Robert
" Speedie, Thomas
Sgt. Sprott, Robert
" Steele, Martin
" Stewart, William
R'man. Sterling, David
" Storey, David
" Storey, Joseph
" Straitt, Samuel
Cpl. Swann, James
R'man. Tate, William Hy.
" Thompson, Jonathan
" Thompson, Robert K.
" Thompson, Samuel
" Thursby, James
" Taggart, Andrew
" Tate, John
" Thompson, John
" Toman, Henry
" Totten, Joseph
" Turner, Samuel

"   Thompson, Samuel
"   Tolerton, Robert
"   Tollerton, Thomas
"   Verner, Thomas
"   Walker, George F.
"   Wallace, George
"   Wallace, William
"   Walsh, David
"   Walsh, William Hy.
Sgt. Waring, Geo. Dickson
R'man. Waring, James Banks
"   Waring, James
"   Waring, William
R.S.M. Watson, John
R'man. Watson, William
"   Webb, Herbert
"   Webb, Joseph
"   Weir, Thomas
"   Welch, Alexander
"   Wilkinson, Hugh
L/Cpl. Williamson, Hy.
Sgt. Williamson, Joe
R'man. Wills, James
"   Wills, Samuel
"   Wilson, Robert
"   Woods, Clements, Alex.
"   Woods, James
C.S.M. Woods, William Fdk.
R'man. Wright, Alexander
"   Wright, Edward
L/Cpl. Tate, David
Cpl. Tate, James
R'man. Taggart, Thomas
"   Thornton, John
"   Todd, Francis
"   Todd, John
"   Topping, Hy.
"   Topping, Samuel
"   Totten, William
"   Vogan, William

" Walker, Isaac
" Walker, John
" Walker, Robert
" Wallace, William John
" Ward, Samuel
" Ward, Thomas
" Waring, Alfred
Sgt. Waring, Samuel
R'man. Waring, William
" Watson, Alexander
" Whiteside, Samuel
" Wilson, Samuel
" Windsor, Charles
" Woods, James
L/Cpl. Wright, William
R'man. Woods, Samuel
" Woods, William
" Wright, Adam S.
" Walker, John
" Wallace, Joseph
L/Cpl. Wallace, James
R'man. Wallace, Joseph
" Watt, Robert
" White, Robert
Sgt. Whiteside, Albert
R'man. Wilkinson, William
" Williamson, Fredk.
" Wilson, Francis
" Wilson, James
" Wilson, Joseph
" Woods, Robert
L/Cpl. Walker, Henry Alb.
R'man. Wallace, John
" Wallace, William
" Waring, John
C.Q.M.S. Waring, Thomas
R'man. Watson, Joseph
" Watt, Samuel
" Weir, William
" Williamson, Andy

"   Williamson, Jos.
"   Williamson, Samuel
"   Williamson, Wm. John
"   Wilson, David
"   Wilson, James
"   Wood, Walter
"   Wylie, William
"   Yendall, William
"   Young, Thomas
"   Young, John
"   Young, John
"   Young, William

ALSO FROM LEONAUR
AVAILABLE IN SOFTCOVER OR HARDCOVER WITH DUST JACKET

THE 9TH—THE KING'S (LIVERPOOL REGIMENT) IN THE GREAT WAR 1914 - 1918 by Enos H. G. Roberts—Mersey to mud—war and Liverpool men.

THE GAMBARDIER by Mark Severn—The experiences of a battery of Heavy artillery on the Western Front during the First World War.

FROM MESSINES TO THIRD YPRES by Thomas Floyd—A personal account of the First World War on the Western front by a 2/5th Lancashire Fusilier.

THE IRISH GUARDS IN THE GREAT WAR - VOLUME 1 by Rudyard Kipling—Edited and Compiled from Their Diaries and Papers—The First Battalion.

THE IRISH GUARDS IN THE GREAT WAR - VOLUME 1 by Rudyard Kipling—Edited and Compiled from Their Diaries and Papers—The Second Battalion.

ARMOURED CARS IN EDEN by K. Roosevelt—An American President's son serving in Rolls Royce armoured cars with the British in Mesopatamia & with the American Artillery in France during the First World War.

CHASSEUR OF 1914 by Marcel Dupont—Experiences of the twilight of the French Light Cavalry by a young officer during the early battles of the great war in Europe.

TROOP HORSE & TRENCH by R.A. Lloyd—The experiences of a British Lifeguardsman of the household cavalry fighting on the western front during the First World War 1914-18.

THE EAST AFRICAN MOUNTED RIFLES by C.J. Wilson—Experiences of the campaign in the East African bush during the First World War.

THE LONG PATROL by George Berrie—A Novel of Light Horsemen from Gallipoli to the Palestine campaign of the First World War.

THE FIGHTING CAMELIERS by Frank Reid—The exploits of the Imperial Camel Corps in the desert and Palestine campaigns of the First World War.

STEEL CHARIOTS IN THE DESERT by S. C. Rolls—The first world war experiences of a Rolls Royce armoured car driver with the Duke of Westminster in Libya and in Arabia with T.E. Lawrence.

WITH THE IMPERIAL CAMEL CORPS IN THE GREAT WAR by Geoffrey Inchbald—The story of a serving officer with the British 2nd battalion against the Senussi and during the Palestine campaign.

AVAILABLE ONLINE AT **www.leonaur.com**
AND FROM ALL GOOD BOOK STORES

www.ingramcontent.com/pod-product-compliance
Lightning Source LLC
Chambersburg PA
CBHW031617160426
43196CB00006B/162